# Jung in Context

The University of Chicago Press   Chicago and London

# Jung in Context

Modernity and the Making of a Psychology

## Peter Homans

The University of Chicago Press, Chicago 60637
The University of Chicago Press, Ltd., London

Library of Congress Cataloging in Publication Data

Homans, Peter.
  Jung in context.

  Bibliography: p.
  Includes index.
  1. Jung, Carl Gustav, 1875–1961.   2. Psychoanalysis.
I. Title.   [DNLM:   1. Psychoanalysis—Biography.
2. Psychoanalysis—History. WZ100 J945HA]
BF173.J85H63        150'.19'54        78–27596
ISBN 0–226–35108–4

Photograph on title page courtesy of the
Bettmann Archive.

Peter Homans is associate professor of religion
and psychological studies in the Divinity School
at the University of Chicago. He is the author
of *Theology after Freud,* the editor of and a
a contributor to *Childhood and Selfhood: Essays
on Tradition, Religion and Modernity in the
Psychology of Erik H. Erikson,* and the editor of
*The Dialogue between Theology and Psychology,*
which is published by the University of
Chicago Press.

For my mother, Dora Miller, my wife Celia, and my daughters Jennifer, Patricia, and Elizabeth

# Contents

# Acknowledgments

I wish to thank the Association of Theological Schools for a research grant that gave me time to write this book, and also my dean, Joseph Kitagawa, for providing me with additional time away from teaching. Without their help it would have been much longer in the making.

# One

## Introduction

### A Contextual Approach to the Formation of Psychological Ideas

Background: The Rise of "Psychological Man"

Since its inception at the turn of the century, psychoanalysis has become increasingly well known and accepted throughout Western Europe and, especially, in the United States. Though it began as the special creation of one man's mind, in the brief span of seventy-five years it has become an outstanding feature of contemporary life.

Psychoanalysis began as a controversial but largely esoteric theory of the mind, exploring its abnormalities and patterns of change. It has undergone revisions, alterations, and even, in the hands of the human potential movement, fundamental transformations. Nonetheless, it retains its hegemony in the contemporary panorama of psychotherapies and has even penetrated to the institutions of education, politics, and law. As America has become more and more a middle-class society, psychoanalysis has been established as a guiding set of ideas woven into the fabric of its institutional life.

From the beginning, psychoanalysis has also been an interpretation of culture—of art, history, and religion. In this it started as the property of a small group of isolated physicians and intellectuals. Today, however, psychoanalysis has penetrated the academies, permanently influencing the way professionals articulate intellectual ideas. One might expect it to have influenced the social sciences, and indeed it has. But, surprisingly, Freud's psychology has made just as strong an impression on the humanities. One of its earliest manifestations in the academies was psychoanalytic literary criticism, and more recently a new school of historiography—psychohistory—has come into being. Even philosophy, for which Freud had only contempt, has had a go at Freud: existential, phenomenological, and analytic schools have engaged psychoanalysis, though there is of course no "psychoanalytic philosophy."

Besides being a therapeutic and intellectual system, psychoanalysis has been from the first a theory about the transactional immediacies of everyday life—a mode of understanding the interrelations between "the I" and "the social other" by interpreting such ordinary phenomena as dreams and slips of the tongue. Even in this, its least-recognized aspect, Freud's work has made its mark. Psychoanalytic ideas have also made their way into entertainment, the media, and political life and thus have become part of everyday social existence—a series of vague, unrecognized, and often unspecifiable assumptions about social life.

The rise of psychoanalytic thinking is coming to be recognized as an outstanding feature of contemporary life, and this serves as the starting point, though not the subject, of this book. Surprising as it may be, disciplined reflection on this phenomenon has not come from moralists and social critics, who seem too caught up in the processes of modernity to inquire into its structure. Nor has it come from those most influenced by psychoanalysis. If a literary critic uses this theory to analyze a novel, he is satisfied if his interpretation faithfully portrays both the work of art and the theory. He does not stop to reflect upon the broader cultural significance of his effort— upon what it means to make a psychoanalytic interpretation in the first place. The same can be said of the psychoanalytically trained anthropologist studying, say, child-rearing in a traditional culture. Least of all do we expect such reflection from the psychoanalysts themselves, who are concerned to make the theory work and who usually believe it simply evolved as part of the history of science.

Recognition of the way psychoanalytic ideas have flowed from their very circumscribed origin into the many levels and sectors of contemporary life has come instead from a small, widely scattered group of social scientists, for the most part uninterested in each other's work, but all preoccupied with defining the nature and origins of modern culture and all convinced that psychology is a central feature of that modernity. It is to their writings that we must turn for guidance in understanding the phenomenal penetration of psychoanalysis and its consolidation into a new image of the person. I refer to this as the literature on "psychological man."

An anticipation of the concept of psychological man appeared in David Riesman's famous book on the sociology of modern culture, *The Lonely Crowd*. The book appeared in 1950, a propitious time in the history of psychology, for during World War II academic psychology became professionalized, and after the war psychoanalysis left the training institutes to become part of American life. Riesman divided the history of Western culture according to three types of social character, using as his measure the sort of authority and the mode of relating to it that each type took as normative. The tradition-directed type listened to the voices of the past, the inner-directed to the voices of parents in the nuclear family, and the other-directed to the voices of peers. Cut off from both past and family life, modern men huddled together to form a crowd; but the crowd was lonely because its members no longer had the rootedness and autonomy essential to genuine social relations.

In its most obvious sense Riesman's work does not really deal with the phenomenon of psychological man—he used psychology to interpret contemporary culture rather than engaging in cultural reflection upon psychology. Yet in a deeper way Riesman did anticipate the rise of psychological man, for he assigned Freud and psychoanalysis a crucial role in the formation of the other-directed person, who uses psychology to free himself from the restraints of the past and the family. But Riesman never followed up this implication of his work.

Credit for the direct recognition of psychological man belongs to another sociologist, Philip Rieff (1959), who coined the term at the end of his brilliant and controversial study of the influence of Freud's thought on modern Western culture. Rieff argued that there is a fundamental and irreconcilable difference between the image of man that developed in traditional Christian culture and the image of man in modern culture. Freud's psychology was a theory not just of the mind or of therapy, but of morals as well. His "new morality" created a different image of man as self-sufficient in relation to the past and to the existing social order and as capable of relating to both without commitment or loyalty because he is equipped with psychological ideas.

Other sociologists have recognized the phenomenon of psychological man without using the same language. For example, Edward Shils (1972) believes that the outstanding feature of modernity is the movement of masses of people from the periphery of society to its center, producing a loss of regard for the authority of tradition and a greater sense of individuality—a personal sense of well-being, an enlargement of inner space, a preoccupation with enriching personal experience. Without saying it outright, Shils accepts the profoundly psychological character of modern life. Peter Berger (1965, 1967) and Fred Weinstein and Gerald Platt (1973) have developed elaborate and sophisticated theories—by no means compatible—dwelling upon the changes in contemporary social structure that have evoked the psychoanalytic-psychological theory of man.

There is some evidence within psychology itself of this new image of man. As early as 1940, E. C. Tolman spoke glowingly of the prospects of a new type of person (whom he called "psychological man") who could reconcile his "id-wants" and "superego-wants" with his "ego-wants" (Tolman 1966). More recently Erik Erikson (1963) has put forth the view that a transformed version of psychoanalysis is necessary if modern man is to come to terms with the inner conflicts created by industrialization and rapid social change. The psychoanalyst Allen Wheelis, in his important book *The Quest for Identity* (1958), has analyzed the tension between inner, personal cohesion and social change, arguing that contemporary man needs more psychological-moral strength if he is to resolve this tension. And more recently the psychiatrist Robert Lifton (1968) has described an emerging type of person, "protean man," whose experience of himself or his self-process is so diffuse that he is engaged in an interminable series of ideological experiments with himself and is unable to settle on a firm basis for ethical behavior. Lifton cites historical dislocations and social change as major causes of protean man.

These discussions of a new type of person are all different, and no one orientation within sociology or psychology addresses this question in a sustained way. But the very presence of similar analyses in various quarters lends plausibility to the hypothesis. Furthermore, these very different analyses agree on several major points. Above all, they tell us, psychological man is characterized by inner diffuseness: he can organize or structure the inner, personal, and private dimension of his experience of the contemporary world only through psychology, and meaning thus tends to be realized in the personal sector of life. As a result, his relation to social institutions is precarious; there is no firm, synergic connection between personal identity and the social order. This inner diffuseness and this inability to commit oneself wholeheartedly to socially derived norms is rooted in the decline of the power of religious thought and institutional practices to organize the forces of personality and society.

### Psychological Man and Psychological Ideas

While all these analyses have something to say about the nature of psychological man, the sociological discussions go beyond description and reflect on origins. They make several basic points. First, they create a fundamental distinction between traditional Western culture and modernity, identifying psychological man with modernity. Second, they associate tradition with religion and modernity with lack of religion—so they view psychological man as originating in conjunction with a break with religion. Third, and most important of all, this literature links the rise of psychological man as a social phenomenon with the emergence of psychological ideas. Psychological man is coexistent with the discipline of psychology itself.

Because of its strong emphasis upon a surrounding social environment, the sociological approach constitutes one of three elements in what I call a *contextual approach* to the rise of psychological ideas. It stands in sharp contrast to the predominant, conventional view found in psychology's own self-interpretation. I call this prevailing view the *ideational,* or *theoretical,* or *systematic* approach. It consists of two major types of treatment of psychological thinking.

There is first the *historical* approach, of which E. G. Boring's *History of Experimental Psychology* (1950) is an outstanding example. Similar to Boring's book are the studies of such figures as Gardner Murphy (1949), Edna Heidbreder (1933), and Duane Schultz (1974). Second is the *systems-summary* approach found in the works of Calvin Hall and Gardner Lindzey (1970), Salvatore Maddi (1968), and Robert Woodworth (1964). Lying midway between the contextual and ideational approaches is that of *intellectual history* as applied to psychology, of which H. Stuart Hughes's studies (1958, 1975) of Freud, Jung, Erikson, and Hartmann are representative.

The ideational approach makes two assumptions about the emergence of the discipline of psychology. First, the influences that led to the formation of the first psychological systems are conceived in purely conceptual terms as antecedent ideas. Hence the history of psychology is concerned entirely with systems of *ideas,* whether religious, philosophical, medical, or social. Second, this approach is modeled after the history of physical science: the history of psychology is but one chapter in the history of science. And, by implication, the rise of psychological man is simply the enlightened social appropriation of scientific-psychological ideas. This is the view taken by many historians within the psychoanalytic movement itself, and it was also Freud's own view of the origins of his work.

This juxtaposition of contextual and ideational approaches represents, of course, a very old debate, the debate about the relation between society and thought. And with psychology, as with other types of thought, the debate cannot be resolved simply by favoring one or the other pole. The contextual literature makes a very convincing portrayal of the social forces that underlie psychological ideas, so that no charge of crude reductionism can be leveled at it. On the other hand, the emergence of psychology as a discipline testifies with equal strength that this discipline has considerable intellectual integrity and is not simply a vague body of free-floating ideas embraced by diverse groups.

Although these approaches cannot be either simply opposed or simply wedded, it is still possible to bring them into relation to each other. Neither one has yet worked out its implications for the other at any great length—a double failure. The contextualist literature has been content to work only with a few psychological constructs. The ideational approach has faintly hinted in the direction of the sociological—Boring's concept of *Zeitgeist* being one example. The genesis of psychological ideas, unlike the sociology of science, is based on innovation and creativity at the very center of consciousness itself. The massive literature on the sociology of physical science cannot simply be transplanted and applied even to the sociology of social science, much less to the sociology of psychology.

Despite the failure of the two discussions to penetrate each other—or, rather, on the basis of this failure—it is possible to work with both sets of materials, not by expanding one into the other, but by recognizing that both ignore a crucial dimension of analysis and by exploring that dimension. Contextual and ideational analyses share a common fault: both ignore the dimension of personal experience in the formation of psychological ideas.

Attention to personal experience forces the debate between social and ideational factors in the rise of psychological ideas into the sphere of the personal life situation of the originative psychologist, relieving it of its exclusive emphasis on collectivism or intellectualism. The study of personal experience engages the social conditions that are the context for the life of the individual psychologist and thus constitutes "microsociology." Personal experience also is important in the formation of new ideas. Such an approach might be called the psychology of knowledge, after the fashion of a sociology of knowledge. I believe that the great and innovative psychologists created their systems partly as a response to social conditions and partly as a response to their intellectual heritage, as the two forces were mediated through the double movement of experience and reflection in their personal lives. Because personal experience acts as a context for the formation of ideas alongside that provided by the analysis of social forces, I use the term "contextual approach" to include both.

The analysis of such personal experience, often called the psychohistorical or psychobiographical approach, has focused mostly on literary and political figures, aiming to clarify their personality structures. It has not been directed toward originative figures in the social sciences, nor has its potential for clarifying the origins of ideas been explored. But some recent work has moved in the direction proposed by this book, and while that work may not provide an exact model, it does include promising anticipatory investigations.

In addition to his psychohistorical work, Erikson (1964) has analyzed the origins of Freud's leading psychological ideas in light of the concept of identity-formation. Heinz Kohut's recent work (1976) on the psychology of narcissism in relation to Freud's creativity complements Erikson's study. The psychiatrist Henri Ellenberger (1970) postulated that both Freud and Jung went through a period of "creative illness" during which they reflected upon their inner struggles, then produced their unique psychological systems. Studies by David Bakan (1966) and Paul Creelen (1974) of the behaviorist John Watson have linked the creation of behaviorist theory to Watson's personal struggle with Puritan moralism. Dorothy Ross (1972), a historian of American psychology, examined the rich internal evidence of G. Stanley Hall's personal life and concluded that his psychological thought emerged from a series of conflicts—with the Puritan heritage of his parents, with secular modes of life, and with philosophical ideas. Cushing Strout (1968) has explored William James's personal identity crisis in relation to his formulation of the idea of free will. Taken together, all these studies convincingly demonstrate the interplay between personal and intellectual factors in the lives of originative psychologists.

### The Importance of Religion in the Rise of Psychological Ideas

Many of these studies, in exploring the social and personal contexts of psychological ideas, have been forced to examine religion. In doing so they open up a fresh dimension in the rise of psychological ideas and, inadvertently, provide a new framework for analyzing religion in relation to psychology. Both the broad sociological approaches and the ideational approaches to psychology often give attention to religion, but both of these must be considerably modified by the dimension of personal experience.

Sociological analyses place both psychological man and psychological ideas within the Western tradition, as religion energizes and forms that tradition. Psychology has arisen in direct proportion to the decline of the power of religion. Thus a substitutive relation obtains between the two: psychology is modern man's "invisible religion.'' According to the ideational understanding, the emergence of psychology is but one more victory in the chronic warfare between theology and science. Psychology results from the conscious, active repudiation of religion.

It is also important to consider theological understandings of psychology. Since theologians are by profession deeply committed to defending a religious point of view, their estimates of religion in relation to psychology may be even more trustworthy than those of other disciplines. In point of fact, however, theologians' views about the role of religion in the rise of psychological systems follow the same pattern already established by the sociological and ideational approaches. Orthodox theologians insist there is no relation between religion and psychology—psychology is simply secular and atheistic. In this they support the ideational view. But liberal theologians, in seeing psychology as a cryptoreligion, follow the sociologists: there is something religious, in a substitutive sense, about psychology. What is most important is that both positions ignore the role of personal religious experience in the life of the originative psychologist.

If left to themselves, theological writings on the nature and rise of psychology generally view it simply as one system of belief. But the psychobiographical approach permits a fresh perspective on the role of religion. It takes the question of the nature and rise of psychology out of the realm of faith and belief—Is psychology ''really'' a substitute for theology, or is it ''really'' secular and atheistic?—and recasts it in a form accessible to believer and nonbeliever alike. The psychobiographical approach asks: What is the role of the personal experience of religion in the formation of a psychologist's key ideas?

Such inquiry views religion as a historical force, one factor alongside other historical factors. Religion becomes an entity that the originative psychologist finds himself facing and must respond to. He can respond by repudiating religious ideas, practices, and pieties or he can assimilate them. In either case his psychological ideas will be affected, insofar as religion was a force with which he had to contend. And all the originative psychologists did have to contend with religion.

In short, originative psychologies are formed through complex processes including many kinds of forces. The contextual approach thus uses social, personal, and religious factors to understand the genesis of psychological ideas.

### The Object of the Contextual Approach: Dynamic Psychology

The existing contextual literature has focused almost entirely upon the psychoanalytic tradition. Both the sociological literature on psychological man and psychobiographical studies of psychologists have been preoccupied with Freud and his followers, although some investigators have begun to explore figures outside Freud's influence. But this literature—especially in its sociological side— does not recognize the great variety in psychological systems; nor does it recognize that psychological ideas associated with Freud and his followers may have in fact arisen in times or places outside Freud's influence. Some continuity can be found between Freud's psychoanalysis and such diverse orientations as those of his immediate followers, the neo-Freudians, ego psychology, humanistic psychology, existential psychology, and even the human potential movement. But there are also great differences between Freud himself and these other psychologies, a point that representatives of both groups make again and again.

To clarify both the discontinuities and the continuities between different psychologies, I use the term "dynamic psychology" to indicate a genre of psychological thinking that owes much to Freud yet departs from his teachings at crucial points. The contextual approach can be applied to this as well. The nature of dynamic psychology can be illustrated by noting the "family resemblances" between Freud and the American humanistic psychologist Carl Rogers. Dynamic psychology is a family of psychologies. To those within the family, its psychologies seem more different than alike; to those outside it, the reverse is true. The literature within psychoanalysis and the literature within Rogerian psychology clearly accent the differences. This is particularly so for Rogers's own writings, which distinguish his psychology point for point from Freud's. Rogers wants his readers to know that there are no likenesses, no parallels. He perceives Freud as paternalistic and rationalistic and associates psychoanalytic theory and methods with religious authoritarianism. But if we look at Freud and Rogers from a perspective outside this family dispute, the two psychologies are remarkably similar: Rogers's concept of "conditions of worth" closely resembles Freud's superego; the Rogerian concept of experience denied to awareness is very similar to Freud's understanding of repression; and, like Freud's, Rogers's developmental perspective on the organism emphasizes early childhood experience. There is, in short, a family resemblance between the two. Both are dynamic psychologies.

A psychological system belongs to the dynamic family, I argue, insofar as it is preoccupied with the following minimal conceptual themes. It assumes first that the mind is the seat of conflicting forces that are accessible only to disciplined introspection and self-observation; second, that these conflicting forces are mounted on a developmental axis that extends back into early childhood experience and forward into adult life; and, third, that this developmental axis is situated in the context of a social environment within which a structure of individuality (self, person, ego, I, or the like) exists in a conflictual relationship to social, institutional forces such that the self constantly struggles alternatively to appropriate these forces and to free itself from them. A fourth characteristic is sometimes present: the dynamic psychologist tries to distinguish between experimental and experiential modes of knowing.

While these criteria for a dynamic psychology may appear to originate entirely in Freud's work, they can be applied much more broadly. In addition to characterizing the early followers of Freud, the neo-Freudians, and the ego psychologists, they also can be found in varying degrees and combinations in the works of early American functional psychologists (e.g., G. Stanley Hall and William James), the American humanistic psychologists (Allport, Rogers, Maslow), and the existential psychologists (e.g., Boss and Binswanger). Insofar as a psychological system incorporates one or more of these ideas, to that extent it is a dynamic psychology.

The notion of a dynamic psychology cuts across different psychological systems, including not only Freudian but non-Freudian figures and extending over two continents and some seventy-five years. It thus suggests the possible emergence of a "psychological tradition." Robert Nisbet (1966) has used the phrase "sociological tradition" to refer to the formative period in sociology, from 1830 to 1900 in Europe, which was populated by great sociologists such as Weber, Marx, Durkheim, and de Tocqueville. During this period and through the works of these men were shaped the basic ideas that constitute the modern discipline of sociology, and these are the ideas that still preoccupy the now far more empirically oriented research of the profession. Nisbet refers to the key ideas in the sociological tradition as "unit ideas," taking the term from the historian of ideas Arthur Lovejoy, as he developed it in his famous book *The Great Chain of Being*. Unit ideas are issues or categories that unite very different formative figures and their even more independent followers into a coherent and consistent tradition of speculation and inquiry, so that together they establish a discipline of modern thought.

Nisbet believes that five "unit ideas" compose the foundations of the discipline of sociology, and he casts these in terms of tensions: community and society, caste and class, authority and power, sacred and profane, and alienation and progress. Each of the great thinkers was preoccupied with these issues or tensions, but in no sense are their renditions to be seen as similar. For example, the tension between community and society, more often recognized as the tension between *Gemeinschaft* and *Gesellschaft,* is central to both Weber and Marx, though they differ in how they state the problem, how they assess its significance, and how they resolve it. It is a nuclear, conceptual theme in sociological thinking.

The sustained and thorough preoccupation with these unit ideas distinguishes sociology from its antecedents in social and political philosophy, ethics, and the like. They define the sociological "outlook" or sociological "imagination." To be concerned with them is to take a particular stance with regard to modern society—to adopt a particular kind of consciousness—that had not previously been formalized in systematic thought.

If we take the publication of *The Interpretation of Dreams* in 1900 as a starting point, the ideas that make up the dynamic orientation within psychology are now three-quarters of a century old—roughly the same age as Nisbet's demarcation of the sociological tradition. Although there is no reason to assume that Nisbet's analysis of the rise of sociology is somehow definitive for psychology, it does suggest that enough time has passed to permit speculation on whether a "psychological tradition" is now being formed—a reservoir of key ideas embedded in the investigations and reflections of originative figures. If so, then the key concepts associated with the dynamic psychologies are "unit ideas" in psychology. Following Nisbet's use of polarity to define his ideas, we can reformulate the unit ideas in dynamic psychology as follows: the tension between conscious and unconscious conflict; the tension between childhood and self-hood; the tension between self and society; and—sometimes—the tension between experimental and experiential modes of under-standing.[1] These fundamental questions have preoccupied many psychologists at different times and places and have inspired much recent empirical research. They are not found within the traditions of inquiry of philosophy or sociology. These new ideas complement and define each other, making psychology a separate thing, not just an elaboration of something else.

This book does not treat the concept of unit ideas in psychology as a whole, for the question of a psychological tradition is broader than the orientation of dynamic psychology. If we use as a starting point James and American functionalism, or experimentalism, the forma-tive period becomes longer. The breadth of orientations in psychol-ogy goes considerably beyond the dynamic—the experimental and the behavioral must also be included. But one could argue, for example, that the specific unit ideas of dynamic psychology extend over into behavioral psychology. Just as Marx and Weber were both preoccupied with the problem of an emerging impersonal social order, though they wrote of it in strikingly different ways, so Freud and Watson were both preoccupied with the problems of conscious-ness and with the childhood origins of adult behavior. But to pursue such questions would deflect energy and interest from the genesis of a specific set of psychological ideas.

The view that psychology includes a dynamic orientation com-posed of several unit ideas bears upon this study in two ways. First, it

1. One could also argue—perhaps should argue—that the tension between the sacred and the profane, or between the religious and the secular, is also a unit idea in psychology, as it has been in the sociological tradition. But since much of the argu-ment of this book is intended to demonstrate that this is so in Jung's psychological theory, I prefer not to assert the presence of this tension at this point but will instead introduce it later, at a number of appropriate points.

expands the range of materials that can be analyzed by the contextual approach beyond the psychoanalytic tradition narrowly defined. Second, it has a limiting effect, for the unit ideas mentioned here appear more obviously in the writings of some psychological figures than others. The contextual approach need not account for the full range of orientations within psychology; it best explains those ideas I have called dynamic. Therefore we need to study a figure or group of figures whose work lies within the dynamic orientation, so as to broaden the application of the contextualist literature that already exists on Freud.

### A Contextual Approach to Jung's Analytical Psychology

Jung's analytical psychology is an excellent subject for contextual analysis because his work provides an outstanding example of psychological man. Like Freud's, Jung's thought has penetrated the industrialized and urbanized middle classes. But whereas psychoanalysis and some of its offshoots have become institutionalized as systems of treatment, Jung's work continues to be very explicitly and openly a theory of how to live in the contemporary world—a world in which religion no longer organizes personal and social life. Jung's ideas are widely disseminated in modern culture. In addition to enjoying a modest but sustained place in the contemporary therapy market, they are studied in high schools and colleges and have a visible readership among the educated public. Internationally distributed training centers are staffed by experts who, in addition to their therapeutic responsibilities, also organize public workshops and lectures in the general area of self-understanding. When a person who attends such meetings thinks to himself, "I accept many of Jung's ideas" or, more simply, "I am a Jungian," he becomes an instance of psychological man.

But Jungian psychology is not simply a movement to be labeled by sociologists as psychological man. It is also a rich and complex system of sophisticated psychological ideas. Taken together these ideas fall very much within the dynamic psychology orientation, containing as they do the three major "unit ideas" of the dynamic psychologies: the mind as the seat of conflicting forces (in Jung, the tension between conscious ego and the unconscious); the developmental context of this conflict (in Jung, the process of individuation, which extends back into childhood and forward into maturity and old age); and the situating of these two tensions in the context of a third, the tension between personal fulfillment and an oppressive social order (in Jung, the tension between the ego and the persona, which sets the stage for the beginning of individuation). Jung was also preoccupied throughout his life with the scientific status of his observations, being concerned with what I have called the tension between experimental and experiential forms of understanding. In all of this, Jung's work provides an intellectual-ideational counterpoint to the social fact of psychological man. To study it, and especially to explore its origins, is to understand more thoroughly the genesis of psychological man.

The rich autobiographical literature surrounding Jung's work provides another reason for focusing on him. The very nature of the contextual approach demands a substantial body of autobiography to augment the macrosociological approach with specific details drawn from the microsociological, personal, psychobiographical sphere. Like most of the originative figures in the dynamic tradition, Jung was by nature introspective. But he was also peculiarly modern in his willingness to reveal his private life to his readers. Furthermore, in addition to the autobiography and his correspondence with Freud and many, many others, Jung's formal writings are rich in personal allusion. James included one of his own experiences in the *Varieties,* and Freud discussed his own dreams in *The Interpretation of Dreams,* but Jung often introduced his personal thoughts in the midst of his official thinking.

The contextual approach recognizes the importance of religion in the rise of psychological ideas. Its sociological component emphasizes that the decline of religion as a cultural force has led to the rise of psychology, while the psychobiographical component focuses upon the psychologist's personal experience of religion. All the originative psychologists—men as different as Freud, James, and Watson—wrote about religion in either a personal or a professional way. All the originative psychologists believed that their theories reinterpreted Western religion or even replaced it entirely. But no discussions of them have examined in detail the interface between the personal experience of religion and the creation of psychological ideas. I believe that religion was not just a phenomenon psychologists interpreted; it was also, in varying degrees, a generative force in the rise of psychological ideas—either through repudiation or through assimilation. Jung's psychology provides a unique arena for studying this process. He was personally exposed to religion and wrote about it at length throughout his life. Most important, Jung was introspective about religion. His autobiographical remarks allow us to explore the extent to which religion—through the mechanisms of repudiation and assimilation—contributed to the formation of his psychology.

Any attempt to approach Jung's psychology contextually, however, quickly meets with a formidable obstacle—the secondary literature. Commentary can come to be inseparable from primary sources, a kind of lens through which the original writings are seen. This effect can be true for contemporary writers as well as ancient figures when, as with Jung, their writings themselves tend to be vague, obscure, and even self-contradictory. In Jung's case this secondary literature is entirely noncontextual. Instead of being open to the possibility that Jung's ideas are rooted in social and autobiographical processes, it assumes—and communicates to readers—that his thought is a static array of isolated ideas about the origins and nature of the psyche.

At the root of this noncontextualism lies a style of scholarship I call "specialist appropriation," wherein specialists in different disciplines use various aspects of Jung's thought not to clarify that thought, but to clarify their own work. Consider, for example, the concept of the unconscious. Sociological perspectives emphasize the role of changing social structure in the formation of this key psychological idea. People construct the concept of the unconscious, one can argue, in part so that they can explain to themselves more convincingly the nature of social reality. A psychobiographical approach can hypothesize that, through reflection, a period of great personal crisis could become a source for this crucial concept. In the hands of the specialists, however, Jung's concept of the unconscious has become virtually "ontological," existing with no derivation whatsoever. Of course there is no reason a specialist interested in a particular feature of Jung's thought should abandon his own interests and take up contextual questions. Specialist appropriation, however, not only ignores these questions but creates an atmosphere in which contextual issues become, intentionally or otherwise, "unthinkable."

By surrounding Jung's writings with an anticontextual ethos, the secondary literature has polarized views of Jung into warring camps, creating the impression that he must be understood in terms of one camp or another and thereby deflecting the curious reader from entertaining nuances of meaning that undercut simple "either-or" alternatives. The literature on Jung is polarized in at least two ways. Jung tends to be viewed either as an irresponsible deviant from Freud or else as a gifted and autonomous thinker who abandoned Freud's dogmatism. Or Jung is viewed by some as very much in the Christian tradition, whereas others believe he experienced this tradition as utterly unacceptable and created his psychology accordingly. The contextualist approach employed here will disclose a far more complex—and interesting—relation between Jung and Freud and between Jung and Christianity, one that cannot be contained by simple polarities.

Specialist appropriation not only militates against understanding the origins of Jung's thought, it also obscures its structure. It creates the impression that it has no leading ideas that constitute a center and that, though they may have been modified as Jung's work developed, nevertheless persisted to give the writings an overall coherence. If there is obscurity about the origins of Jung's thought, however, and if this obscurity extends to its inner structure, then it may well be that clarifying origins will bring clarity to the structure.

At first glance the literature surrounding Jung seems formidable, if not awe-inspiring. One is impressed by the spectrum of points of view that have found Jung a sympathetic figure. But surely no one figure, even though he writes for that intellectual democracy the "modern mind," can support the diverse and contradictory positions critics claim to have found in Jung: quantum physics, psychotherapy, Christian theology, Eastern mysticism, and even Durkheimian sociology.

Most of the sustained commentary on Jung can be reduced to four groups of specialists, each of whom has claimed him as especially amenable to their interpretation: theologians, humanists, Jungian psychotherapists, and anti-Jungian psychologists. Hans Schaer

(1950), a Protestant pastor, David Cox (1959), a Protestant theologian, and Victor White (1952), a Catholic theologian, have created one axis of Jungian scholarship by arguing that through his analysis of the dynamics of the collective unconscious Jung gave psychological explication to Christian doctrine and practice. Jung's creation of his psychology—both its sheer presence and its particular contents—is taken as a daring and brilliant attempt to rediscover in the modern world the lost essence of the Christian view of person and society. But another group of theologians has argued exactly the opposite. Raymond Hostie (1957), a Catholic theologian, and two Protestant theologians, H. L. Philp (1958) and William Johnson (1974), have insisted that Jung subverts the authority of Christian revelation. By rendering that experience in psychological terms, Jung has reduced the objective reality of the Christian God to the subjective contents of the psyche and has thereby taken from revelation and given to man the responsibility and the means of choosing between good and evil, denying the primacy of good over evil essential to the Christian world view. Two issues vex the theologians, then: the very presence of psychology as a new type of consciousness, and the moral commitments of that psychology.

The humanists have no interest in theology and are less divided among themselves, because they see in Jung's thought the structure of a universal experience. Historians of religion such as Joseph Campbell (1956), Erich Neumann (1962), and Joseph Henderson (1963) believe Jung discovered those psychological dynamics that are universal throughout the cultures and religions of the world. Myth is the primary category of religion, and they use the intricacies of the individuation process to interpret the mythologies of the world. The internecine warfare of theologians is but a species within the wider genus of religion.

Some literary critics have not found it difficult to apply to art Jung's analysis of the universal dynamics of human experience. Writers such as Herbert Read (1965), Northrop Frye (1957), and especially Maud Bodkin (1934) have found in Jung's concept of the unconscious and his analysis of the archetype the key to the way symbol and language represent human experience in the work of art. In doing so they have created a new form of criticism—"archetypal" or "myth" criticism.

Within the more strictly psychological sphere are the Jungians and the anti-Jungians. Investigators such as Marie-Louise Von Franz (1975), Jolande Jacobi (1967), and in America June Singer (1972) have in effect viewed Jung's psychology as a "way"—a new point of view or world outlook that explains the otherwise opaque nature of contemporary society, politics, religion, and especially inner personal life. They have taken Jung as an authoritative guide who has pointed this "way." In so doing they have much in common with the humanists, firmly rejecting any suggestion that Jung was primarily Christian and emphasizing the universal applicability of his thought. Countering them are the anti-Jungians, usually Freudians, such as Ernest Jones (1955), Edward Glover (1956), and Philip Rieff (1966), all of whom see Jung as a truculent, malevolent meddler who tampered with Freud's pure science, converting it into an ersatz religion, a "theogonic" process. Two recent biographies of Jung have captured this extraordinary polarization regarding the significance of his work: Laurens Van der Post (1977) presents Jung's life as a contemporary hero's journey of the intellect, and Paul Stern (1976) portrays Jung as a small-minded, mean little man who hid behind an obscurantist vocabulary, was supported by wealthy but aimless Americans, and wrote for a confused, meaning-hungry public.

Very recently the classical or orthodox Jungian approaches to symbol and myth (Campbell, Neumann) and specifically to the psyche (Von Franz, Jacobi) have been augmented—perhaps I should say challenged—by the emergence of a new orientation within Jungian psychology. I refer to what has come to be called "archetypal psychology" (Hillman 1975; Miller 1974). This approach gives special attention to Jung's later writings, such as the alchemical texts, and emphasizes a plurality of selves and gods in the structure of the psyche. It represents a fresh stream of creative energy in the evolution of Jung's psychology, although it is too early to assess the precise nature of its lasting contribution. Its very presence, however, testifies further to the diverse and often contradictory character of the secondary literature on Jung.

Clearly Jung's work did possess the interests, ideas, themes, and characteristics that this literature of specialist appropriation exemplifies. No one can quarrel with such a view. But equally clear is the utterly contradictory character of these images of Jung. Taken as a whole and at face value, these writings describe a scene of total centerlessness. But this impression is due to the wholly non-contexual—really anticontextual—character of the literature: the question of derivation is "unthinkable" as long as one views Jung along such lines. Yet if one steps back from this literature, and for the moment from the question of internal consistency, and asks about context, the answers one obtains can "cue" a reassessment of whether there are consistent central, leading themes in Jung. The question of origins gives a very different picture of Jung's work as a whole.

It is instructive to compare the secondary literature on Freud in this regard, because scholarship on Freud is so much more advanced. Commentary by and on the psychoanalytic movement has gone through several stages. During the first phase, from its beginnings until the early 1940s, when it was establishing itself, psychoanalysis made vigorous interpretations of the major spheres of culture, and these interpretations were just as vigorously debated by the rightful occupants of these spheres. Owing to the novelty of psychoanalysis and the intensity of the claims and counterclaims of this debate, the central core of Freud's ideas remained obscure. Then in the 1950s and 1960s psychoanalysis underwent considerable inner develop-ment, and at the same time cultural criticism of it shifted away from emphasizing Freud's "position" on particular issues and toward at-tempting to understand the whole of the Freudian texts in relation to the whole of the Western past. Most recently, in its third phase, psychoanalysis continues its internal development but has also be-come interested in its own origins. And cultural criticism of psychoanalysis has also shifted away from total assessment and to-ward exploration of its historical and sociological origins.

The existing literature on Jung roughly parallels the first stage of the literature on Freud, the stage during which vigorous, sometimes acrimonious interpretations and counterinterpretations are made, and there is little effort to view the psychology as a whole, in its historical-cultural context or in terms of its origins. Just as this specialist appropriation eventually broke down for Freud's thought—as a result of the different perspective created by sustained familiarity, the passage of time, and persistent scholarship—it is also beginning to break down for Jung's. Even though the internal de-

velopment of Jung's psychology is in no sense as extensive or profound as the development of Freud's—Jung's psychology is younger
by twenty years—it has evolved enough so that new questions about
it are possible. And if the evolution of cultural commentary on
psychoanalysis is any guide (there is no reason to think it is not), one
can ask two questions unfamiliar to the current literature on Jung:
How are we to understand the origins, the formation, and the context
of Jung's ideas? And what is the significance of Jung's thought in
relation to Western culture?

In pursuing these questions I am not suggesting that Jung needs to
be "rediscovered." Nothing in this book seeks to defend the "Jungian" point of view. I simply argue that much of the sociological and
psychological literature on the origins of psychoanalysis and the
psychoanalytic movement can profitably be extended to Jung's life
and thought and that these tools, so alien to the secondary literature
on Jung, reveal a more complex, more accurate picture of his life and
work—in particular his relation to Freud and to Western Christianity.

In sum, the central thrust of this book is the creation of a contextual approach to the formation of Jung's psychological ideas—an
analysis of the psychobiographical, religious, and sociological factors as these are intertwined in the incredibly complex genesis of his
thought. This analysis, which constitutes the body of the book, is
contained in chapters 3 and 4 (psychobiographical factors), chapter 5
(religious factors), and chapter 6 (sociological factors). Jung's ideas
took their definitive shape over a period of roughly twenty years,
beginning in 1900 when he first entered medical practice and ending
in 1920, by which time he had undergone a major life crisis stimulated to a considerable extent by his early affection for and subsequent "break" with Freud. Contrary to most of the secondary
literature on Jung, I argue—and the evidence here is remarkably
clear—that the leading original ideas that make up Jung's psychology were consolidated at the end of this critical period; that they
were intimately related to Jung's personal experience at that time,
especially his relationship with Freud; and that they underwent little
significant change thereafter. Chapter 7 extends the contextual approach to its most far-reaching conclusion by discussing the major
themes in Jung's mature thought (from 1920 onward), demonstrating
that the formative forces structured or cued the particular contents of

his thought. In the concluding chapter 8 I return to the concept of psychological man as it has been developed here and reflect on it in the light of the contextual analysis.

Unlike most studies of Jung, which pass hastily over the formative period and Jung's personal experiences during it—especially his relationship with Freud—to dwell at length on the mature writings, my study analyzes in depth the personal dimensions of the formation of Jung's thought and accords far less attention to his mature work.

Because my major emphasis is upon the genesis of Jung's thought, particularly upon the role of personal experience in the genesis, and also because I attempt to order Jung's writings in relation to his personal experience, it is important to have a general overview of the relation between his life and his thought and also a clear understanding of the texts that constitute the basis for interpreting that relation. I will therefore begin by discussing the advantages, liabilities, and general nature of the materials employed in the ensuing contextual analysis.

# Two

## How to Read Jung

To disclose the forces that gave rise to an originative figure's key ideas, one must have at hand two fundamental sets of documents: the primary texts that are to be analyzed, and the theoretical frameworks used to interpret them. For Jung there are three primary texts: the *Collected Works;* his autobiography, entitled *Memories, Dreams, Reflections* (1961a); and his lengthy and intimate correspondence with Freud, the *Freud-Jung Letters* (McGuire 1974). These materials are rich and complex. At times their interrelation is strikingly clear, but frequently it is obscure, even conflicting. Not only is the relation among the several texts often confusing, but each text is in itself often obscure and therefore each work needs to be situated in some sort of overview. I shall therefore introduce two concepts that at this stage are only hypotheses: the concept of Jung's ''core process'' and the ''three themes'' of his mature thought.

All dynamic psychologies depict a type or paradigm of personal experience that I refer to as a ''core process,'' described by the central concepts of the psychological system in question. Freud's elaborate theories of the unconscious, of psychosexual development, of mechanisms of defense, and of methods of treatment, when taken together, isolate and describe a form of experience that he believed was fundamental to all experience. Harry Stack Sullivan's complex analysis of self-processes, with its highly idiosyncratic nomenclature, is another example. The same can be said of Carl Rogers's psychology: the self, experience denied to awareness, the necessity for the therapist to enter the client's internal frame of reference, the organismic valuing process—all go to disclose what Rogers sees as paradigmatic in both treatment and life.

Carl Jung's analytical psychology defines its core process in the most general sense as the process of individuation. It begins in a psychological context wherein the ego or center of consciousness is relatively untouched by the contents of the collective unconscious. Under these conditions, the ego is shaped largely by the persona or collective consciousness, a condition of rational or instrumental adaptation to social reality. The onset of individuation is marked by a weakening of the persona—of the relation of rational consciousness to daily life—and the subsequent appearance of archetypal images, most notably the shadow and the anima. As individuation continues, these archetypal images are, through interpretation, assimilated into the consciousness of the ego. Then, as a result of this assimilation, the self gradually comes into being, so that the ego and the contents of the collective unconscious achieve a balanced relationship. The achievement of individuation or true individuality is often accompanied by images of a quaternity or mandala, in dreams, fantasy, and imaginative productions.

The notion of the core process is, however, only the center or foreground of Jung's psychological thought. Although it is present in virtually every mature essay or book he wrote, it does not of itself clarify his writings beyond a certain point. It must be seen in relation to the broader ranges of his thought as well. The core process is really a frame of interpretation that Jung continually applied to specific phenomena, largely cultural in character. It is true that Jung's interests seem boundless, but they are only apparently so. I suggest that throughout his mature thought Jung applied his core process primarily to three major areas: to clinical work, which included his estimate of Freud's psychoanalysis; to religion—in particular to the Christian religion and Christian dogma—and to the problem of modernity or contemporaneity. I call these three areas the three major themes of the mature Jung. The core process and the "three themes" together give form to Jung's massive and, it seems, endlessly varied writings. Accordingly, the question of how Jung's thought was formed can be posed as follows: When did the core process take shape? In what personal circumstances did it emerge? Were there early anticipations and later developments of it? And how and where in his writings did Jung apply the core process to the three themes?

The eighteen volumes of the *Collected Works* present a formidable challenge even to the most ambitious and willing student. The *Standard Edition* of Freud's works is in strict chronological order, and so the reader can follow, step by step, the development of Freud's ideas. Nor is it particularly disconcerting to find clinical and nonclinical discussions close together—such was the genius of Freud and the nature of his psychoanalysis. On the other hand, the editors of the *Collected Works* felt a conflict between a strict chronological ordering of Jung's works and an ordering by subject matter. Their solution—to be guided by what they have called (rather vaguely, I think) Jung's "interests"—has produced a corpus that only generally follows chronological development and that contains some strategic exceptions. But the variety of subject matter in Jung's writings was not the editors' only problem. What is equally confusing about the *Collected Works* is Jung's relentless penchant for seemingly endless revision of the works he deemed most valuable. Just where, chronologically, does one place a work that has been revised—especially if it has been revised more than once? And, if one prints the revision, what does one do with the original? Although the arrangement of the *Collected Works* is ostensibly sensitive to chronology, it at times obscures the development of Jung's thought—even sometimes the fact that it had a development—and makes some of the correlations between his personal experience and the unfolding of his ideas difficult, though not impossible, to establish.

In his autobiography Jung gave an interesting overview of the major stages of his life and their relation to his thought, and there is no reason we should not accept it, at least in its most general and comprehensive sense, as have biographers both friendly and hostile to Jung (Hannah 1976; Ellenberger 1970; Jaffe 1972; Stern 1976). Jung spoke of his early years, his student years, his university years (which included medical training), his early psychiatric activities at the Burghölzli Mental Hospital, his years of collaboration with Freud, and then a period of personal, inner crisis following the famous break with Freud, a period he described as "confrontation with the unconscious." Jung believed that this critical period of painful loneliness coincided with the production of his unique psychological ideas. The rest of his life was spent, he said, in refining these ideas and applying them to cultural phenomena.

By combining Jung's descriptions of the major phases of his life with the conceptions of the core process and the three themes, it is possible to order the *Collected Works*. According to this schema, the first three volumes, respectively entitled *Psychiatric Studies* (1970a), *Experimental Researches* (1973a), and *The Psychogenesis of Mental Disease* (1972), belong to his period of early psychiatric activities. The fourth volume, *Freud and Psychoanalysis* (1961b), represents Jung's intellectual work during his collaboration with Freud. The fifth, *Symbols of Transformation* (1967a), is, as I shall show later, a transitional work that is more anti-Freudian than genuinely Jungian in content. The major ideas in volume 7, *Two Essays on Analytical Psychology* (1966a), were conceived in 1916 and 1917, during Jung's crisis period, although their final dates are 1943 and 1928. The ideas produced during the crisis period were consolidated— indeed, they were cataloged—in volume 6, *Psychological Types* (1971), originally published in 1921. The essence of the core process lies in these last two works.

The rest of Jung's writings (volumes 9–18) contain very little that is new in the sense of originative psychological ideas, but rather consist of refinements of the core process and applications of it to various therapeutic and cultural phenomena, which I call the three themes. Volume 8, and volume 9, parts 1 and 2, respectively entitled *The Structure and Dynamics of the Psyche* (1960), *The Archetypes and the Collective Unconscious* (1959a), and *Aion* (1959b), consist of essays in which the core process is further embellished, refined, and deepened. In volume 10, *Civilization in Transition* (1964a), Jung applied the core process to the view of modern man as mass man living in a mass society. In volume 11, *Psychology and Religion: West and East* (1963a), he interpreted the Christian tradition in the light of the core process. Volumes 16 and 17, *The Practice of Psychotherapy* (1954) and *The Development of Personality* (1964b), apply the core process to clinical and developmental phenomena, and in these we find Jung's persistent criticism of Freud. Volume 15

(1966*b*) contains several essays on art and literature and two important papers on Freud. And the volumes on alchemy, volumes 12 (1953), 13 (1967*b*), and 14 (1970*b*), constitute the final phase of Jung's work, through which he was able to find an intellectual movement in history that anticipated his own ideas—anticipated, that is, the core process.

This breakdown of Jung's *Collected Works* and their correlation with major periods in his life, however valid it may be in a broad sense, is confusing at several important points. And titling each volume as if it were a self-contained—indeed, almost timeless—work, combined with Jung's penchant for revisions, has at points obscured the way the development of his work relates to his personal experience. For example, *Symbols of Transformation,* volume 5 of the *Collected Works,* published in 1967, was originally published in 1912, when Jung's relation to Freud had become increasingly complex and conflicted. Jung has repeatedly said that the contents of this book—his ideas about the libido and his theory of religion—were the source of his break with Freud. The letters contain extensive reference to the 1912 version, and the two must be read closely together. The 1967 version (the "official" version of *Symbols of Transformation*) is an extensive revision in which the mature Jung thoroughly reinterpreted the 1912 text in the light of the core process, which was, as we have noted, formulated in the crisis period 1913 to 1918, after the original version was published. Hence the 1967 text tells us nothing about Jung's thought at the crucial time when he was beginning to differ significantly from Freud. The 1912 version, which tells us a great deal about his thought at this time, does not appear in the *Collected Works.* The original version has, however, been translated into English (Jung 1965). It is a key text in the study of the formation of Jung's ideas, for when it is read in conjunction with the correspondence with Freud it sheds great light not only upon Jung's intellectual orientation at the time, but also upon his personal and psychological condition. Oddly enough, the 1912 version is rarely studied, even by Jungians. All my references to *Symbols of Transformation* are therefore to the English translation of the original version (1965).

Similar circumstances limit access to the key ideas constituting the core process, found in the famous *Two Essays on Analytical*

*Psychology* (1966*a*), published in 1966 as volume 7 of the *Collected Works*. The first version of the first essay was published in 1912 and is included in the volume just mentioned. But a 1917 revision (the second of several), written toward the end of the crisis period, contains for the first time the bulk of Jung's truly original ideas. Although a much later revision was published in the *Collected Works*, the crucial 1917 version is not included. However, it too has been translated into English (Jung 1917). The very important paper "The Transcendent Function" (1958) described for the first time the essence of Jungian psychotherapy. Like the already-mentioned version of the first of the *Two Essays*, this document was completed in the midst of Jung's critical period, in the year 1916. But it is buried in volume 8 of the *Collected Works*, in which all the other papers date from 1926.

The organization of the *Collected Works* also somewhat obscures the origins of the "three themes" in Jung's writings. As I will argue in detail below, these themes were first experienced as tensions or intellectual forces that—stimulated by contact with Freud—contributed to the formation of the core process. Once the core process was formed, Jung turned back to these tensions—Freud's psychoanalysis, the Christian tradition, and the view of modern man as mass man—and interpreted them. The essay entitled "The Role of the Unconscious" contains Jung's first consolidated effort to interpret cultural phenomena in the light of the core process. Because it was written in 1918, while Jung was still struggling with his critical experience, it testifies to the intimate relation between these themes and tensions and the core process. However, the essay appears in *Civilization in Transition*, volume 10 of the *Collected Works*, (1964*a*), whereas all the other papers in this volume belong to the later period of mature production.

Just as the organization of the *Collected Works* both supports and distorts a clear understanding of the formation of Jung's psychological system, so does the autobiography support and distort the role of his personal experience. *Memories, Dreams, Reflections* (1961*a*) is a vital document for such a study, but it is also an extremely ambiguous text and must be treated accordingly. Two recent biographies, by Hannah (1976) and by Stern (1976), both based substantially upon the autobiography, have created entirely dissimilar portraits of

Jung's life—the first demonstrating that Jung's thought flows unin-
terruptedly from his sensitive and profound emotional life, the second asserting that his thought is to a considerable extent a massive
defense against intrapsychic and interpersonal conflicts. What can be
said about the value and limitations of this document?

At one level this text gives a rough and very general overview of
the objective circumstances of Jung's life. In this sense its fundamental value lies in its division of his life into several stages, which I
have already identified. But this is not its central importance. Jung
remarked in its prologue that all memories of outer circumstances
paled before the facts of his inner life. The autobiography is the more
remarkable for its impoverishment in the sphere of external life and
for its rich and detailed portrayal of Jung's inner life: the emotional
tone and the fantasies, dreams, and visions of his early childhood and
adolescence; his sharp feelings about his father and mother; the intense emotionality and vivid imagery of his personal experience of
religion; his personal reactions to Freud; and, perhaps most important of all, the inner details of his critical period of anguish, loneliness, and creativity after his break with Freud and its role in the
formation of his truly original ideas. In all this the autobiography
offers a rich harvest to one studying the psychological origins of
Jung's thought.

But there are equally strong reasons to be wary in approaching this
book. It was written entirely from the standpoint of Jungian psychology: hardly an experience does not receive a Jungian interpretation.
Jung and his editor, Aniela Jaffe, even found it necessary to include
an elaborate glossary of complex Jungian terminology. The implication is clear: Jung's experiences are to be interpreted in terms of the
technicalities of Jungian psychology. While all autobiography involves self-interpretation, this document is less an autobiography in
the conventional sense than a special genre of its own—what I would
call "automythology." Indeed, Jung referred to it as his search for a
"personal myth."

Other features stand out. We might expect such a document to be
poor in outer detail: Jung was in his early eighties when he wrote and
dictated the book; he was extremely introspective all his life; and
Jungian psychology is an extremely introspective system of ideas.
Still, does this really account for the remarkable fact that only three

personal relationships in Jung's entire life are discussed in detail—
his relations to his father, his mother, and Freud? Jung does not
describe his relation to his sister (except to note her birth and death in
a coldly detached manner); to friends of his childhood and adolescence; to colleagues during his early or later professional years; to his
wife; to his mistress and collaborator, Toni Wolff; or to his children
and friends during his mature years. Yet we know from other sources
that Jung had active friendships as a university student, during his
professional work both before and during the psychoanalytic years,
and later in life as well. Despite these limitations, it is still possible to
use the autobiography at length to reconstruct the relation between
personal experience and theory formation. A key stabilizing resource
for this task lies in the correspondence with Freud, which was
completed before Jung devised his core process during his crisis
years.

The correspondence between Freud and Jung (McGuire 1974)
consists of 359 letters the two men exchanged during the period 1906
to 1914.[1] They portray in great detail the turmoil, excitement, and
innovation that occurred during a decisive phase of the psychoanalytic movement. And while these letters also contain considerable important information about the intellectual development of the theories
of both Freud and Jung at the time, they primarily provide the
psychologically attuned reader with a rich sequence of glimpses into
the emotional lives of the two men. This dimension of the correspondence is enhanced because the development of psychoanalytic
thinking is itself an intensely introspective process, in which new
ideas and inner experiences are necessarily closely interrelated in the
same person. Thus, when the two pioneers of the early phase of the
psychoanalytic movement chose to share their thoughts, they shared
not only these ideas but also the feelings each had about himself, and
this led to sharing the feelings they had about each other. So the
letters must be read at different levels: the intellectual level of
Freud's ideas and Jung's ideas; and the level of Freud's emotions,
Jung's emotions, and their emotional interaction as each man interpreted it. But there is a third level, that of retrospective psychological
reflection: there were factors in the relationship of which neither was

1. One final letter was written in 1923.

aware, but which we, from the vantage point of today and with more refined psychological tools, can discern in it. Forces at this level are not self-evident in the correspondence and therefore demand interpretation.

It is common knowledge that Freud believed Jung emotionally resisted his sexual theory and fled from it into religion; equally well known is Jung's view that Freud was emotionally overattached to his sexual theory and thus made a dogma of it. These views belong to the respective lore of the two ''camps'' and to the first two levels of the correspondence. There is indisputable truth to these views. But the letters also reveal an entirely new dimension that accounts for the intimacy of the relationship between the two men—at first intensely positive, then bitterly negative. And, with regard to Jung, they also provide evidence for a view that other sources do not suggest—that from Jung's vantage point Freud, the only person treated in detail in the autobiography besides Jung's parents, not only was central during the so-called psychoanalytic years but also played a key part, unbeknown to both men, in the subsequent formation of Jung's mature thought. This extremely complex effect and ''aftereffect'' of Freud on Jung (the reverse is also true, but to a lesser degree) sheds light on how personal experience shaped Jung's thought and accords the letters a privileged position among the primary texts.

Because the *Collected Works* at times obscures the line of development of Jung's ideas, because the autobiography is at best an ambiguous document, and because the correspondence with Freud has extraordinarily subtle psychological ramifications, without interpretation none of these sources—essential as they are—can alone clarify the effect of personal experience on Jung's original psychological ideas. No effort has yet been made to define the relation between these disparate but obviously related materials. They must be taken together and supplemented by comprehensive theoretical frameworks, neither classically Freudian nor classically Jungian. Then it will be possible to gain distance and understanding and not only to undercut the tiresome, polarized claims of the Freudian-Jungian debate but to disclose knowledge that the debate has obscured.

To accomplish this task I begin by setting forth three psychobiographical theories—those of Henri Ellenberger, Erik Erikson, and

Heinz Kohut. None of these theories is strictly Freudian in the classic sense. Each has been applied to Freud's creative period, and Ellenberger's has been applied to Jung as well. These theories serve as "grids" that coordinate the *Collected Works,* the autobiography, and the *Letters* and in doing so help us understand the psychological origins of Jung's thought.

# Three

## Psychological Factors in the Formation of Jung's Thought: The First Three Phases, 1900-1913

### Prologue: Three Psychobiographical Hypotheses

Henri Ellenberger's Concept of "Creative Illness"

Ellenberger's massive study *The Discovery of the Unconscious* (1970) centers upon the history and evolution of dynamic psychology from its origins in Mesmerism at the end of the eighteenth century to the consolidation of dynamic psychiatry at the end of World War II. In the midst of this rich panorama he gives extensive attention to Freud and Jung, for he believes that their lives and thought illustrate with special forcefulness his central thesis: that the origins of dynamic psychiatry are to be found not in scientific-experimental advancement of historically transmitted ideas—what I have called the ideational or systematic approach to the origins of psychological ideas—but in what he calls a "creative illness."

While Ellenberger's vision of the rise of dynamic psychiatry is immensely rich in historical detail, his concept of creative illness actually is rather easy to formulate. In every case the following events occur: the illness begins with an intense preoccupation with a single idea or a search for a single truth; it is accompanied by symptoms of emotional and sometimes physical illness such as depression, psychosomatic ailments, even psychotic productions; and in some cases there is a need for a mentor or guide. The individual thus isolates himself from his social world and undergoes an intense inner experience that forces him to create self-imposed techniques and exercises to reduce his symptoms. The illness terminates with the appearance of a new vision of truth that the now-creative individual feels obliged to communicate to the world, a new sense of euphoria or psychic well-being and energy for work, and a new intellectual movement inspired by the new ideas and infused by the new energies.

Ellenberger believes that Freud underwent such a creative illness. In the latter part of the 1890s he was intensely preoccupied with the problem of neurosis and unconscious motivation. During this period he suffered from heart symptoms, shortness of breath, and brooding depression. He developed an intense relationship with one man, Fliess, but was otherwise greatly isolated from his social world. These conditions produced his self-analysis, resulting in the development of techniques for analyzing his own dreams and other mental productions. Freud's illness terminated in 1900 with the publication of his *Interpretation of Dreams,* which contained the foundations for the new science of psychoanalysis. He also felt a sense of personal exhilaration that gave him the energy to take steps for himself and to lead his new movement.

Jung's situation as described in the autobiography was very similar to Freud's. Shortly after his break with Freud, Jung became intensely preoccupied with the nature of the unconscious. He withdrew from the psychoanalytic movement and from his teaching at the University of Zurich. His imagination was flooded with disturbing dreams, fantasies, and visions. Under their pressure he derived techniques for their analysis and interpretation—for translating them from the unconscious into consciousness. Gradually he emerged from his "experiment" equipped with the major ideas of his new science, analytical psychology. By 1919 he was the head of a new school of psychology, had acquired an international reputation, and was infused with a need for activity. From his "journey" into the unconscious he came back with enough material for the rest of a life's work.

Ellenberger's analysis of the creation of Jung's psychological ideas gives a broad overview for speculating about possible correlations between the inner events reported in the autobiography and the development of Jung's thought in the *Collected Works.* Beyond this, however, it lacks specificity at important points. Ellenberger does not recognize the importance of Jung's relationship with Freud in the process and outcome of Jung's creative illness. He wrote his book before the correspondence between the two men was available to him. He also ignores Jung's painful relationship with his parents, his emotional impoverishment in childhood, and the role religion played in the actual forming of his psychological ideas. Moreover, he does not build specific linkages between experiences in the critical period and the texts in which the new ideas were first articulated.

### Erik Erikson's Concepts of "Psychological Discovery" and "Identity"

Historians of psychoanalysis, often but by no means always working within the psychoanalytic tradition itself, have produced a rich and now widely read literature analyzing the personal aspects of that period in Freud's life during which he produced his key originative ideas in *The Interpretation of Dreams*. Erik Erikson's contribution to this literature (1964) is of central importance for our discussion of Jung, because he provides categories of analysis applicable to figures besides Freud, and also because his psychology asks questions that give specificity to Ellenberger's generalizations. Hence I have drawn on Erikson's analysis of Freud rather than on his better-known general discussions of identity-formation.

Erikson refers to this period in Freud's life as a time of "psychological discovery." During this time Freud was beset simultaneously by crises in three different areas, and his original ideas emerged as he responded to these crises in an innovatively integrative way. Freud underwent a crisis in therapeutic technique, a crisis in his conceptualization of clinical experience, and a personal crisis. The cumulative resolution of these three crises eventuated in his major psychological discoveries and in his personal identity as "the first psychoanalyst."

As a medical doctor at the end of the nineteenth century, Freud had inherited the work techniques of the "cult of the paternal male"—the role of the all-knowing father-physician whose task it was to explain to his patients the nature of their illness and to prescribe a cure. But in his therapeutic work Freud gradually allowed himself to focus more and more on the possibility that the causes of his patients' distress were unknown or, if known, then known first to them, not to him. He found it necessary to abandon his role as omniscient doctor and surrender to the possibility that hidden meanings were embedded in his patients' communications. His readiness to do this made it possible for him to conceive of a new, essentially psychological stance toward his patients. This stance forced him to put aside the cathartic and suggestive methods, and he discovered a new therapeutic role, that "evenly hovering attention" that was to be the key to all further psychoanalytic inquiry.

A crisis in therapeutic technique could not be separated from a crisis in the conceptualization of clinical experience. Freud began with the neurological model of his day, which emphasized quantities of mental energy, and he spoke of these in a mechanical way, as can easily be seen in the "Project." Freud began to believe, however, that the mechanical model was not adequate to the kind of phenomena he was observing, and, when combined with the exigencies of clinical investigation, this belief forced him to abandon the quantitative model and devise a new conceptual system. Thus he began to think in such terms as "libido," "psychosexuality," and "psychical reality" and finally formulated the key to all this new thinking, the universal unconscious itself.

These two crises coincided with a third, in his personal life, centering on his relation to his friend, the Berlin physician Wilhelm Fliess. It was a relationship of overestimation and dependency, in which Freud confided both personal and professional thoughts. As he did so he gradually discovered some of his personal conflicts and was able to further work out his intellectual questionings. In this relationship Freud first recognized his own father transference to Fliess and subsequently his infantile relationship to his mother. Then, combining these, he discovered the oedipal complex and recognized it as a dominant theme in literature and mythology throughout the world. It is possible to think of these three dimensions of psychological discovery as a threefold crisis in the spheres of work, thought, and person, all interrelated in the life of a creative individual. According to Erikson, Freud's resolution of these three crises had the cumulative effect of consolidating a new sense of personal identity.

Erikson's analysis of Freud's creative crisis can be extended, with appropriate modifications, to the formation of Jung's ideas. Jung too underwent a threefold crisis. While his thought was being formed, from 1900 to 1920, he went through a series of formidable intellectual changes, which then culminated in his unique system of psychological ideas. But these changes at the intellectual level were accompanied by a personal crisis that centered largely on his relationship with Freud. And both of these changes were inseparable from shifts in work techniques: Jung was first trained in experimental and descriptive psychiatry; then he became a psychoanalyst; then, finally, he developed his own special therapeutic techniques. For Jung as for Freud, therefore, there was an interplay between the dimensions of thought, person, and work, all of which were resolved during a crisis period. It is thus possible to interpret the critical period as a time of breakdown and rebuilding of identity, composed of a struggle to reintegrate the three dimensions of psychological discovery.

Erikson's schema allows us to ask another question: If Freud had a special transference relationship during his creative crisis, was Jung's relationship to Freud also based on transference? There is considerable evidence for the view that the oedipal drama accounts for their initial rapport and for the final breakdown of the relationship. Not only did Freud expressly understand Jung's relationship to himself this way, Jung too accepted it and dutifully struggled with his "father complex"—as the letters clearly state. Furthermore, the two most important historians of the psychoanalytic movement, Ernest Jones (1955) and Paul Roazen (1975), have used this psychological framework to interpret the Freud-Jung relationship, although their conclusions regarding the role of each man in the struggle are quite different.

The psychological forces in the Freud-Jung relationship were not, however, entirely those of the regressive transference neurosis of classic psychoanalysis: rivalry with a father figure, jealousy, aggressivity, rebelliousness against authority, competitiveness, guilt, and frustrated object love. In addition there were the themes of narcissism: the self and its objects; empathy and its absence; self-esteem, shame, and inferiority; idealization and grandiosity; and the desire for and fear of psychic merger. The Freud-Jung relationship was a transference, but it was a narcissistic transference. This hypothesis, which I shall develop first in relation to the correspondence, also sheds great light upon Jung's childhood experiences and upon his psychological condition and intellectual development after the break with Freud.

## Heinz Kohut's Psychology of Narcissism

According to Kohut (1975), psychoanalysis stands at a crucial point in its development, and this is related to the psychology of narcissism. Freud and his immediate followers have done their work. They have created careful, detailed elaborations of the core process of psychoanalysis. But the historical evolution of the theory now faces a fundamental challenge. Since Freud's presence no longer pervades the psychoanalytic movement, contemporary theorists and practitioners must decide whether they will remain attached to the personal aura and formulations of its originator or whether—under the stimulus of new clinical problems and new cultural conditions—they will be imbued with a fresh sense of initiative and new ideals.

Freud held several attitudes that the analyst of today need not adopt in order to be faithful to the essentials of his discipline; each of these involves a more forthright engagement of the problem of narcissism and its associated process, empathy. When Freud urged analysts to model themselves after surgeons, putting aside all feelings, even sympathy, he gave expression to a time-bound necessity for the early practitioner. Also, Freud believed that narcissism and object love were inversely related, thereby inadvertently supporting the suspicion that all narcissistic organization is pathological. Freud faced irrational criticism from a hypocritical and high-minded Christian morality and consequently felt he needed to unmask religion. But today's analyst need not assume this attitude in his work. Furthermore, Freud had need to keep an emotional distance from the insane; but this specific attitude does not belong to the intrinsic value system of psychoanalysis. It is of great importance that on all these points Jung strongly criticized Freud; but this observation needs careful clarification.

Easily as important as the bias against narcissism in the early psychoanalytic movement is the cultural climate of today. For Kohut (1972), contemporary life harbors a pervasive attitude that is unfavorable to the acceptance of narcissism as a healthy and approvable psychological constellation. Our deeply ingrained Western value

systems, by extolling altruism and disparaging egoism and concern
for oneself, encourage contempt toward the powerful narcissistic
forces in everyday life, thereby reducing the possibilities of self-
control and social adaptation. The hypocrisy toward narcissism that
pervades life today resembles the hypocrisy toward sexuality in
Victorian times.

While Kohut is critical of classic Freudianism at certain points and
sensitive to the cultural situation of today, he is neither simply a
psychologically attuned social critic nor a revisionist. The psychology of narcissism (Kohut 1971) attempts to clarify a problem Freud
himself introduced but did not explicate fully or clearly. This
psychology is a psychology of the self, which may be defined as the
locus of valuing and esteem-formation—of esteem for the self and
esteem given over to others.

Following Freud's metapsychology, Kohut portrays early
psychosexual development as occurring in three stages: a stage of
autoeroticism or primary narcissism, in which self and other are
undifferentiated; the stage of narcissism proper, wherein a cohesive
self and a definite sense of the externality of objects begins to form;
then the oedipal stage in which ego and object love become realities.
Kohut's work attempts to clarify the second stage, the stage of narcissism. What distinguishes his work from Freud's, and accounts for
his criticism of Freud, is his conviction that narcissism follows an
independent line of development: the sphere of object relations and
the sphere of object love exist side by side, and, further, the narcissistic organization persists into adult life and fuels it with energy.
Just as the oedipal stage appears in the dramas of romance and
enmity in historical movements, art, and religion, so also do the
themes of self-esteem and valued others.

Hence the psychology of the self, addressed to the early stages of
the self's intimacy with others, is crucial to understanding such introspective, like-minded, and creative men as Freud and Jung. As Kohut
tellingly notes, when a man enters a phase of creativity, he with-
draws from his love relations and centers his energies upon the
self—in other words, he reenters the stage of narcissism. Here we
already have an important clue to the psychological meaning of
Jung's break with Freud and of his thought processes at this time.

Although our goal is knowledge of how these infantile stages—in a modified form—intrude upon adult life in the shape of narcissistic transferences, it is important to have some knowledge of their developmental vicissitudes. In the first stage of development (primary narcissism), the baby experiences the mother and her ministrations not as "you" independent of himself but from within a view of the world in which the I-you differentiation has not yet been established (Kohut 1966, pp. 245–46). He is in a state of infantile bliss and perfection. This equilibrium, however, is unavoidably disturbed by the inevitable shortcomings of maternal care. Hence the baby develops a new twofold system of perfection: he replaces the earlier perfection with a grandiose image of himself (the beginnings of a coherent self) and a powerfully idealized parent imago (the beginnings of a sense of "the other"). But because the separation is at first not complete, the grandiose self experiences the idealized parent imago as part of itself—a condition Kohut refers to as the experience of the other as a "self-object"—as part of oneself.

Under optimal conditions of child care, in which parental empathy is tempered by the demands of reality, a transmutation of the narcissistic stage occurs. Grandiosity in the self undergoes gradual disappointment and taming, so that the child begins to develop a wholesome and realistic sense of self-esteem and self-enjoyment. And, in the sphere of the idealized other, the parent imago gradually becomes internalized in the form of mature ideals, goals, and visions of what reality ought to be.

If trauma intervenes and the child's narcissistic needs are not gradually embraced and tamed, however, the wish for an idealized, powerful parent imago will become split off or repressed, as will the child's grandiosity. Both will persist unresolved into later life, producing a variety of symptoms: feelings of emptiness and despair, feelings that one is not fully real, excessive self-consciousness and feelings of inferiority (depletion of the self), or an intense and persistent desire to merge with a powerful source of self-esteem. Lack of interest in sex, work inhibitions, inability to sustain significant relationships, moments of uncontrollable rage, lack of humor and empathy, and hypochondria are also common.

One consequence of the failure to integrate the grandiose self is of special importance for our effort to understand the Freud-Jung relationship. Kohut believes that "a persistently active grandiose self, with its delusional claims, may severely incapacitate an ego of average endowment. A gifted person's ego, however, may well be pushed to the use of its utmost capacities and thus to a realistic outstanding performance, by the demands of the grandiose fantasies of a persistent, poorly modified grandiose self'' (1971, pp. 108–9). Kohut also believes that the narcissistic organization is neither ill nor evil, for a special talent for empathic perception is related to narcissistic problems—an observation applicable to Freud and Jung, who in their professional lives, though not always with each other, displayed profound capacities for empathy.

Like the oedipal disorders, the narcissistic disorders also produce transferences. In fact, the presence of a narcissistic transference permits the best differential diagnosis for distinguishing these personalities from the pathology of the borderline and schizophrenic conditions. Persons beset by these latter conditions do not possess the outlines of a cohesive self and hence cannot form a transference relationship. In narcissistic disorders, with a properly empathic analyst, one of two types (or even a mix of the two types) of transference occurs. On the one hand there is the therapeutic reactivation of the omnipotent object—of the idealized parent imago. The patient experiences the analyst as the sum of psychic perfection he once attributed to the idealized parent. Kohut calls this the ''idealizing transference.'' On the other hand there is the ''mirror transference,'' wherein the grandiose self is reactivated and the analyst is experienced as an extension of the self, producing a condition of psychic merger or, in less intense forms, of twinship or alter ego. As we shall soon see, the Freud-Jung relationship was fraught with the language of idealization and merger, and these powerful emotions, when interrupted by complex intellectual factors, caused the breakdown of the relationship between the two men and accounted in large part for their subsequent lifelong animosity.

Even a brief description of Kohut's analysis of the treatment process is out of place here, since Freud and Jung did not attempt to work analytically with each other—although on their trip to America they did briefly analyze each other's dreams and Freud did from time to time offer soothing, echoing responses to Jung's reports of his inner turmoil. But since we do wish to assess the process by which, and the extent to which, Jung extricated himself from his transference to Freud, we should note that Kohut believes that the internal transformations of growth consist in strengthening ideals (resolving the idealizing transference) and transforming the grandiose self into realistic self-esteem. Jung did undergo such transformations in his lonely, critical period, but he did so in extremely complex and ambiguous ways: he created his own unique thought system (the sphere of ideals), and he formed a threefold identity of himself as therapist, as moralist and social critic, and as prophet (the sphere of self-esteem).

In applying the psychology of narcissism to the Freud-Jung association, I am not simply reducing the relationship to its pathography; indeed, the dilemmas of narcissism feed into the central psychological dilemmas of the most fully human aspects of adult life. But several additional transformations of narcissism exist alongside the strengthening of values and self-esteem. Empathy is a transformation of narcissism: it refers to one's ability to discern others' basic inner experiences that are similar to one's own. Like empathy, creativity is also related to narcissism—it is the capacity to be empathic to one's innermost unique, productive experiences. The presence of humor connotes the capacity to view the grandiosity of the self from a wider frame of reference. And wisdom relates the self and its newly won perspective upon itself to the transience of cherished ideals and objects and, most important, to its own transience. We want to know the extent to which Jung, particularly after his critical years of aloneness and originality, both achieved and did not achieve these virtues.

The *Collected Works,* when placed in proper chronological order, give a clear picture of the development and transformations of Jung's thought. The autobiography provides rich introspective material scattered throughout his life. And the *Letters* record in great detail Jung's inner processes during the years with Freud. Although they cover only part of the period when Jung's thought was taking shape, the *Letters,* as will be amply shown, provide the fundamental psychological evidence for basic insight into Jung's personality. Unlike the autobiography, they trace a close relationship over a period of time, not reinterpreted in the light of Jung's core process.

For these reasons it makes sense to treat first the formation of Jung's thought—linked so closely to Freud's person, work, and ideas—and to analyze its relation to the letters, using supplementary material wherever possible. This analysis provides the basic psychological argument. Then, with some firm evidence in hand, we can undertake retrospective reflection upon Jung's early years, and especially upon the way religion shaped his thought. In one sense this procedure mars the developmental continuity of Jung's life. But in another, psychological sense it is more appropriate to begin with the years when his ideas were developing, after his personality was already well formed; to draw conclusions about this phase; then to reflect retrospectively on the early years. By good fortune, the nature of the materials supports this procedure. The correspondence with Freud says so much about the adult Jung and his thought that we can use it as a source of insight for its own time, then generalize backward into the earlier years and forward into the crisis years—phases of Jung's life that are only episodically covered by the autobiography. This exploration is far more circumscribed, of course, than would be the conventional "life and thought," for which there is insufficient evidence.

## The First Phase: Anticipations of Freud and the Early Professional Years, 1900–1907

Jung's psychological thought took shape over almost twenty years (1900–1918), a major segment of his middle life. Jung has reported that throughout his childhood and adolescence he was beset by painful and primitive fantasies, by introspective musings, and by struggles with religion. But when he entered adult life these states had, at least for the time being, lost their hold upon him. He became an active and energetic young psychiatrist, though without any ideas of his own. After the period when Jung produced his original ideas, his inner life was under the constant interpretive control of his unique psychological thought. He became the leader of a new school of psychology and was on his way to becoming internationally known as a moralist and social critic. He interpreted the nature of modernity to his contemporaries and, in the process, reinterpreted his own Christian tradition. The key to this transformation lies in the formative period.

During these twenty years Jung went through an extraordinary series of intellectual changes. He began his work as a research psychiatrist at the Burghölzli Hospital in Zurich (first phase) and wrote papers along lines already established by the disciplines of clinical and research psychiatry. Then his writings shifted and became openly psychoanalytic in character (second phase) as his acquaintance with Freud deepened and then became strained. There followed a transitional period (third phase) during which Jung criticized Freud but nonetheless continued to depend heavily upon his ideas. At the end of this period he broke entirely with Freud, both intellectually and personally. Then Jung entered his fourth and final phase, the critical period—a time of great personal and intellectual complexity. His inner life became increasingly turbulent, and toward the end of the phase he constructed his unique new system of ideas. In all this the figure of Freud looms far larger than previous scholarship has led us to believe.

Jung entered the professional world of clinical and research psychiatry and began to work within the approaches others made available to him. This phase began with the publication of his medical dissertation, *On the Psychology and Pathology of So-called Occult Phenomena* (1902); was filled out by twenty-two papers on clinical psychiatry, word association experiments, and the new orientations of Freud, Janet, and Binet (Freud's principal works known to Jung at this time were the *Studies on Hysteria* and *The Interpretation of Dreams*); and concluded in 1907 with his much-heralded—at the time—monograph on schizophrenia, *The Psychology of Dementia Praecox* (1907). All these works demonstrate that Jung easily absorbed the literature of his field but was also capable of making contributions to it. At the beginning of the period Freud was one of several innovative figures whom Jung, as a young man beginning a new profession, felt might contribute to his work. By the end of the period he considered Freud the single outstanding investigator.

The psychiatry of the time classified patients' states of consciousness according to previously established descriptions of disease entities. Thus these doctors spoke of such diagnostic states as hereditary inferiority, epilepsy, neurasthenia, and hysteria. In his medical dissertation Jung took up the problem of somnambulistic states—dreamlike states, bizarre acts, visions, hallucinations, and lapses of memory. To understand these phenomena he drew on writers like Janet and hypothesized an unconscious or subconscious personality, concluding that ideas that were once in consciousness sink below its threshold and through dissociation go on working in the unconscious. The subject thus attempts to mediate between two subconscious personalities and represses one of them; but these thoughts lead an independent existence. Toward the end of this study Jung wondered whether these processes were identical to Freud's concept of repressed thoughts. Thus, in his earliest work he postulated the concept of the unconscious and drew, tentatively, upon Freud's analysis of its fundamental mechanism, repression.

In the papers that immediately followed, Jung pursued this problem and so moved closer to Freud's theories. Writing on such varied topics as simulated insanity (1903), hysterical misreading (1904), cryptomnesia (1905a), and the nature of memory (1905b), he spoke more and more frequently of Breuer and Freud, of the Freudian mechanism of repressed affect, of Freud's theory of hysteria, of an unconscious mind and its repression, of free association as a link between conscious and unconscious, and of the relation of all of these to dreams and symptoms. By 1904 Jung had established a laboratory to develop research on the word association test. The examiner read a list of words to the subject, who was instructed to reply as quickly as possible with the first word that occurred to him. The examiner noted the word and the reaction time. By 1906 Jung had written papers stating that the psychological processes revealed by the word association test were identical with those Freud had described in his theories of the unconscious, repression, dreams, and hysteria (Jung 1906).

In addition to giving experimental proof to Freud's theories, Jung added a concept of his own—the complex. He said a complex was a feeling-toned idea or train of thought. There was an ego complex— our conscious state of mind—and there were also morbid or repressed complexes, often sexual. In hysteria a conscious complex split off from the ego complex and became an unconscious complex. Jung also began at this time to defend Freud. He spoke of the need for attention to the doctor's mental condition that Freud's methods presupposed, and he would often add that the new technique took patience. Jung's perception of the introspective, self-reflective character of psychoanalysis was unique for its day.

Jung's monograph on schizophrenia (1907) synthesized in an impressive and commanding way the major interests of his first phase—his clinical work, which had come to focus more and more upon hysteria, his work on the word association test, his interest in Freud's theories of the unconscious, hysteria, and dreams, his own concept of the complex, and his researches on schizophrenia, although he had not previously published on this last subject. The book was really a general theory of psychopathology. The foreword is dated July 1906, indicating that the work was complete before Jung's first letter to Freud in October. In the foreword Jung praised Freud, asserted that only those who had, like himself, used his methods could judge Freud, and concluded by likening the greatness of Freud's psychoanalysis to that of Galileo's telescope.

Jung began by summarizing the existing research on hysteria and dementia praecox, giving special attention to the works of Binet, Janet, Breuer, and Freud. He restated the concepts of the unconscious and repression and deepened his definition of the complex. The paranoid form of dementia praecox, he surmised, followed use of the mechanism of hysteria. But then he questioned why paranoia was stable and resistant, while hysteria was mobile. The burden of the study was an attempt to differentiate between these two forms of illness.

In the normal person the ego complex was in effect the center of personality. It was linked to the powerful feeling tone of bodily sensation. But the ego complex could be threatened. The affect of a new complex could impinge upon the stability of the ego complex. Under such conditions the ego complex was no longer the whole of personality; the new complex acted as an independent center of will and feeling. In hysteria the unconscious complexes were mobile— they could be replaced by other, more reality-oriented complexes, because they could be influenced by emotional rapport in the treatment relationship. The complexes of dementia praecox, however, remained rigid because of metabolic defects, and they could not be influenced by the treatment relationship. Thus they exercised absolute control over the ego complex.

Jung concluded with a case study, asserting that his case analysis was no different from the analysis of a dream. Toward the end he remarked that one of his conclusions was "known to all psychoanalysts" (p. 127), thereby suggesting that he had begun to identify with this work role. Clearly he was ready—if only on intellectual and clinical grounds—for a personal relationship with Freud.

## The Second Phase: Jung's Friendship with Freud and the Psychoanalytic Years, 1907–11

From the perspective of the chronological development presented in the *Collected Works,* it is clear that 1907–11 constituted the "psychoanalytic years." During this time Jung's intellectual efforts shifted entirely, moving from his synthesis of descriptive psychiatry, experimental research, and Freud's theories to a comprehensively Freudian orientation. Thus, though he displayed considerable intellectual activity at this time—and even more organizational activity—in the publications of this period he was still working with other people's ideas. This phase contained not only a shift in thought but also a shift in work techniques: Jung became a practicing psychoanalyst. It is hard to tell which came first.

But changes in the dimension of person are far less easy to describe than changes in thought and in work techniques. Outwardly, Jung's personal identity was even more stable than before: his work as a doctor and his life as a family man were further consolidated and were enhanced by his new relation to a great, though controversial, man—Freud—and by his new responsibilities in the advancement of the psychoanalytic movement. But this period also contains all the personal circumstances that led to the break between Jung and Freud and that also established the conditions for the subsequent lonely, anguished, and creative crisis. For this reason, and also because Jung's writings during these years are his least original, I will center first and primarily on the personal relationship between the two men and will consider its associated circumstances—family life, friends, colleagues, conferences, publications, and the like—only as they bear on this relationship and in particular upon its role in the formation of Jung's thought.

The outer circumstances of this relationship are well known. It began with enthusiastic mutual rapport, which came to a climax on the trip to America in September 1909. The close relationship encouraged the exchange of ideas and fostered collaboration. After the trip several new factors emerged: the organizational expansion of the psychoanalytic movement, Jung's interest in applying the theory to mythology and religion, and Jung's later innovations in the libido theory. Freud worried about the extent to which Jung's ideas began to differ from his own. He objected not so much to Jung's interest in religion as to what he believed was Jung's careless application of psychoanalytic theory to religion. Also, he feared Jung's tendency to spiritualize his thought. But he was even more concerned about Jung's reluctance to work regularly and energetically for the advancement of the psychoanalytic movement. Jung was not suited to the role of psychoanalytic entrepreneur. As he became more and more engrossed in his practice, in his study of mythology, and in his theoretical innovations, he became resentful of Freud's demands for conformity and activity and fearful of his criticism. By the end of 1911 the two men had become so unfriendly that the stage was set for the final break.

In the letters, Freud tended to account for these developments by means of his own psychological theory: Jung was acting out his "father complex"—he displaced onto Freud unconscious feelings and attitudes of rebelliousness originally directed toward his father. In a later publication Freud spoke of Jung's relentless desire to further his own interests (Freud 1914c, p. 43). The letters also contain Jung's conviction that Freud became increasingly dogmatic and authoritarian about his sexual theory and that he tried to control and dominate Jung by treating him as a neurotic patient with unresolved conflicts. To free himself intellectually and personally from Freud, Jung said, he had no choice but to go his own way. Much later, in his autobiography, Jung added that Freud had made a religious dogma of sexuality.

Thus, at bottom both men viewed the relationship as a kind of transference, each assigning blame to the other. This basic view is supported by later analyses of the relationship and its breakdown. Jones (1955) supports the general trend in Freud's view, arguing that Jung resisted Freud's sexual theories. Roazen (1975) also sees the relation as a father-son conflict, but he faults Freud for authoritarianism and gives more credit to the genuineness of Jung's struggle for autonomy. Jung had less personal need to make sex all-important, and Freud's repudiation of religion may have been linked to the passive meaning Judaism held for him. A recent article by Stepansky (1976) cogently points out that from the very beginning of the relationship Jung never accepted Freud's libido theory in toto, nor did he ever accept the role of mere disciple—he always envisioned the relationship as one of collaboration between independent investigators. What Erikson has called the "cult of the paternal male" accounts for Freud's belief that it was the duty of age to correct and admonish younger followers. Despite his disclaimers, he wanted loyalty—both intellectual and organizational.

Two features of the correspondence, however, are not taken into account by these understandings of it. The first is the prominence of the language of idealization, psychic merger, and self-esteem. The second is the subtle way these phenomena became intertwined in Jung's mind with his personal experience of religion. To account for these crucial but till now ignored features of the correspondence, I argue that the Freud-Jung relationship was not simply—perhaps from Jung's point of view, not at all—an oedipal conflict, in which over-intense rivalry exists between a father figure and a son figure. Instead, drawing upon Kohut for theory and upon his colleague John Gedo for application at specific points, I propose that the relationship between the two men was a narcissistic transference and that it underwent a number of the vicissitudes that characterize this type of relationship. This transference was pivotal not only in Jung's personal struggle with Freud, but also in his later intellectual formulations—for, as Kohut has suggested, narcissism and creativity are closely related.

At first Freud and Jung idealized each other, becoming participants in a mutual psychic merger or narcissistic transference. This phase of their relationship was consolidated at the time of their trip to the United States, when they were together constantly for six weeks. They analyzed each other's dreams, and Jung thus experienced himself as in analysis with Freud. After his return from America the deepening of this transference activated his own grandiosity. He became excessively invested in his own self-esteem and, fueled by Freud's admiration and promises, increasingly dependent upon Freud's empathic investment of him. Then this grandiosity took a wholly unexpected turn: it became associated in a very complex way with his personal experience of religion, and he began to write *Symbols of Transformation*. This book was in part an attempt to integrate his experience of religion with his concurrent experience of Freud and of Freud's ideas; but it was also an intellectual attempt to reflect upon the implications of Freud's psychoanalytic ideas for traditional religious values in the context of modernity.

When in 1900 Freud completed his masterpiece, *The Interpretation of Dreams,* he received little acclaim from the world. So when Jung presented himself in 1906—obviously gifted, admiring, forthright, and ready to learn—Freud's own esteem needs were engaged. But as time progressed he was able to modify them, although even at the end of the relationship Freud to some extent experienced Jung's defection as an injury to his own narcissistic organization. Freud's subsequent demands for intellectual conformity and administrative activity interrupted Jung's narcissistic transference with him. Carrying out the dynamics of an interrupted narcissistic transference, the result was a growing propensity for narcissistic rage. The conditions for cycles of demand and angry resentment became established, although as late as the end of 1911 both men were struggling to maintain a positive relationship. In all this the association was a constant interplay of realistic factors—what I have called outer circumstances—that existed alongside and exacerbated the deeper psychological dynamics.

But the psychology of narcissism casts light not only on the relation between the two men, but also upon their thought, for in Freud and Jung thought and person were intimately related. After the break, the basic psychological task of both men—but of Jung especially—was to extricate themselves from the merger and reestablish their damaged self-esteem. As a result of this "psychological mandate" both men turned their thoughts to the problem that had pervaded their lives—the problem of narcissism. Freud threw himself into this problem shortly after the break (e.g., 1914b),[1] and Jung's writings on introversion and the moral task of individuation, as I shall argue below, betray a preoccupation with what can only be called a "struggle with narcissism."

The correspondence of the first eight months (December 1906 to July 1907) is devoted to the relationship between the two men and to the discussion of psychoanalytic ideas in that context. It is rich in the

1. See the final pages of chapter 4 for further development of this point.

language of idealization and of merger and, on Jung's part, in confidences. In December Jung discussed with surprising frankness one of his dreams concerning his marriage and his sexual feelings (McGuire 1974, #9).[2] After his visit to Freud in March 1907, Jung wrote that the visit had aroused his complexes (#17). In the next letter Freud spoke of his conviction that Jung would continue and complete his work (#18), and Jung replied that he had made considerable "inner progress" since he had come to know Freud personally, adding that an understanding of psychoanalysis was inseparable from knowledge of Freud's personality (#19). In May Jung reported the change his ideas had undergone: there had been a reformation in his psychological thinking. He now viewed his earlier (pre-Freudian) days not only as intellectually wrong and defective but as "morally inferior" as well (#26). At the end of May Freud had referred to the "riches" they should share, and in early June Jung replied that he lived "from the crumbs that fall from the rich man's table" (#29). A month later he once again confided to Freud some personal experiences he could not understand (#35). The intense immediacy and rapport of this early stage is not contradicted by the aged Jung's sober reflection on their first meeting. They talked for thirteen hours without pause: "Freud was the first man of real importance I had encountered; in my experience up to that time, no one else could compare with him. . . . I found him extremely intelligent, shrewd and altogether remarkable" (1961a, p. 149).

That Jung's enthusiastic idealization of Freud continued to develop—and was reciprocated—is seen in their exchanges regarding Jung's participation in a psychiatry conference in September 1907, in Amsterdam. Jung presented a paper defending Freud's ideas—a typical performance for Jung during his psychoanalytic years. Freud's soothing and admiring tones at this time expressed his own idealizing transference: "My personality was impoverished by the interruption in our correspondence," he began, and he added that Jung's lecture would be a "milestone in history." Then he declared his own sense of merger with Jung in an extraordinarily concrete

2. The following discussion makes extensive reference to the correspondence between Freud and Jung. Rather than cite editor, date, and page each time I refer to it, I have simply cited the letters by the numbers assigned in McGuire 1974. This also helps emphasize the fundamentally epistolary nature of the relationship.

image: "And when you have injected your own personal leaven into the fermenting mass of my ideas . . . there will be no further difference between your achievement and mine" (#38).

While Jung was in Amsterdam Freud wrote again. This time he told Jung of the loneliness that had accompanied his creative years while he was writing *The Interpretation of Dreams,* adding that only then had a sense of certainty finally come over him, a sense that "bade me wait until a voice from the unknown multitude should answer mine. That voice was yours" (#42). Freud's letter stirred Jung. The day after he returned to Zurich from the conference he thanked Freud for the letter, saying it "came just at the right moment," and added "it did me good to feel that I was fighting not only for an important discovery but for a great and honorable man as well" (#44).

During the following six months (September 1907 to February 1908) the relationship intensified. Jung continued to entrust personal confidences to Freud. He spoke of his envy of a colleague's "polygamous instinct" (#46), and he sought Freud's advice about a patient who was erotically attracted to him (#48). He confessed to Freud that his veneration of him was like a " 'religious' crush" and that he found this disgusting and ridiculous because of its erotic undertone (#49). This confession produced in him "all the agonies of a patient in analysis" (#50). Several months later Freud began to address him as "Dear friend." Jung thanked him profusely for this gesture but added that he wished to be treated not as an equal but as a son, noting with some perceptiveness that this would avoid misunderstandings between "two hard-headed people" (#72). Some months later, after the two men had met in Salzburg, Freud wrote of his confidence in their alliance, saying that "it probably springs from a feeling I have when I look at you. But I am satisfied to feel at one with you and no longer fear that we might be torn apart" (#87), thereby reiterating his own sense of merger with Jung.

The strong sense of mutual appreciation, esteem, and intimacy continued into the time of their trip to America. Jung spoke again of his "polygamous tendencies" and even referred to an "urge for identification" with Freud that had—fortunately, he said—subsided (#133). Freud must have sensed Jung's idealization, for he had remarked earlier that Jung was to be his own master and that his

(Freud's) fatherhood would not stand in the way (#118). Later he confessed that he did not wish to fall back into the father role (#139). Jung's letters to Freud up to this time conflict with his later estimate of this period as recorded in the autobiography. There he reflected on his first meeting with Freud, concluding that Freud had made a dogma of his sexual theory and that this struck at the heart of their friendship (1961a, p. 150).

Jung's autobiographical account of the trip to America (1961a, pp. 156–61), like the account of the first meeting, contradicts the correspondence, although it also contains some important evidence corroborating the hypothesis that a typical oedipal transference relationship existed alongside the narcissistic merger. In the autobiography Jung reported several conversations with Freud and through these created a highly ambivalent estimate of Freud at this time. In Bremen, before sailing, Jung and Freud became involved in a discussion of a recent news item: mummified corpses had been discovered in peat bogs in northern Germany; this fascinated Jung, and he spoke at length about them. Jung's enthusiasm for this topic got on Freud's nerves, and in the midst of the discussion he suddenly fainted. Later Freud informed Jung that his interest in corpses signified death wishes toward Freud, a view Jung of course did not accept.

Freud also spoke frequently about his plan for Jung to be his successor. Jung said that this embarrassed him, for he knew he could not uphold Freud's views, but that at the time his respect for Freud was too great to permit disagreement. During the trip they analyzed each other's dreams. At one point Jung asked Freud for further personal information about one of his dreams, but Freud declined, saying, "I cannot risk my authority"; Jung added, "at that moment he lost it altogether" (1961a, p. 158).[3] And, last, Jung had an

3. Jung has said more about this episode than he reported in his autobiography. In May 1957 he granted an interview to a friend, Professor John Billinsky of Andover Newton Theological School in Massachusetts. The purpose of Billinsky's interview was to inquire into the reasons why Jung had broken off his relationship with Freud, and he published the contents of the interview. Jung told Billinsky that, during his 1907 visit to Freud in Vienna, Freud's sister-in-law confided to him that "Freud was in love with her" and that "their relationship was very intimate." Then, Jung went on, during their visit to Clark University he and Freud analyzed each other's dreams. Freud had dreams in which his wife and her sister played important parts. Accordingly, Jung asked Freud for associations to the dreams, but Freud declined, saying, "I

elaborate dream of a house of several stories with two skulls in the
basement. Freud was convinced that the skulls signified death wishes
concerning him. Jung, unwilling to risk open disagreement—to have
done so would have required renouncing the psychic merger with
Freud—claimed that the skulls symbolized his wife and sister-in-
law, although he inwardly rejected this interpretation.

In reporting these incidents Jung created a cumulative image not
only of Freud but of himself. Freud is pictured as hopelessly trapped
in his own authoritarian dogmatic system of ideas and eager to impose these upon his colleague. Jung, on the other hand, appears as an
open person who is superior because he is capable of seeing through
the limitations of Freud's dogmatism. Two observations upon this
episode are in order. The charge of dogmatism is to be understood
psychologically as an accusation of narcissism and grandiosity.
Jung's sense of Freud's powerful confidence in his own ideas and in
his own person may have activated a feeling of uncertainty—of
narcissistic vulnerability—in the younger man. Second, Jung's portrait of Freud is identical to the view he repeatedly expressed about
his father, whom he pitied for being hopelessly trapped in dogmatism, not of psychoanalysis but of Christian theology. This retrospective view of Freud is not at all the view of the correspondence—
although a much later letter does allude to Freud's authoritarianism
during the trip to America.

But Jung also acknowledged deep involvement with Freud at this
time: "I would never have wanted to discontinue our dream
analyses . . . they meant a great deal to me and I found our relationship
exceedingly valuable" (1961a, p. 158). The correspondence directly
following Jung's return from America supports this view. Jung
wrote: "On the journey back to Switzerland I never stopped analys-
ing dreams" (#155), and two weeks later he referred to feeling

---

cannot risk my authority." Jung also told Billinsky that during the trip Freud developed "severe neuroses" and that he suggested further analysis, which Freud refused. Jung concluded that "it was my knowledge of Freud's triangle that became a
very important factor in my break with Freud . . . . I could not accept Freud's
placing authority above the truth . . . . This led to further problems in our relationship" (Billinsky 1969). That the phrase "I cannot risk my authority" occurs
both in the Billinsky account and in the autobiography at least strongly suggests that
the former is an elaboration of the event reported earlier.

homesick for Freud and added: "The analysis on the voyage home has done me a lot of good" (#157). Jung clearly experienced himself as having been in analysis with Freud. Freud's reply to the first letter reflected once again his own predilection for psychic merger with Jung: "The day after we separated an incredible number of people looked amazingly like you; wherever I went in Hamburg, your light hat with the dark band kept turning up. And the same in Berlin" (#156). This was, however, the last time Freud was to use the language of merger with Jung, and his eventual withdrawal of it was of great consequence.

After the trip to America and up to December 1911, the correspondence indicates two changes in Jung's situation, which together set the stage for the eventual break and—after that—for Jung's lonely, anguished, and finally creative years. Jung continued to intensify his merger with Freud: he confided that he was "plagued by complexes"; that his wife had staged a number of jealous scenes; but that he had used Freud's psychology to analyze himself and his wife successfully. He concluded, cryptically, that the prerequisite for a good marriage was the license to be unfaithful (#175). He reported to Freud that he was ordering his daily affairs by following the basic principles of "the psychoanalytic way of life" and that he religiously analyzed his dreams (#204).

Second, Jung's letters also spoke of what can only have been the emergence of an intense personal involvement—he called it an obsession—with mythology and religion: "mythology . . . has me in its grip" (#173); "my dreams revel in symbols" (#180); "my mythology swirls" (#196); and "mythology . . . [is] eating me alive" (#254). These remarks, which reflect a kind of grandiose excitement, suggest that the fantasy processes so characteristic of the critical period 1913–17 were already asserting themselves. As a result of this shift in Jung's psychological condition he began to write *Symbols of Transformation,* the book that was to figure so prominently in the breakdown of his relationship with Freud.

The conventional views of the break between the two men—that Jung "resisted" Freud's theories or that Freud could not tolerate Jung's innovations—address only the surface of their relationship. The letters reveal that a far richer, more complex situation also existed—alongside the intellectual differences—and the psychology of narcissism clarifies what this material reveals. John Gedo (1974), applying Kohut's theory to the *Freud-Jung Letters,* has cogently argued that there was a relation between Jung's idealization of Freud and his thoughts about religion. Jung's need to idealize Freud became so strong that he idealized Freud's psychoanalytic ideas into the dimension of a religion. Jung tried to endow Freud and psychoanalysis with religious powers (Gedo 1974, p. 38). Freud repudiated these idealizations, provoking responses of narcissistic rage from Jung (p. 41), and it was Jung's deep disappointment that, according to Gedo, led to the break between the two men.

Gedo has clearly put his finger on a critical point in the Freud-Jung relationship. In a letter of February 1910, Jung's idealization of Freud and his fusion of Freud's ideas with religion is plain. Freud had asked Jung to comment on whether the psychoanalytic movement should join an ethical fraternity. Freud liked the idea because he felt it would protect psychoanalysis from the state and the church. Jung replied that a mere fraternity was "artificial," then lyrically proclaimed that psychoanalysis was the historical fulfillment of the Christian gospel: "I imagine a far finer and more comprehensive task for psychoanalysis . . . we must give it time to infiltrate into people from many centers, to revivify among intellectuals a feeling for symbol and myth, ever so gently to transform Christ back into the soothsaying God of the vine. . . . A genuine and proper ethical development cannot abandon Christianity but must grow up within it, must bring to fruition its hymn of love, the agony and ecstasy over the dying and resurgent god" (#178). Gedo cites other letters that contain expressions of Jung's idealization of Freud—#113 and #168.[4]

Freud, however, did not accept this idealization of himself and his ideas and their fusion with mythology and religion. His reply began on a soothing and echoing note: "Yes, in you the tempest rages." Then he frankly stated his feelings: "But you mustn't regard me as the founder of a religion. My intentions are not so far reaching. . . . I am not thinking of a substitute for religion; this need must be subli-

---

4. Jung's own remarks confirmed that he fused an idealization of Freud with religion. In October 1907, as I have noted, he had said: "my veneration for you has something of the character of a 'religious' crush" (#49). And a month later he confided in Freud again: "My old religiosity had secretly found in you a compensating factor" (#51).

mated'' (#179). In his reply Jung apologetically referred to his own letter as ''another of those rampages of fantasy'' (#180).

It is difficult to judge from the correspondence whether Jung's narcissistic transference was of the idealizing sort or whether it was predominantly a mirror transference. Gedo considers it to be the former, although he emphasizes grandiosity as well as idealization. Kohut states that some narcissistic transferences contain a mix of the two—idealization of the object and grandiosity in the subject (1971, p. 221). It is clear from the correspondence that Jung held both attitudes. But the presence of grandiosity is associated not only with his idealization of Freud but also with Jung's reports of the emerging prominence and importance of mythology in both his personal and his intellectual life. However, there are sources for Jung's preoccupation with mythology that are independent of his relation to Freud and that also fed into the writing of *Symbols of Transformation*, which Gedo does not mention. Furthermore, though Gedo does speak of Jung's grandiosity during his critical years—a point that must be made—he does not discuss the extent to which Jung's psychological system is also an attempt to come to terms with narcissism. And, by identifying Jung's psychology with religion, Gedo fails to recognize the extent to which Jung's psychology—here quite similar to Freud's—was also a repudiation of Christianity. This point, which I shall take up in chapter 5, is of fundamental importance in understanding Jung's relation to his religious past—both developmentally and intellectually.

The presence of both attitudes—idealization of Freud and grandiosity in the self—and the association of the second with mythology provides the following account of this phase of Jung's life. His merger with Freud, consolidated during the trip to America, persisted and even intensified immediately thereafter. Then the intensity of this relation activated Jung's own grandiose needs. He began to idealize Freud, but also to invest his own thoughts with increasing narcissism. In more colloquial language, he romanticized and absolutized his thoughts. That this ''self-idealization'' (my term, not Kohut's) took a religious turn can be accounted for, in part, by three further observations. First, Kohut notes that one of the forms of regression a narcissistic transference takes is that of ecstatic religious feelings and hypomanic excitement (Kohut 1971, p. 97). Jung's references to his "rampages of fantasy" were clearly states of excitement in which religious feelings predominated. But, far more important than this, it seems inevitable that Jung's many unresolved childhood and adolescent religious experiences would emerge under the impact of a regressive relationship such as he had established with Freud. Finally, since myths embody what a society considers supreme and ultimate, it seems logical that Jung's heightened need for self-esteem should force a fusion between his own mental productions and these cultural objects. This fusion of grandiosity and personally experienced mythology accounts for the contents and also the well-nigh unreadable style of *Symbols of Transformation*. In it Jung transposed his own fantasies and thoughts onto a cosmic level.

The exchanges in the closing months of 1911 contain Jung's reports of his forthcoming writings on mythology, some criticisms of them by Freud, and evidence of Jung's increasing apprehension over these criticisms. Then, in October and November, Emma Jung wrote several letters to Freud. In the second she stated that her husband was fearful of Freud's rejection of part 2 of *Symbols of Transformation,* and she accordingly asked Freud not to think of Carl "with a father's feeling: 'He will grow but I must dwindle' " (McGuire, p. 457). She thereby reiterated the oedipal estimate of their relationship that both Freud and Jung held. But in her next letter (pp. 462–63) she retracted this view and gave a surprisingly insightful interpretation of the matter: Jung's fear of Freud's opinion was only a pretext for his own resistance to writing and, further, *Symbols of Transformation* was a form of self-exploration. More than either of the two men she had discerned what was afoot between them and what was happening in the writing of *Symbols of Transformation*. Jung was under stress, and the book was not a detached discussion of the psychology of religion. It was a personal document through which he first attempted to work out the crisis that began with Freud and that, despite his writing this book, broke out even more fully in 1913–17. Even then it was not to be resolved with finality.

The writings Jung published from the end of 1907 up through 1911 are the work of what are rightly called his psychoanalytic years. These papers of course were prepared months before publication—in some cases a year or more. But on the whole they are remarkable for their inner consistency and for the way they match the positive side of Jung's involvement with Freud's ideas, even though not all are published in *Freud and Psychoanalysis,* volume 4 of the *Collected Works* (the volume purporting to cover the period of Jung's involvement with Freud's thought). With only an occasional exception, all these papers express Jung's thoroughgoing appropriation of Freud's psychoanalytic ideas, his enthusiastic commitment to Freud's psychoanalytic method, and his confidence in the integrity of Freud's person. Thus they contrast sharply with Jung's murky inner life at the close of this period.

Three papers on hysteria (1908*b*), dreams (1909), and rumor (1910*b*) are little more than summaries of what Jung took to be Freud's central ideas on these subjects. Although in his three Clark lectures of 1909 Jung spoke on such non-Freudian topics as the association method and the family constellation, in them he referred to himself as part of the Freudian school and clearly indicated that he felt himself part of the psychoanalytic movement. In two papers— one on Bleuler (1911*a*) and the other on Morton Prince (1911*b*)—he went beyond summarizing Freud's views and actively defended them. Bleuler had proposed that the term ambivalence be used to describe the negative attitude of the schizophrenic patient. Jung countered by saying that one should psychoanalyze ambivalence, for the Freudian concept of resistance gave a better account of the pathology than did the concept of ambivalence. Jung cited Freud's paper "The Antithetical Meaning of Primal Words" to indicate what he had in mind. Jung concluded that Freud's dream psychology and theory of neurosis should be brought to bear on schizophrenia.

In the paper on Morton Prince Jung took a much more aggressive attitude. Prince had questioned the validity of Freud's theory of dreams, particularly the notion that all dreams are wish fulfillments, and had published his own analysis of a patient's dreams to prove his point. Jung reanalyzed the dreams of Prince's patient, demonstrated that they were indeed wish fulfilling, then went on to show the sexual roots of these wishes. He said Prince was "prudish" and "unscientific" and added that an understanding of psychoanalysis was "a function of analytical self-knowledge," that "where self-knowledge fails, psychoanalysis cannot flourish" (1911*b*, p. 58). He concluded that "to practice psychoanalysis one must subject one's ethical concepts to a total revision" (1911*b*, p. 68). It is interesting that the paper criticizing Prince appeared alongside part 1 of *Symbols of Transformation.*

During this period there are two suggestions of ideas that differ from Freud's. In "The Content of the Psychoses" (1908*a*) Jung argued that the psychoses must be seen not as biologically rooted but as distortions of problems that beset everyone. Using case material, he illustrated how his patients had suffered disappointments in life and had developed their illnesses to compensate for these setbacks. Their symptoms sprang, he said, from normal conflicts and frustrated wishes. And in his Clark lecture on psychic conflicts in a child Jung spoke for the first time of "introversion." He described how a child had become mournful and dreamy as a result of the birth of a sibling: part of the love that formerly belonged to a real object became introverted; it was turned inward into the subject and there produced increased imaginative activity (1910*a*, pp. 12–13).

In the paper criticizing Bleuler Jung used the concept of introversion a second time: in schizophrenia introversion mechanisms predominate. He also spoke of "autism," "life-wound," and "autoerotism" (Freud's term), thereby anticipating much later discussions of "narcissistic injury." Indeed, introversion was Jung's term for narcissism.[5] In *Symbols of Transformation* he spoke of schizophrenia as an introversion neurosis and contrasted it to hysteria and transference. The concept of introversion may have resulted from some not inaccurate introspection on his own personal predicament with Freud. As I will show in the next chapter, a central issue in Jung's delineation of his core process was the problem of narcissism—he called it "inflation" and "godlikeness"—and how to come to terms with it.

### The Third Phase: Jung's Break with Freud and His Neo-Freudian Writings, 1911–13

During the period 1911–13 the deeper psychological forces that had already become constellated intensified and led to the final break between the two men. Jung's idealization of Freud and his association of Freud's ideas with religion had been repudiated by the older

---

5. See discussion and footnote, p. 70.

man. This grandiosity had been activated by a series of circumstances and was deeply linked to Jung's interest in mythology and religion: he was convinced of their central importance and thus was excitedly absorbed in writing *Symbols of Transformation*. Freud saw only the surface of this: Jung interpreting religion and the libido theory more and more extravagantly. He genuinely felt betrayed by the man to whom he had promised the future of psychoanalysis. Jung, his self-esteem now inseparable from his mythological investigations, experienced Freud's criticisms as arbitrary and authoritarian and, above all, as a withdrawal of valued empathy. The closing period focused overtly on intellectual differences and upon the two men's psychologically reductionistic interpretations of each other's behavior. The narcissistic forces in their relationship asserted themselves silently.

In the early months of 1912 Jung continued to tell Freud about his state of mind. He was "grappling with the endless proliferation of mythological fantasies" (#295); he spoke of his "grisly fights with the hydra of mythological fantasy," adding, "sometimes I feel like calling for help"—a possible allusion to his need for Freud (#297); and he talked about his descent "to the realm of the Mothers" (#300). Personal resentments cropped up followed by efforts at reconciliation (#301 and #303). In March through May they once again disagreed about religion. Jung explained his theories of matriarchy and incest (#313, #315), and Freud confessed "strong antipathy towards your innovation" (#316). Jung's reply displayed his own skill in the art of psychological reductionism: "I am grieved to see what powerful affects you have mobilized for your counter-offensive against my suggestions" (#318).

The Fordham lectures added fuel to the fire. Jung claimed he had success in America because his new views won over people who had been offended by Freud's emphasis on sexuality. Freud's famous reply followed—the further you remove yourself from psychoanalysis the more certain you will be of applause—and added that he did not understand part 2 (#324). In this letter Freud also abandoned his customary greeting (Dear friend) and addressed Jung as "Dear Dr. Jung." Jung sought to protect his sagging esteem and autonomy by distancing himself: "Since you have disavowed me so thoroughly, my collaboration can hardly be acceptable . . . let us give

the well-meant error its rightful place" (#326). Of the Munich conference in November Freud wrote to Putnam: "I shall hardly be able
to accept his [Jung's] modification of the libido theory" (McGuire
1974, p. 522).

At this conference Jung achieved a surprising insight into his
relationship with Freud. A letter to Freud immediately after the conference indicated that he in effect understood that the phenomenon of
psychic merger was at the root of their dissension: "I am glad we
were able to meet in Munich, as this was the first time I have really
understood you. I realized how different I am from you. This realization will be enough to effect a radical change in my whole attitude. . . . I hope the insight I have at last gained will guide my conduct
from now on" (#328). Jung had achieved, I think, a momentary
sense of his own separateness from Freud, and his self was temporarily enriched by it. But the insight was too intellectualized to
withstand Freud's reply, which really precipitated the break.

Freud thanked Jung for his friendly letter and even conceded that
"one always finds it rather irritating when the other party insists on
having an opinion of his own," referring to his own "bit of
neurosis." Then he reversed his field and cut at the heart of Jung's
endeavors. Of the *Symbols of Transformation* he said: "I now believe that in it you have brought us a great revelation, though not the
one you intended" (#329). Jung raged against this remark, accusing
Freud of using his own neurosis as a means of rendering his colleagues passive, dependent functions of himself (#330). But the
theme of his letter is not simply anger over differing intellectual
views derived by two autonomous individuals. The theme of the
letter—its key words are "underestimation" and "devaluing"—is
Jung's injured self-esteem and associated narcissistic rage. Had he
not been trapped in a psychic merger with Freud, he might have
simply withdrawn with dignity and composure from the overbearing
older man.

Days later Jung committed a slip of the pen (#335) and Freud
called attention to it (#337). Jung's reply (#338) was even more
furious than the one described above. Freud's technique of treating
pupils like patients produced "slavish sons and impudent puppies."
He saw through Freud's "little trick." Freud, he said, sniffed out
symptomatic actions while remaining on top as the father, "sitting

pretty." His own symptomatic actions were nothing compared with the beam in Freud's eye. He protested that he was not neurotic, that he had undergone an analysis more thorough than Freud's self-analysis. Underlying the accusations of this letter is an emotional tone identical with that of the previous angry letter: injured self- )) esteem, fear of abandonment, and associated narcissistic rage.

Two weeks later, in January 1913, Freud broke off personal relations. For the next several months Jung continued to write to him about official matters. Both attended the Munich conference in September 1913, where Jung presented some ideas about psychological types that were his first, embryonic effort to construct a theory of his own—Freud was an extravert, Adler an introvert—and which was very much rooted in the psychological task of achieving a sense of his own self, independent of Freud. In October Jung resigned from the *Jahrbuch*. In April 1914 he resigned as president of the International Psychoanalytic Association and also from his position as privatdocent at the University of Zurich.

During the past five years Jung's intellectual efforts had been directed entirely by Freud's thought, his professional work had become exclusively psychoanalytic, and he had become intensely involved with Freud at a personal level—it is worth repeating that Freud is the only nonparental figure discussed in detail in the autobiography. Now, with all of this taken from him, it is not surprising that he would undergo a major personal crisis. )

The biographical discussion of this brief period has disclosed the centrality of Freud's person and ideas for Jung, the narcissistic dimension of this relationship—in the form of psychic merger and then the painful interruption of that merger—and the way these psychological processes became entangled with religion in Jung's mind. These circumstances are reflected in Jung's writings of this time. Although the period was brief, it forms a distinctive transition between the relatively stable and uncomplicated psychoanalytic years and the frightful critical-creative period when Jung was totally alone and constructed his original psychological system.

Jungians sometimes hail this period, especially the publication of *Symbols of Transformation* in 1912, as the time of Jung's definitive "break" with Freud. They are only partly right. It is far more correct to say that this was Jung's "neo-Freudian" or "revisionist" period.

All his ideas at this time were simply negatives of Freud's; none were original. It was a time of rebellion, not of creativity. Jung had not yet psychologically separated himself from Freud enough to engage in originative reflection. Freud's mind was still present in Jung's writings, although it was now being repudiated.

Despite the personal turmoil of this period, Jung was intellectually active. The important works of this time comprise the *Symbols of Transformation,* published in 1912; the Fordham lectures, published as *The Theory of Psychoanalysis* in 1913 (1913*b*); two papers, "New Paths in Psychology" (1912); the first edition of the first essay of the famous *Two Essays on Analytical Psychology* (1966*a*); and "A Contribution to the Study of Psychological Types" (1913*c*). Taken together, these papers not only embody the main ideas of this period but also provide the earliest evidence of three basic "tensions"— pressing intellectual questions that Jung encountered and could resolve only by creating the core process. These tensions formed a triangle of incompatible intellectual forces: Freud's psychoanalysis, which Jung rightly recognized as a new mode of consciousness in the West; its unbridgeable estrangement from Western Christianity; and the confusion this tension created for modern man, whom Jung later described as "mass man." Although these tensions were all to some extent present in all the writings of this period, each "tension" also received extended treatment in specific writings: *Symbols of Transformation* represented Jung's struggle with religion; *The Theory of Psychoanalysis* his struggle with Freud's thought; and "New Paths" his first attempt to work as a social critic and moralist concerned with the fate of modern man. The essay on types signaled Jung's awareness of the persisting centrality of Freud's thought for the eventual emergence of his own distinctive ideas.

*Symbols of Transformation* is not simply a psychological study of religion; it is Jung's early attempt to resolve these tensions, particularly the tension between psychoanalysis and Christianity. It also clearly illustrates the intensely personal character of Jung's writings at this time and their intimate relationship to Freud's person, as well as to his thought and work. Furthermore, despite the deviant flavor of its theoretical-psychological apparatus, its assessment of traditional religion is remarkably similar to Freud's: in it Jung created a psychological interpretation of Christianity, thereby clearly placing it in the past and judging it unsuitable for the modern temper. Jung never abandoned this repudiation of traditional Christianity—a fact many theologians and also psychoanalysts fail to recognize— although he did also affirm some aspects of the Christian tradition. Freud's refusal to recognize this may have been an additional source of narcissistic injury to Jung.

The book purports to consist of two sources that are easily recognized and described. First, Jung revised his conception of the libido. Second, in 1906 the Swiss psychologist Theodore Flournoy published a report of several dreamlike experiences written for him by a young American student, Miss Frank Miller. The article consisted of fifteen pages—nine described the experiences, and the remaining pages were an account of their origins in Miss Miller's everyday life. Equipped with an alarmingly simplistic theoretical framework—the libido theory was only sketchily developed—Jung proposed to interpret Miss Miller's very brief report of her several mental productions. But the book is more than five hundred pages long. In effect it simply uses the libido theory and the Miller fantasies as stimuli for a full-scale, grandiose foray into the myths, rituals, symbolism, and practices of Judaic, Christian, Hellenic, Eastern, and primitive cultures.

Jung argued that his knowledge of the structure and dynamics of the libido, derived from his own and Freud's psychoanalytic investigations, allowed him to penetrate into the hidden processes whereby past civilizations constructed their self-defining images, myths, and symbols and to disclose their "real" meaning. The climax of his discussion centered on the figure of the hero, which Jung believed occupied a privileged position in the mythologies of the past. The life of the hero was a symbol of the dynamics of the libido. Through his struggles with various mythological figures the hero regressed to a state of primal conflict with the mother, who threatened to devour him. His heroic qualities lay in his capacity to extricate himself from this encounter with the "terrible mother" and to break free from the regressive libidinal bond between them. Thus for Jung the drama of the hero symbolized the renunciation of mankind's universal infantile wish to return to the mother. Jung referred to this renunciation as "the sacrifice." The hero, symbolic of a reactivation of a longing for the mother, sacrificed this aspect of himself—this "infantile personality"—in order to become a fully distinct individual wholly adapted to present life circumstances. So it was that the libido theory decoded the message of the past.

But the book is not a careful, detached study in the psychology of ancient mythologies. It is an incredibly grandiose effort to compress the complexity, richness, diversity, and contradictoriness of ancient symbolism into the mold of the simplistic libido theory. Its manner of execution is, furthermore, easily as grandiose as its method and conclusions. It presents the reader with a multiple series of free associations and flights of ideas in which one image or thought leads to another, and this to another, for pages on end. In Jung's own words to Freud, it is a "storming," a "rampage of fantasy." It is, in short, a record of Jung's own fantasies, not an interpretation of the myths and symbols of the past.

One example will suffice (1965, pp. 234 ff.). In the midst of one of her reveries Miss Miller imagined a "city of dreams." This provoked Jung to a discourse on cities in ancient cultures and mythologies—cities in the Old Testament and Egypt; then he noted that cities and women are related; but women are also related to land; this led him to reflect on the movement of the sun over "maternal" waters; which reminded him of Frobenius's concept of the night-sea journey; that stimulated Jung to think of Noah's journey; but, he then added, journeys are an expression of the wish for rebirth; this prompted a discussion of the Book of Revelation; and so on. Not until page 263 did Jung return to the next phrase in Miss Miller's brief report.

Jung himself was aware that powerful emotional factors accompanied the writing of this book. After his visit to America, he reported (1961a, pp. 162–63), he began reading mythology "like mad . . . with feverish interest." It was, he said, as if he were "in an imaginary madhouse" trying to interpret the mythological figures of the past as if they were his patients. In the midst of his excitement he came upon Miss Miller's fantasies, which "operated like a catalyst upon the stored-up and disorderly ideas within me." In his 1950 foreword to the revision he wrote of the original: "It was written at top speed . . . without regard to time or method. I had to fling my material hastily together . . . the whole thing came upon me like a landslide." He referred to the book as fragments strung together. It was, he concluded, "the explosion of all those psychic contents which could find no room . . . in the constricting atmosphere of Freudian psychology" (1967a, p. xxiii).

But the final paragraph of the foreword indicated that Jung himself was partially aware of the deeper psychological forces that had descended upon him at this time: "I was acutely conscious then of the loss of friendly relations with Freud and of the lost comradeship of our work together" (1967a, p. xxvi). In *Symbols of Transformation* Jung grandiosely and narcissistically idealized his own mental processes. In doing so he urged upon the reader his conviction that his own "mythological fantasies" provided the key to the meaning of the past, and he fused his own mental processes with ancient cultural productions. He thus demonstrated a lack of experiential perspective upon his mental life at the time—what Kohut has called an "experience-distant" mental attitude.

Because Jung's sense of Freud's person and his writing of this book were so closely related, it is interesting to speculate on his remarks about the writing of the last chapter, "The Sacrifice." Jung reported in the autobiography (1961a, p. 167) that he delayed writing it for two months because he knew that the ideas in it would cost him his relationship with Freud. Through this concept Jung advanced his own interpretation of incest: the child, like the hero in mythology, sacrificed his infantile relation with his mother in order to adapt to his own world. Finally, Jung said, he understood his own reluctance. Writing the chapter meant sacrificing himself to the fate of being misunderstood. But the idea of sacrifice may have had emotional significance for Jung in another sense: in putting forth his own ideas he would have to renounce—sacrifice—the narcissistic transference to Freud.

But the intellectual heart of this book is not the revised libido theory, or Jung's interpretation of the Miller fantasies, or even his analyses of the mythologies of the world. It is the fate of Christianity in the light of modernity and in particular the new science of psychoanalysis. Jung's libido theory may have been a departure from Freud's, but it still added up to a secular, non-Christian view of the present. In the introduction Jung pointed out how Freud had shown—by establishing the ubiquity of the oedipal complex—the way the ancient past reflects present-day conflicts. He informed the reader that his book was an extension and application of Freud's work—he likened it to a recently published book on Leonardo da Vinci. In his own book Jung relentlessly interpreted Christianity: "The phenomenon, well-known to every psychoanalyst, of the unconscious transformation of an erotic conflict into religious activity is something *ethically wholly worthless* and nothing but an hysterical production" (1965, p. 82). And he spoke on behalf of "a conscious recognition and understanding with which we can take possession of this libido which is bound up in incest and transformed into religious exercises so that we no longer need the stage of religious symbolism . . . man could without compulsion wish that which he must do, and this from knowledge, without delusion through belief in religious symbols" (1965, p. 262).

But an element of quest also permeated Jung's book: through the psychological analysis of the past, "we win that stable point of view outside our own culture" that leads to "an objective understanding" of that culture (1965, p. 5). And, in reflecting upon the problem of belief, he said: "I think *belief should be replaced by understanding;* then we would keep the beauty of the symbol, but still remain free from the depressing results of submission to belief" (1965, p. 263; his italics). But the anti-Christian tone of the book wins out. Jung's quest for a "stable point of view" and for the "beauty of symbol" are expressions of nostalgia, not achievements of interpretation. They point up the "problem of our time" and the dilemma of "modern man." Their absence became for Jung the central intellectual predicament of his critical period, and served—as I shall point out below—as the sociological matrix out of which he conceived his core process.

Just as *Symbols of Transformation* gives evidence of great inner stress, there is also evidence of coherence in the second work of this period, the one given over to Jung's assessment of Freud's psychology. Jung's outer life remained orderly, and his Fordham lectures were written in a clear, matter-of-fact style. Jung did not mention them in his autobiography. The lectures ran 140 pages and covered most of the major points in Freud's psychology at the time. In fact, every innovative suggestion is simply a negation of one of Freud's ideas.

Jung expanded the concept of libido beyond the sexual meaning it had for Freud to include psychic energy in general, and he referred to this as the energetic theory of libido. Then he divided the development of libido into three stages: a presexual stage in which nutrition and growth predominate (birth to age four); a prepubertal stage (age five to puberty); then a stage of maturity, in which the libido is gradually desexualized and adapted to the demands of social reality. Jung was convinced that the psychoses, especially schizophrenia, could not be explained simply in terms of a withdrawal of erotic interest. There was also in this illness a withdrawal of interest in reality, and hence a person's reality sense is not entirely erotic. In schizophrenia the libido does not adapt to reality but undergoes introversion, thereby regressing inwardly and attaching itself to fantasies of very early life.

These formulations led to other innovations. Jung believed that his concept of sacrifice gave a better account of the oedipal situation than did Freud's notion of a castration complex. Thus he cast Freud's concept of castration in a moral context. He also modified Freud's views by stating that the boy's oedipal rivalry with his father and love for his mother were merely "childish" demands for love. He believed, further, that the cause of neurosis was in the present, not the past, and spoke of the etiological significance of the present.

Jung also proposed several modifications in treatment. Of great importance was his notion of "active participation" by both patient and therapist in the patient's fantasy material. The analyst urges his patient to enter into his mental productions consciously and intentionally—in a spirit of thinking, not passively or dreamily—so as to bring them into the light of day for analysis and integration. Active participation takes place, however, in the context of transference. In medieval times priests guided their parishioners by manipulating the transference, but modern men and women wish to be free, autonomous and independent of parental substitutes, of which the priest is one. Hence the task of treatment is to analyze the transference. But here Jung again juxtaposed himself to Freud. Freud's method was historical and reductive. Jung proposed a prospective, teleological view in which dreams, when properly interpreted, presage the future tendencies of the patient's life. He did not, however, explain how such principles of interpretation actually worked out in treatment.

The psychology of narcissism not only can be used to interpret the deeper personal aspects of Jung's personal relation to Freud but can also clarify, to a limited extent, Jung's intellectual and conceptual work at this time. Such a viewpoint becomes plausible if two factors are considered. First, Jung had been participating in a narcissistic transference with Freud that was now breaking down, causing anxiety and stress. Second, throughout his Freudian years Jung had trained himself, with great effort and persistence, to be introspective about his own personal relations; and from time to time he had been successful in gaining insight. From this it follows that he might well have been introspectively focusing upon narcissistic factors in his own experience, and his thoughts at this time could be expected to articulate aspects of the phenomenon of narcissism. Some of the ideas in *The Theory of Psychoanalysis* provide evidence for this view.

When Jung spoke of a presexual stage given over to a sense of reality not composed entirely of sexual desire, he was referring to preoedipal, narcissistic phenomena. His concept of an introversion neurosis, which he juxtaposed to transference and hysteria, also pointed to a stage of development during which the self/other relation was incompletely formed. And his association of all this with the mother rather than the father anticipates Kohut's assertion that the narcissistic stage of development fundamentally involves mother and child. Kohut has also told us that creativity is linked to the stage of narcissism. Toward the end of *Symbols of Transformation* Jung spoke of *"the willed introversion of a creative mind,"* in which the mind "dips . . . into the source of life, in order there to wrest a little more strength from the mother." It was, he said, "a mother-child play with one's self . . . *a Narcissus state"* (1965, pp. 336–37; Jung's italics).[6]

6. According to the Jungian analyst Murray Stein, narcissism is directly linked to introversion in Jung's system, and it is the key to experiencing the archetypes. Stein writes: "Narcissus gazing in the pool becomes an image for imaginative activity . . . . To reach imagination . . . requires the functioning of Narcissus in the psyche; the psyche moves toward imagination and the imaginal realm through the functioning of narcissism." Commenting on Jung's discussion of introversion in *Psychological Types,* Stein continues: "When introverted thinking runs toward the extreme of its natural direction . . . it loses its contact increasingly with facts and objective data and

Unfortunately, however, probably because of the turbulent, un-settling, and extraordinarily painful loss of Freud's empathic inclu-sion of Jung in his world, at this time in his life Jung did not possess the requisite inner strength for sustained, accurate, introspective ob-servation, reflection, and subsequent collation of his findings. The phenomenon of introversion never became integrated into the theory of psychosexuality. Instead, he proposed that overcoming narcissis-tic grandiosity was a moral and ethical task—the sacrifice of the infantile personality to the demands of social adaptation.

Jung's early preoccupation with the problem of modernity, the third "intellectual tension"—while it is inseparable from and there-fore also appears in the two preceding works on religion and psychoanalysis—received its first focused statement in the essay "New Paths in Psychology" (1912). This essay is important because it shows very clearly that, at the time of his break with Freud, psychoanalysis possessed cultural as well as religious and clinical significance for Jung. He was taking on the role of moralist and social critic, a role that, along with those of therapist and prophet, was to become a key element in his mature identity.

After summarizing the sexual theories of neurosis of Freud and Breuer and reviewing some of his own clinical work, Jung stepped forth upon his "new path": the clinical problem was in fact a cultural one. Cultural forces such as urbanization, the specialization of labor, industrialization, and loss of contact with nature all created a social need to discharge energy, which took the form of sexual tension. But this need was censured by the hypocritical and narrow traditional morality. Thus neurosis was bound up with what Jung called "the problem of our time"—it was an unsuccessful effort by individuals to solve "the general problem." And psychoanalytic therapy was therefore a cultural, not a medical problem. Through it modern man could "fit into this scheme of things" and acquire "a working philosophy of life" (1912, p. 267).

Writing in the following year, Jung again indicated how the prob-lem of modern man was shaping his thought. Religious and philo-

---

develops 'ideas which approximate more and more to the eternal validity of the primordial images'. . . . As thought and fantasy lose themselves to Narcissus . . . they penetrate through to the archetypal world'' (Stein 1976, p. 46).

sophical forces must receive positive consideration in therapy, he wrote: "There must be built up in him [the neurotic] that same psychological attitude which was characterized by the living belief in a religious or philosophical dogma . . . a religious or philosophical attitude is not the same thing as belief in a dogma . . . it gives rise to incentives . . . [for] creative work and . . . sacrifice" (Jung 1913*a*, p. 241). Clearly psychoanalysis had "seen through" traditional religion. But under the pressures of modernity—as Jung understood the diagnosis—it had to be replaced by something else. At this time, however, Jung did not know what that something else would be.

In his paper "A Contribution to the Study of Psychological Types" (1913*c*), Jung consolidated—though only at the conceptual level—his separation from Freud. The two men had broken off personal relations in January 1913, and the paper was presented at the Munich conference in September, the last time they were ever to meet. It suggested considerable introspective effort, combined with resentment, composed as it was in the midst of Jung's painful and turbulent loss of psychic merger. In it he advanced the notion of types, a key idea that was to receive extensive elaboration at the close of his creative years—but at this time he was able only to present it as a problem.

The ideas in the paper are sketchily developed and, like those in the other papers in this period, are negatives of Freud's ideas. But here Jung achieved his first modicum of distance from Freud. He argued that in the main psychopathology presented two types of illness: hysteria, characterized by intense feeling toward the object, and dementia praecox, characterized by apathy toward the object. These were two contrary movements of the libido. As such they suggested two different psychological types: extraversion, wherein interest is given to the outer world, and introversion, wherein there is a devaluation of the object world. Jung supported his views by likening them to William James's notions of toughmindedness and tendermindedness. Then he put Freud in his place. Freud's theory was extraverted, reductive, causalistic, and objective; Adler's was introverted, finalistic, and subjective. But the key to the paper—and to Jung's relation with Freud and to this period of his work—lies in the final sentence: "The difficult task of creating a psychology which will be equally fair to both types must be reserved for the future'' (1913c, p. 509).

Little wonder that Freud found the atmosphere ''fatiguing and unedifying'' (McGuire 1974, p. 550). In one stroke Jung had pronounced Freud's person and thought incomplete. In doing so he irrevocably established the psychological and conceptual conditions for his critical years of loneliness and intellectual confusion. But, surprisingly, as he left this period, new thoughts—Jungian thoughts—came to occupy a central place. And the key to the new system was the theory of types.

# Four

## Psychological Factors in the Formation of Jung's Thought: The Fourth Phase, 1913-18

### The Struggle with Narcissism during the Critical Years

By the close of 1913 Jung had consolidated, though only outwardly, his break with Freud. It was a break in every possible way—not only personally but also professionally, in terms of work techniques, and intellectually, in terms of theory. Total as it was, the break with Freud was also part of a wider, general withdrawal from the social world of everyday life. Not only did Jung resign from the *Jahrbuch* and the International Psychoanalytic Association, he renounced his position as privatdocent at the University of Zurich. As a result he entered a phase of life characterized by an intense, long-term inner crisis—a period of turmoil and confusion in which he was beset by bizarre visions, dreams, and thoughts that he at first could not in the least comprehend. Then, gradually, he developed techniques for understanding these mental productions. He referred to this process, which took place over a period of several years, as his "experiment." As he began to gain mastery over these initially overwhelming experiences, he reflected further upon them, broadening them to include observations on his patients. By the end of 1918 these reflections became consolidated in two major papers (1916, 1917), which were subsequently revised to become the *Two Essays on Analytical Psychology* (1966a). They compose what I have called the core process.

In its broadest and most general sense Jung experienced what Ellenberger has called a creative illness. But Erikson's scheme makes possible a more specific analysis of the psychological forces at work in Jung's life at this time. He underwent an identity crisis composed of major interlocking changes in the spheres of work, person, and thought. During his years with Freud, Jung had unified his own sense of self by becoming a practicing psychoanalyst, by adopting Freud's ideas, and by forming an intense personal relationship with Freud himself. Then, in the critical years, all this psychological work was undone. Jung reported that after parting with Freud he found it necessary to develop a "new attitude"—an attitude different from the one Freud had taught him—toward his patients (1961a, p. 170). For three years, he wrote, his scientific reading was at a standstill (1961a, p. 193) and "beyond Freud, after all, I knew nothing" (1961a, p. 199). And he noted that after parting with Freud he felt personally disoriented (1961a, p. 170). But by the end of the period Jung had devised a clearly articulated set of new techniques for psychotherapy; he had created a new system of psychological ideas; and he possessed a new sense of himself as a person separate from Freud.

But the most specific interpretive schema applicable to Jung's crisis period is Kohut's psychology of narcissism. Even though the letters end in 1914 and hence primary evidence for the nature of the crisis must be drawn solely from the autobiography, the two sources are at points sufficiently consistent to permit drawing upon them both. Jung's central problem during the neo-Freudian years was the interruption of his psychic merger with Freud, and it follows psychologically that the focus of the critical years had to be a struggle with narcissism: the loss of an idealized other, grandiosity in the sphere of the self, and resulting periods of narcissistic rage. Despite its episodic and generalizing character, the autobiography provides evidence of two trends: an initial phase wherein Jung internally separated himself from Freud's person; and a second phase given over to a reconstitution of his self apart from Freud. The view of Jung's critical years as a struggle with narcissism receives added support from the fact that his core process displayed narcissistic themes: it contained affirmations of narcissism and was also directed toward overcoming narcissism.

Studies of Freud's creative crisis place great importance on the presence of Wilhelm Fliess (Erikson 1964; Ellenberger 1970; Kohut 1976; Schur 1972) as a special other person upon whom Freud played out and through whom he consolidated strong emotions and new ideas. According to the autobiography, there is no such "other" in Jung's case. But two recent biographies contradict this view. Barbara Hannah (1976, pp. 103, 117), a Jungian analyst and a longtime friend of Jung, reports that a young woman named Toni Wolff came to Jung as a patient in 1911; the analysis lasted until 1914 and they later became lifelong friends. Paul Stern (1976, p. 135) dates their first meeting to 1909. Stern's account is probably more accurate, for we know that Jung recommended Toni Wolff to Freud in August 1911 as a participant in a conference (#269). Presumably his therapy with her was by then, if not over, at least well along the way.

According to both accounts their relationship combined elements of treatment, romance, and friendship, although neither biographer discloses which element was dominant during Jung's crisis years. Hannah adds, however, that Toni Wolff "accompanied" Jung on his journey into the unconscious, and she offers the further observation that Toni Wolff's presence was experienced by Jung during those moments of the critical years when he struggled with female images. Van der Post (1977, pp. 168–75) assigns her great importance during the crisis years and implies that without her Jung might never have arrived at his new and creative system of ideas. It is unlikely that we will ever know the true nature of their relationship, for after her death Jung destroyed all their letters. But, because these biographers associate Toni Wolff with the critical period, it is not idle speculation to suppose that she served as a "merger figure" for Jung: a person to whom he could confide his most disturbing thoughts and whom he could rely on for support.[1]

At the beginning of his critical period Jung paused and took stock of his situation: "After the parting of the ways with Freud, a period

---

1. Consider, for example, the following remarks by Kohut: "during periods of intense creativity (especially during its early stages) certain creative persons require a specific relationship with another person . . . which is similar to that which establishes itself during the psychoanalytic treatment of one major group of narcissistic personality disorders" (Kohut 1976, p. 399; see also p. 404).

of inner uncertainty began for me. It would be no exaggeration to call it a state of disorientation. I felt totally suspended in mid-air, for I had not yet found my own footing" (1961a, p. 170).[2] He went on to describe, as I have already noted, how he also felt it necessary to develop a new attitude toward his patients. He did not, however, introduce a well-formed theoretical framework, but at first simply remained open to their imaginative productions. If these two remarks are viewed in the light of the psychology of narcissism, it is clear that the cause precipitating Jung's crisis was the need to separate himself psychologically from Freud. It was not an easy task.

From Christmas 1912 to summer 1914, Jung had several dreams and visions that, despite their exotic imagery, can be related to this task. At the end of November 1912, Freud had insulted Jung by saying that *Symbols of Transformation* had brought a great revelation, but not the one Jung had intended; and shortly thereafter Freud had interpreted psychoanalytically a slip of the pen Jung had made. Jung's replies—the second reply was dated 18 December (#338)— are the only truly rage-filled letters of the entire correspondence. The autobiography reports (1961a, pp. 171–72) that about Christmas 1912 Jung dreamed that he was sitting on a gold Renaissance chair high in a tower, surrounded by objects of rare color and beauty. His children were seated near him. It is possible that the aristocratic opulence and the quiet, regal grandeur of this dream embodied a theme of narcissistic reinstatement whereby Jung, the former "crown prince," reendowed himself, in imagination, with the valued self-esteem he had lost through the breakdown of his relationship with Freud. If this is true, the dream can be understood as initiating in the unconscious a process of restitution whereby Jung began the long task of bringing coherence to the self that had been so injured by the loss of connection with Freud and the psychoanalytic movement.

A year later, in September 1913, the Munich conference was held.

---

2. It is worth noting Gedo's interpretation of Jung's reference to being suspended in midair: "This candid self-description bears striking resemblance to the reports and imagery of those patients who, after establishing an archaic narcissistic transference in analysis, find themselves cast suddenly upon their own resources. In conformity with the state of present-day technology, they typically imagine themselves to be in orbit around the Earth, without any means of re-entry from outer space" (Gedo 1974, p. 49).

A month later Jung wrote to Freud saying he had heard that Freud doubted his "bona fides" (#357) and that he could no longer, for this reason, edit the *Jahrbuch*. In December 1913, Jung dreamed (1961a, pp. 179–80) that he was on a lonely, rocky mountain when he heard Siegfried's horn and knew he had to kill him. He was armed , with a rifle, and when Siegfried appeared he shot him. The dream ended on a note of disgust and unbearable guilt over having destroyed something so great and beautiful. When he awoke he was obsessed by an urge to kill himself unless he could understand the dream. He pondered, then decided that the figure of Siegfried represented "what the Germans want to achieve . . . to impose their will, have their own way" (1961a, p. 180) and that he had done the same—that he was imposing his own will upon himself. Hence to Jung the heroic attitude of Siegfried symbolized his conscious effort to dominate his own mental life. This effort had to be abandoned; for, he concluded, there were in life things higher than the will of the ego.

Despite the epic and romantic imagery of this dream, which distances its surface aspects from the mundane circumstances of the psychoanalytic movement in which Jung had been deeply immersed, the structure of conflict in it is identical to Jung's perception of his relationship with Freud at the time of the break. Siegfried, the German, wanted to impose his own will, have his own way, just as Jung felt that Freud was imposing his own theory on Jung's innovative efforts. Jung rebelled against this by killing Siegfried (Freud) and so separated himself, internally, from Freud. But he also turned the question of "having one's own way" back upon himself—that is, he did not simply project all the blame upon Freud. The dream instructed him to give up his own heroic idealism, through which he imposed his own will upon others, but particularly upon himself. By means of his own introspective efforts Jung was able to renounce some portion of narcissistic grandiosity and associated rage— without, however, identifying the internal forces in this fashion—that had been activated by the interruption of the psychic merger with Freud. As a result, he was somewhat less omnipotently inclined to attempt to control the contents of his own consciousness, and thus was willing to admit that unconscious forces were at work within him.

Then several months later, in April 1914, Jung withdrew as president of the International Psychoanalytic Association (#358). At approximately the same time (spring and early summer 1914) he reported a thrice-repeated dream (1961a, p. 176). My interpretation of all the preceding evidence argues that the outward and inner events can be related. In his dream an Arctic cold wave descended and turned the land to ice—all green, living things were killed by frost. The third dream had an unexpected end. In it there stood a leaf-bearing tree that Jung referred to as his tree of life. The frost had transformed the leaves of the tree into sweet grapes. Jung plucked the grapes and gave them to a waiting crowd.

The cold, ice, and frost, I suggest, symbolized the sense of abandonment and narcissistic vulnerability that Jung experienced in relation to Freud and to the psychoanalytic movement and that he inflated to cosmic proportions in the dream. As a result of this deprivation Jung's sense of self was depleted. The positive ending of the dream—that frost should cause the growth of sweet grapes—represented Jung's desire and emerging capacity to affirm his inner self. And that he should give the grapes to a waiting crowd indicates an emerging sense of identity that has prophetic and ideological coloration.

The psychoanalyst John Gedo (1974, p. 50) has argued that the ending of this dream, in which Jung gave grapes to the crowd, indicates that he had himself become the "soothsaying God of the Vine" (#178), a role he had originally hoped might be filled by Freud and by Freudian psychoanalysis. Accordingly, Gedo believes that Jung became the prophet of a new religion. My own argument agrees with this point but places it in a wider context. Gedo does not discuss the fact that Jung rejected traditional Christianity as strongly as Freud did. Nor does he mention Jung's astute perception that the rise of psychology is related to the decline of religion. Hence the relation between psychoanalysis and Christianity is more complex than simple substitution. I will argue below that Jung's personal identity was threefold: psychotherapist and critic of Freud, moralist and social critic of modernity, and prophet or reinterpreter of Christianity. This composite identity matches the three "tensions" of his early thought and the three "themes" of his mature thought, which I will discuss in detail in chapter 7. But the identity of prophet was an important element in Jung's final consolidation of his ideas.

Ideological concerns were clearly present in the early phases of

Jung's critical years. In July 1914 he read a paper in London entitled "On Psychological Understanding" (1914), in which he addressed the problem of dream formation and interpretation, especially in dementia praecox. The contents of the paper strongly reflect the type of experience he was undergoing, as reported in the autobiography. Jung expanded upon what he had only recently come to call the constructive or prospective standpoint. Then he advanced the notion that delusional patients—primarily those he called "introverts"—try to construct, by means of their mental productions, "a new world-system . . . a Weltanschauung" (1914, p. 189). This system enables them to adapt to their own inner, psychic situation, but it also serves as a necessary transition to adaptation to the world in general. Jung concluded that one of the needs of men is to adapt to the world by means of a system of ideas about the world as a whole. The argument fits, hand-in-glove, the situation of the anguished Jung, frustrated by Freud's refusal to allow psychoanalysis to become a world view and disenchanted with traditional Christianity. If the paper is read concurrently with Jung's personal predicament, it clearly suggests that he perceived the construction of a world view or ideology to be one of the tasks of the critical years.

By August 1914 Jung had entered the most conflicted phase of his critical years, which terminated only toward the end of the decade. The major portions of the autobiography chapter "Confrontation with the Unconscious," which began with the dreams already described, is given over to reporting the nature of this struggle and provides evidence that links it to the formation of the core process. The fundamental characteristic of this phase was its intense centering upon Jung's innermost self—hence it seems right to conclude that by this time he had at least to some extent separated himself from Freud and entered another, more self-oriented phase, in which he attempted to reconstruct his fragmented self apart from Freud.

However, we must bear in mind that the irruption of fantasy that constituted this period was really an extension and deepening of those mental processes—we can do no better than to use Jung's own phrase, "rampages of fantasy" (#180)—that were activated in him immediately after his return from America and his analytic conversations with Freud in 1909. At that time they existed side by side with his relation to everyday social reality, while remaining split off from it. Now they moved to the very center of his consciousness, demanding his total attention, to the exclusion of everything but the most minimal social relations.

The period began with the appearance of bizarre fantasies and visions, followed by perplexity and an inability to cope with new experiences. Jung's dominant attitude at this time was fear of being overwhelmed by these strange mental productions. He was possessed of strong inner resistances to the process taking place. At one point he feared he was on the edge of a psychosis. Throughout the period he was unable to read scientific literature of any sort. On the other hand, he felt driven by "a demonic strength" (1961a, p. 177) to find the meaning of his experiences and to anchor them in reality.

Gradually he devised ways to cope with his experiences, referring to these as his "experiment." He began by writing down the fantasies and attempting to relate them to existing and childhood psychic conditions. At times he would deliberately induce further imaginative productions. He developed his own form of "play therapy"— building houses out of small stones. At other times it was necessary to calm himself by the techniques of Yoga or to translate turbulent emotions into images, a process that gave him reassurance.

But these were largely ad hoc efforts that produced only temporary relief. The lasting aspect of Jung's experiment with the unconscious consisted of a particular kind of mental activity in which he first projected or objectified specific mental contents and engaged in a relationship with them, then interpreted them. Through this double process he was able to dissolve their psychological force over him and gain a modicum of psychological distance from himself. This process was also the personal experience that provided the matrix for the formation of the ideas that composed his original psychological system.

Jung first did this by imaginatively projecting the images of Elijah, a figure of ancient prophetic wisdom, and Salome, a young woman representing an erotic element. Elijah became transformed into another figure whom Jung named Philemon, and his relation to this figure became the crux of the experiment. Jung first dreamed of Philemon, but this dream image lingered and was taken up into the sphere of everyday fantasy. Jung entered into imaginary conversations with this figure, who, he reported, acted as a guru—as someone

possessing superior knowledge and ability who could help him un-
tangle the chaotic productions of his mind. Jung "learned" from
Philemon that certain contents of the psyche exist independent of his
own center of volition. These conversations "taught me psychic
objectivity, the reality of the psyche. Through him the distinction
was clarified betwcen myself and the object of my thought" (1961a,
p. 183). Thus, through this experience Jung acquired the principle of
psychic distance, which he later called differentiation of the ego from
the collective unconscious. He designated the figure represented by
Elijah and Philemon as the archetype of the wise old man or the mana
personality.

The same process subsequently occurred with a female figure and
then with a visual representation of an objectification of his total self.
After describing the episode with the figure of Philemon, Jung began
to wonder about the nature of his experiment with the
unconscious—clearly it was not science; but, if not, then what was
it? As if in answer to this question, he experienced a female voice
within him proposing that his experiment was genuine art. An argument ensued, and Jung concluded that this figure was attempting to
trick him into overestimating the worth of his endeavors. Through
imaginary conversations with this voice he distinguished his conscious ego from it and concluded that it represented the inner relation
to his unconscious. Later he named this figure the anima.

Beginning in 1916 and later in 1918, Jung reported, the flow of
fantasies and their accompanying disturbing emotionality gradually
diminished, and he began to feel more in control. This experience of
a consolidation of inner life and of relation to the outer world was
associated with the drawing of mandala figures—round designs that
were often divided into four sections and filled in with elaborate
detail. Jung decided that these figures represented the whole of his
being or the wholeness of the self (1961a, p. 196), by which he
meant a balanced integration of alien, unconscious contents into the
consciousness of the moment. With the construction of these designs
and a recognition of their significance, the experiment with the unconscious came to a close.

This description of the deepest level of Jung's experiment, brief as
it is, centers upon the three most important relations in human life: a
guiding male figure, a female figure, and representations of the pure

self.[3] It is not surprising, then, that the heart of the individuation process should consist of an encounter between the conscious ego and the archetypes of the mother, the father, and the self. Although experience of these images formed the heart of Jung's psychology, they cannot be separated from his other key concepts. The experiment as a whole provided the experiential matrix for many of Jung's other central ideas, which were inseparable from it. This continuous process of objectification of alien feelings in the form of images, of engagement with these images, and of consequent interpretation of them made it necessary for him to formulate—to account for his experiences—such concepts as the collective unconscious, the archetypes, differentiation of the ego from the contents of the collective unconscious through active imagination, the shadow, the anima, individuation, and the self.

Recall, too, Jung's condition when writing *Symbols of Transformation*. At that time he had grandiosely and narcissistically fused the contents of his own consciousness with the mythological symbolism of the past. But then, in the critical period, he experienced this fusion in a much more immediate and personal way: his entire consciousness was crowded with these images. By constructing the theory of archetypes and all that goes with it, in one stroke—through the medium of thought itself—he interposed interpretive categories between his own mind and these cultural products, thereby separating himself from them. By naming his inner experiences, he created his system of psychological ideas. In so doing he achieved both personal, psychological distance from himself and his merger with the cultural products of the past and also a new interpretive theory that could be applied to the past.

Jung's descriptions of his deepest and innermost conflicts, wherein he objectified the male figure of Philemon, the female anima figure, and later the experience of the total self, signify an inner struggle that

---

3. In his analysis of Luther, Erikson asserts that man's religious life consists of three "objects": a wish for unity with a maternal matrix, the paternal voice of guiding conscience, and the pure self, which he calls "the unborn core of creation" (Erikson 1958, p. 264). Erikson's description of the three religious objects can be applied to Jung's crisis period and indicates how closely interwoven were the psychological and the religious in this phase of his life. The role of religion in the formation of Jung's ideas will be taken up in the following chapter.

is predominantly narcissistic in character. Narcissism refers to the psychological task of forming a cohesive self, a process that occurs primarily in relation to a significant "other" person: the problem of narcissism is the problem of the "other" or, more generally, the problem of "otherness." More precisely, the task of the stage of narcissism is to differentiate a sense of self from the sense one has of another, whom the self has previously idealized or with whom the self has previously merged. Jung's experiences were struggles to establish a sense of "otherness" and, conversely, a sense of a coherent self.

The experiment forced him to focus upon the task of identifying objects in his consciousness, then upon discerning the nature and source of these objects. As a result of this he was able to "draw a line" between what was internal and what was external, what was self and what was other. As I have already noted, he said this specifically of his experience of the archetype of the guru, Philemon: "Through him the distinction was clarified between myself and the object of my thought" (1961a, p. 183). Jung concluded that the image of Philemon and other images experienced initially as part of himself were in fact "other" than himself. They were universal images, not personal, individualistic images. The capacity to develop such clarity about this distinction brought Jung considerable relief.

On the whole, however, Jung's negotiation of this struggle with narcissism was ambiguous and open to criticism. He had concluded that these images were other than himself. But although he rightly concluded that such images could not be understood in terms of Freud's theory of the repression of sexual fantasies, he did not open himself to the possibility that they might still have had a basis in personal experience. He did not raise the question whether these experiences might be developmentally earlier than the oedipal conflict, a hypothesis I will present below when I review Jung's core process, which also reflects at the level of thought his struggle with narcissism. Instead Jung assumed that, because these images were not then accessible to introspection oriented to the oedipal stage of personal development, they were collective and nonpersonal. Therefore, alongside the thrust toward differentiation and self-cohesion in this experience, Jung retained solipsistic components in

his thinking—he rendered as external and objective some mental
processes that were in fact internal and subjective.

The theme of the struggle with narcissism appears not only in
Jung's descriptions of his innermost conflicts but also in his own
reflections on their significance. He described how he needed to
bring his fantasies back to reality (1961a, p. 188), and he strove to
translate the unconscious into ethical forms of behavior (1961a, p.
193). As a result of the struggle he ceased, he said, to belong to
himself alone (1961a, p. 192) and instead "aimed at *this* world and
*this* life" (1961a, p. 189). And he reintroduced one of his favorite
ideas, which was to capture much of the moral thrust of the core
process and whose narcissistic nature has already been noted—the
abandonment of the superordinate position of the ego (1961a, p.
196). Such reflections suggest a struggle to reduce the archaic claims
of the grandiose self. But Jung's reflections also indicated that he
always viewed his experiment with the unconscious as the source of
important new ideas for the world at large and therefore as the source
for a new personal sense of identity: "until it was completed I could
not appear before the public" (1961a, p. 193).

While Jung's descriptions indicate that his struggle was primarily
internal and devoid of references to real-life figures in his social
world, there is some evidence—admittedly slender—that this was
not entirely true. Barbara Hannah has reported that Jung shared his
disturbing experiences with Toni Wolff. Hannah describes her as
someone who had no ability to experience the unconscious firsthand.
This may have been just what Jung needed most at his critical hour.
Hannah believes that their relationship was represented in Jung's
fantasies of the wise old man accompanied by the erotic young
woman. Freud too may have been represented in Jung's fantasies.
Jung's encounter with the "other" occurred in relation to the fantasy
figure of Philemon, who derived from an earlier vision of Elijah and
who served the confused Jung as a guide or guru. Jung reported that
he desperately wished for a real human guide during this period, and
according to Hannah Jung had hoped Freud would serve as that guide
(1976, p. 122). In later years Jung likened Freud to an Old Testament
prophet who shattered idols (1934, p. 36), and he may have entertained this view of Freud as early as the critical years. Therefore I am

inclined to believe, judging from all the evidence already presented, that, although he did not self-consciously reflect in such a way upon this phase of his life, Jung was psychologically engaged at the deepest level at three points: his relation to Freud (guiding paternal figure), his relation to Toni Wolff (companion, courtesan, and maternal matrix), and his own self (the pure self).

Jung's descriptions of his experiences—which I have tried to separate as much as possible from his own retrospective-theoretical interpretations—indicate that the critical years created an experiential matrix out of which his key concepts or core process grew. And Jung himself explicitly stated that this was true. He referred to these years when he was pursuing his inner images as the most important in his life: his later thoughts were only "supplements" and "clarifications" of these experiences (1961a, p. 199). "My science," he said, "was the only way . . . of extricating myself from that chaos" (1961a, p. 192). Jung reviewed his major works in the chapter of the autobiography that follows the description of the crisis years. Here he reported that the stream of fantasies finally ebbed about 1917 and that he then attempted to take an objective view of the whole experience and reflect upon it. This sustained reflection resulted in his writing several key documents: two essays, published in 1916 and 1917, that were later revised to form the definitive *Two Essays on Analytical Psychology;* a short essay entitled "The Transcendent Function" that was completed in 1916; and the book-length *Psychological Types,* published in 1921. These documents contain all the major ideas of the core process.

No discussion of Jung's critical period, so turbulent and in many ways so bizarre, is complete without reference to the question of his sanity. This is a double-edged issue. On one hand, raising such a question can simply be a means of exploring in greater detail and with more exactitude the nature of Jung's crisis. On the other hand, such a question can serve a polemical interest: if Jung was deeply disturbed at this time, and if his major ideas were closely linked to his disturbance, the ideas can thereby be discredited. For a brief period Jung himself feared a psychosis. But he soon abandoned this view and concluded that while his dreams, visions, and fantasies were surely the stuff of psychosis, they were also the matrix of a mythopoetic imagination that had vanished from a rational age. Be-

cause he could take an interpretive perspective upon his experiencing, he not only was able to avoid illness but was also able to achieve
a state of self-understanding far surpassing that of the average modern man.

One might expect that on this point, more than on any other,
Freudians and Jungians would find ample reason to disagree; but
such is not the case. D. W. Winnicott (1964), a British psychoanalyst, believes that Jung's autobiography as a whole described
a successful and creative encounter with schizophrenia. Joseph
Wheelwright (1976), a leading American Jungian analyst who
was trained by Jung, concurs with Winnicott and believes that
every deep Jungian analysis is a psychotic experience in which the
patient is accompanied by someone who has been ''there before''
and from which he emerges more whole. He has noted that John
Weir Perry, another American Jungian, agrees with this view. On the
other hand, the British psychoanalyst Anthony Storr (1973, pp.
16–17) has argued that, though Jung's experiences were of psychotic
intensity, his ego was strong enough to withstand a schizophrenic
break and, further, that his creativity protected him from such massive disorganization.

The psychology of narcissism provides a richer, more complex—
and, I think, more accurate—view of Jung's crisis, one that agrees in
principle with Storr's but differs in the details of actual analysis. The
correspondence with Freud and portions of the autobiography show
that during the psychoanalytic years Jung developed a narcissistic
merger with Freud and that the disintegration of this relationship left
Jung with an acute sense of narcissistic injury and vulnerability. He
was deprived of an important object of idealization and his needs for
esteem and potential for grandiosity, previously met to a considerable degree by his relationship with Freud, were frustrated. He responded by turning more and more into himself, experiencing inner
depletion and fragmentation of self.

This severe regression occurred at two levels. At one level there
were temporary episodes of psychoticlike (but not in fact psychotic)
mental processes, such as are found during particular phases of the
treatment of narcissistic character disorders. But there was also, at a
deeper level, some actual regression into the autoerotic dimensions
of very early life experience. The presence of these two modes of

psychological organization alongside each other accounts for one of the most important features of Jung's critical years—that he could at one moment only stand silently, as it were, and observe the irruption of bizarre mental processes but then, at the next moment, could actively interpret them. Toward the end of the critical period his sense of self recovered sufficient coherence to permit him to maintain a systematic perspective upon his more bizarre mental processes. Gradually his self-unification progressed to the point where he could reenter the world of everyday social life—equipped with a new theory of personal change, a new system of ideas about the modern world, and a new personal identity.

Kohut has stated that injury to self-esteem and to the propensity for grandiosity in the self can actually propel some gifted individuals into creative activity. The form of the experiences reported during the crisis years clearly indicate one experiential source—what I have called the matrix—of Jung's psychological ideas. But he also brought to these experiences a powerful drive or ambition to be creative, an initiator of original ideas. He had a need to become a creative person. The sources of this need derived partly from his relation to Freud, partly from his early childhood and adolescent relationship with his father, and partly from his desire to better himself socially—Ellenberger (1970) has emphasized social ambition as a motive in Jung's (and Freud's) life history. Consider, for example, Jung's telling remark that he could not "appear before the public" until his experiment was complete. We can further suppose that, as creative and original ideas began to appear, they added sorely needed increments of self-esteem. Then, his esteem thus enhanced, Jung was in a better psychological position to feel confident about producing more creative ideas. In this fashion a cycle was produced.

Thus through the psychology of narcissism there is established an important link between psychopathology and creativity. The formation of Jung's original system of ideas was fueled by his personal conflicts; but the ideas themselves, in a circular relationship, also helped lift him out of those conflicts.

Although the critical years consisted, at their deepest level, of a struggle with narcissism, it is possible to expand this interpretive framework and argue that they were at the same time an identity crisis. It is important to recognize some theoretical inconsistency in this proposal. On one hand, Kohut believes that Erikson's descriptions of identity crises constitute only the precipitating external circumstances for what is essentially a crisis in self-cohesion. On the other hand, Erikson has stipulated that identity formation has a "self-aspect" as well as an "ego-aspect" (1959, p. 149), which seems to take into account Kohut's objections. In Jung's case, however, as in the case of some other gifted and creative individuals, the circumstances were so complex and the changes were so radical and far-reaching—the emergence of a new psychology, a new theory of modernity, and a reinterpretation of Christianity—that it seems necessary to introduce a broader framework than the psychology of narcissism. However, such a move does not keep us from recognizing that the dynamics of narcissism constitute the psychological infrastructure, so to speak, of the crisis in identity formation.

Before the crisis years Jung had achieved a sense of personal identity that centered upon his roles as psychoanalyst and teacher. At the peak of the psychoanalytic years the former began to take precedence. Jung more and more employed the work techniques of Freud's psychoanalysis, although he maintained some interest in his word association test and in other aspects of clinical research at the Burghölzli. Also, he came more and more under the influence of Freud's ideas. And his personal involvement with Freud was, as we have seen, intense. All these activities created, as I have suggested, a firm and even exhilarating sense of personal identity—a synthesis of person, work, and thought. That Jung repudiated all these achievements during the critical years clearly indicates that he underwent a radical form of identity diffusion. He emerged from the critical years with a new set of work techniques for personality change, a new theory of personality in general, and a new sense of himself—he was no longer the leading follower/exponent of psychoanalysis; he was C. G. Jung, the founder of a new movement in psychology. These acquisitions suggest an even more radical instance of identity change—a thoroughgoing identity reconstruction.

But Erikson usually speaks of identity-formation in relation to ideology, and the latter concept helps clarify further the nature of Jung's identity crisis. Erikson has referred to ideology in two different, though not inconsistent, ways. On the one hand there is the identity-ideology linkage as it applies to the ordinary developing young person. In this case Erikson stressed the young person's need for a system of ideas, images, and ideals that will make facts amenable to ideas, thereby producing a world image that will support his growing sense of identity. On the other hand, he has discussed ideological innovation. In this case a person creates a new identity that departs from the models society provides, and for this reason he creates a new ideology. Such a person in effect makes new facts amenable to new ideas, thereby creating a world image that supports not only his own new identity but also a new collective sense of identity. We can call this innovative rather than adaptive ideology.

Erikson has also discussed psychoanalysis itself in relation to ideology. In one of his earliest discussions of ego identity he remarked that the early psychoanalytic movement provided Freud's followers with a "psychoanalytic identity" and a corresponding ideology (1959, p. 153). By this Erikson does not mean to diminish the claims that psychoanalysis is a science; but he does insist that it has an ideological dimension. But while Erikson's discussion of Freud's three dimensions of psychological discovery, upon which I have relied so heavily, does associate these dimensions with Freud's identity, he did not mention ideology in that context. However, his consistent and persistent association of identity and ideology leads me to assume that he believes creative discovery—even creative discovery in psychological science—has a dimension of ideology.

There is some evidence that, during his critical years, Jung self-consciously and intentionally participated in ideological innovation. He reported that he resigned from his position at the University of Zurich—and presumably, also, from the psychoanalytic movement—because the intensity of his personal crisis was forcing new ideas upon him. No longer could he confine himself, he said, simply to "generally understandable material." Instead, he had to "find an entirely new and different orientation." The purpose of this search was "to convey to my intimates a new way of seeing things" (1961a, pp. 193–95). In these remarks Jung testified to the ideological character of his new system of ideas. It is important to recognize that the term ideology is not used here in a pejorative sense.

Jung's ideas thus evolved at several different levels simultaneously. At the most fundamental, personal, and intimate level there was the struggle with narcissism, deriving from a merger with Freud, and the theme of narcissism is central to the core process—that process reflects psychological ideas similar to those in the psychology of narcissism, as well as containing imperatives to overcome narcissism. At a second level there was Jung's identity struggle— his efforts at psychological discovery—in which he sought to reconstruct a synthesis between new work techniques, his new system of psychological ideas, and his new sense of himself as the leader of a new psychological movement.

But this synthesis of work, thought, and person—this creation of a new psychology—was not separable, in Jung's mind, from what I have called the three intellectual tensions that perplexed him so much at the initial stages of his critical years and also served as a stimulus for the formation of his core process. Jung's personal identity as founder of a new psychology must be extended to another level to include these wider intellectual interests, in which he had a deep personal investment. In addition to creating a new psychology, Jung's thought also reinterpreted Freud's (and Adler's) psychology, traditional Christianity, and the plight of modern man as mass man. It was a set of ideas that harmonized these contradictory trends. Thus at this third level Jung's personal identity was threefold: psychologist (originator of a new therapy and critic of Freud), social critic and moralist (commentator on the predicament of modern man), and prophet (critic of traditional Christianity). Insofar as his core process was a synthesis of all three—a "new way of seeing things"—Jung's identity must also be understood as a synthesis of these three self-images. In this extremely comprehensive sense his identity was that of an ideologist.

### The Contents of the Core Process That Emerged during the Critical Years: The Narcissistic Aspects

Jung set forth the basic ideas of his unique system of psychological thought toward the end of his critical period, during the years 1916–20. Taken together, the ideas created during this period constitute what I have called his core process—the delineation of a fundamental structure of experience that, he believed, described the inner processes of the lives of all men and women. The works that followed this period, which I refer to as his mature thought, deepened and expanded the ideas of the core process and applied them to a variety of activities, both psychotherapeutic and cultural. But nothing essentially new—nothing that could be remotely likened to the creative activity at the close of the crisis years—was produced during the very long period of Jung's mature life.

The four documents that embody the creative activity of this period varied greatly both in style and in publication history. The two essays—the second version of the first essay, published in 1917 (1917), and the first version of the second essay, published in 1916 (1916)—were just that: essays, one ninety pages long, the other thirty-five, that clothe the individuation process with all the basic Jungian ideas. The brief essay entitled "The Transcendent Function" (1958) was written in 1916 and described one phase of individuation, the psychological work of active imagination by which the conscious ego assimilated unconscious contents. Jung referred to it as a historical document, and, although it was later revised, none of the subsequent writings on psychotherapy contradict its original basic postulates. *Psychological Types* was a book more than six hundred pages long, consisting mostly of lengthy historical and descriptive discussions of the problem of types—it is elaborate, pedantic, and antiquarian in its style of scholarship. Its main value lies in the last hundred pages, which contain more than fifty definitions explaining all the major concepts of Jung's system. This section serves primarily as a reference guide to his thought. First published in 1921 (1921), it was slightly revised for its later appearance as volume 6 of the *Collected Works* (1971).

Each of the four documents describes in its own way the nature of the individuation process, but the two essays are the most important to the aims of this study. More than the others they let the reader see the extraordinary extent to which Jung's theories reflect his inner experiences during the crisis years, because they describe the individuation process step by step, and these steps were reflected from time to time in Jung's crisis experiences. Also, they give more prominence than do any of Jung's other writings to one of the essential features of the core process: its narrative, processive, and developmental character. In this they allow the reader to see how Jung's interpretations of many varied cultural activities were always simply applications of the same core process. This fact, so essential to understanding the logic of Jung's work as a whole, is obscured by many otherwise excellent discussions of it. Three recent summaries of Jung's work—by Edward Whitmont (1969), June Singer (1972), and Anthony Storr (1973)—fail to highlight this feature of Jung's writings. The following brief review of Jung's core process provides an objective sense of its general drift, so necessary for discussing its relation to his personal experience and its narcissistic components, as well as for subsequent analyses of the role of religious experience in its formation and for discussion of the extent to which its origins are also sociological.

In their 1916 and 1917 forms, both essays attempt to describe the individuation process as a whole, and thus they overlap at many points. There is little advantage in simply summarizing both. The second essay is the richer and fuller with one exception. The first essay contains the absolutely essential description of Jung's theory of types and explains how it opens out into the process of individuation, making it both necessary and possible.

The fundamental structure of the individuation process and many of the section titles found in the 1916 and 1917 versions are reproduced in the final version, *Two Essays on Analytical Psychology* (1966a), although the latter provides a far more coherent and deeply nuanced discussion—which unfortunately is also marred to some extent by digressions, elaborate illustrations, and, from time to time, vague prophetic warnings. True, some concepts and explanations in the final version are not found in the earlier editions; but their equivalent meanings do appear in the "Definitions" section of *Psychological Types,* thereby indicating that they had their origins in the critical years. The best procedure, then, is to follow the more developed final version of the two essays, duly noting those few points where it seems to depart from the material created during the crisis years.

When Jung last saw Freud at the Munich conference of 1913, the break had outwardly taken place. At the conference Jung read his paper on psychological types, which developed his theory of extraversion and introversion, linking Freud to the former and Adler to the latter. Jung concluded by announcing that the future task of psychology was to formulate a view that would be "equally fair" to

both types. The implication was clear: it was Jung who would develop this theory and so create a psychological system that would
include and thereby surpass the other two. Jung's decision to make
the problem of types the starting point of his new theory was due
partly to creative intellectual thought and partly to observations of his
patients. But he was also trying to disentangle his sense of self from
his merger with Freud. This psychological conflict received welcome
intellectual expression and support in Jung's conclusion that he and
Freud—and Adler—constituted different types of persons. A
psychodynamic infrastructure stimulated the formation of the theory
of types.

In 1915, in the very depths of his crisis years, Jung carried on a
voluminous correspondence on the subject of types with his friend
Dr. Hans Schmid. Only one piece of this correspondence has been
published, but it is in itself a key document (Jung 1973*b*, pp. 30–32).
In it Jung movingly lamented how destructive of human integrity was
Freud's extreme and exclusive emphasis upon analytical-intellectual
understanding. The tone of the letter is one of personal anguish and
torment. Both its content and its tone suggest that Jung had indeed
attempted to apply Freud's methods to himself and to his patients but
experienced these methods as a form of excessive intellectualization
that snuffed out that mystery of life which is the unique, individual
self. Jung went so far as to link Freud's views with the devil. The
letter demonstrates that Jung's struggle to form an intellectual viewpoint separate from Freud's had a strong personal/psychological
dimension, and we can infer that, because this correspondence
centered on the problem of types, Jung was using this concept to
give intellectual substance to his psychological need to differentiate
himself from Freud.[4]

---

4. Jung wrote: "In wanting to understand, ethical and human as it sounds, there lurks
the devil's will, which though not at first perceptible to me, is perceptible to the other.
Understanding is a fearfully binding power, at times a veritable murder of the
soul . . . . The core of the individual is a mystery of life, which is snuffed out when it is
'grasped.' . . . The symbol wants to guard against Freudian interpretations . . . . With
our patients 'analytical' understanding has a wholesomely destructive effect . . . but is
banefully destructive on sound tissue. It is a technique we have learned from the
devil . . . . The menacing and dangerous thing about analysis is that the individual is
apparently understood: the devil eats his soul away" (Jung 1973*b*, pp. 31–32).

Thus, for both intellectual and psychological reasons it is not surprising that when Jung introduced his unique, creative thought to the world he began with a discussion of types. The problem of types is the point of passage from Freud's views to Jung's. In the first four chapters of the first essay Jung reviewed the origins and history of the psychoanalytic movement, criticized it, and so provided a rationale for his own approach. He argued that psychoanalysis had produced essentially two psychologies, that of Freud and that of Adler, each based on one of two universal attitudes—introversion or extraversion. The extravert quickly forms attachments to objects and is objectively oriented, while the introvert shies away from objects and is subjectively oriented. Thus Jung associated Freud with extraversion: the Freudian theory focused exclusively on the pleasurable relation of the libido to objects in the empirical, sensuously observable external world, and Freud was himself an extraverted person. Jung associated Adler with introversion: according to Adler, the patient does not seek attachments to objects but instead is subjectively oriented and strives for power over objects. Adler was an introverted person and hence produced this peculiar type of psychology. In such fashion Jung relativized both Freud and Adler.

Jung's evaluation of the two theories was a double one. In one sense, he asserted, both Freud and Adler had described important aspects of mental life. Their theories differed only because their psychological makeup differed. But in a more fundamental sense both were mistaken, for both were reductive. In the last analysis Jung brusquely dismissed both theories as mere "caustics" or "auxiliary" concepts. He likened them to medicinal poisons that could interrupt a disease process but could not enhance life as a whole. The psyche not only was reducible to anterior, personal motives but also contained intentional, meaning-constructing capacities that derived from present situations and orientations to the world. Jung believed that at its deepest level neurosis was a positive attempt to construct the meaning of life, and he concluded that Freud and Adler had together presented to the psychological world what he called the problem of opposites. For these reasons he felt that a new psychology—his psychology—was in order.

Jung's exposition of the theoretical reasons why the psychologies of Freud and Adler called for a third point of view is hard to follow.

In one sense it seems that the term "extravert" should apply to psychologists like Wundt and the later behaviorists, in which case the term "introvert" would apply to all the depth psychologies—those of Freud, of Adler, and of Jung. In another sense it seems more appropriate, if one is to call Freud the extravert, to identify Jung himself as the introvert. After all, introversion and its associated processes was one of his favorite, key subjects through which he often identified his psychology. In both cases Adler seems out of place. Possibly Jung's psychological need to repudiate Freud could have been a factor in the creation of his argument. We should remember that, during the psychoanalytic years, Jung deeply feared that Freud might associate him with Adler, and he protested to Freud that he would never go that way. But now, after the break with Freud and by means of the theory of types, it is Freud who is associated with the hated Adler—a comedown indeed for the founder of psychoanalysis who held Adler in contempt.

Fortunately Jung did not dwell on his type theory overlong but turned instead to a concrete case to further illustrate his objections to Freud and Adler. But he did far more than simply present one case history. He also described the most distinctive feature of his own therapeutic work—a feature prefigured in his personal experience. It is what I call the "typically Jungian moment" in therapy and personal life. When such a moment occurs, all the typically Jungian concepts are brought into play to describe it and to account for its origins. Thus this "moment" is the key point in Jung's exposition of his own ideas. It is carefully described in both essays and constitutes the burden of the paper entitled "The Transcendent Function."

In the early stages of psychotherapeutic treatment, Jung said, things proceed very much as Freud described it. A transference relationship is formed, and the doctor takes on various transference roles—father, mother, lover, and the like. At this time, accordingly, Freud's reductive techniques are necessary for interpreting dreams and transference as instances of personal and infantile sexuality. But the time comes when the transference relation takes a new turn, producing fantasies of a more extravagant kind. The doctor is exalted into the role of savior or demon. At times the patient deifies the doctor and at other times he views him with extraordinary contempt. Extravagant attitudes are also produced in the self: either self-deification, which Jung referred to as inflation or godlikeness, or else inferiority and what he called moral laceration. The continued application of Freudian techniques does not help in this new situation, for the patient has already assimilated the contents of these interpretations. According to Jung, the psychoanalytic method has released new sources of psychological energy and so has created a problem it cannot itself solve. Hence a new conceptual framework is required to account for this process.

At this point two observations drawn from the psychology of narcissism are in order. First, Jung's descriptions of the "new" stage of the transference unmistakably resemble certain features of what is now called a narcissistic transference. Such transferences activate the idealized parent imago, in which perfection is assigned to the therapist (in Jung's terms, the therapist as "savior"), or else they activate the narcissistically cathected grandiose self and its associated feelings of shame and inferiority (Jung's self-deification, inflation, and moral laceration). Jung used his own brand of moral and theological language to describe these psychological states—the language of what Kohut calls the "altruistic value systems of the West." Reflecting now from the vantage point of some fifty years of clinical investigation, we can suggest that Jung had encountered a patient population different from Freud's, in which preoedipal, narcissistic problems were predominant. However, the descriptive language he employed both obscured the psychodynamics of these states and also illuminated them.

Second, as Jung's correspondence with Freud, the writings of the psychoanalytic years, and the autobiography all amply demonstrate, Jung had internalized Freud's psychological theory—that is, he sincerely and persistently applied it to his own personal life as well as to the lives of his patients for a considerable time. And, as our analysis of Jung's identity transformation shows, Jung's formulations of clinical processes were closely related to his personal experience. From these two facts we can surmise with some confidence that Jung probably tried at first to use Freud's theory to interpret his own crisis experience; but he was forced to conclude, on introspective grounds, that, just as the theory did not work for his patients, it did not work for him—or vice versa. For, like that of his patients, Jung's personal organization was narcissistic and preoedipal. Thus it may have been a fateful advantage for Jung that Freud was not available to serve as a guide through the crisis years—much as Jung would have preferred it—for it seems that Freud, with his oedipal psychology, could not have helped him.

In the fifth chapter of his first essay Jung presented his own solution to the problem he had been developing in the four preceding chapters—that the therapeutic relationship produced phenomena that the theories and techniques of Freud and Adler could neither explain nor interpret with positive therapeutic effect. The patient's attitudes were extravagant because there were no grounds for them in his personal memories and personal history. Therefore they had to derive, Jung argued, from another source. Accordingly, he postulated a basic distinction between a personal unconscious and a wider collective or impersonal or transpersonal unconscious. The latter had no basis in personal experience but was, instead, a universal characteristic of the mental life of all people at all times. Because it was transpersonal in origin, this dimension of the unconscious could not be comprehended psychoanalytically.

Then Jung introduced what has come to be—along with the concepts of introvert and extravert—his most famous psychological idea: the archetype. The contents of the collective unconscious consisted of primordial images, what in 1916–17 he called "dominants." Thus, when the libido was released by the caustic techniques of Freud and Adler from its attachments to objects in the personal unconscious, it followed its own natural "channel" or "gradient" and flowed into the collective unconscious, where it attached itself to the archetypes, activating these universal forms of human experience. In Jung's mind this process accounted for his patients' extravagant overestimations and underestimations of the therapist and the self, and also for the otherwise bizarre contents of their imaginative life. For when this imagery is linked to the myths and legends of different cultures, which repeat themselves over and over again, it no longer seems bizarre, but instead is eminently sensible.

The emergence into conscious awareness of archetypal levels of experiencing set the fundamental task for the characteristically Jungian therapeutic process. The patient must learn to differentiate what is ego from what is not ego—that is, he must learn to distinguish his conscious ego from the archetypal contents of the collective unconscious. The remaining chapters of the first essay attempted to explain how such differentiation can take place, by adducing such notions as the synthetic or constructive method, the transcendent function, and the method of amplification. This process is described in greater detail and with greater clarity in the second essay, however, and that essay also gives further, more substantial conceptual elaboration to what I have called the typical Jungian "moment" of therapy— largely by way of its lengthy discussion of another famous Jungian term, the persona.

The second essay is divided into two parts. In the first chapter of part 1 Jung repeated his discussion of the necessity for distinguishing between a personal and a collective unconscious, and he explained his reason for this distinction by giving another example of a transference relation that produced an extravagant idealization of the therapist, this time referring to the idealization as a "virtual God-image." He also repeated his criticism of Freud's techniques, which reduced such collective material to personal reminiscence. The second chapter expanded on the processes of inflation and godlikeness as a consequence of the exposure of the ego to the collective unconscious. Then Jung introduced a new concept regarding the nature of "the collective." Just as he had previously distinguished between a personal unconscious and a collective unconscious, he also in effect distinguished between a personal consciousness and a collective consciousness. The link between these was what he called "the collective ideal." This new distinction prepared the way for the discussion of the persona and its breakdown, through which Jung conceptualized in a different way the typical "Jungian" moment in therapy, to which he was led in the first essay by the discussion of types.

Although Jung's mature thought gave little place to the early developmental life of the child, despite the considerable attention he paid to it in, for example, his 1913 lectures *The Theory of Psychoanalysis,* the core process does in fact include this phase of experience. In very early infantile life a differentiated, conscious ego has not yet formed, and therefore the child's mind is in touch with the collective unconscious. As the Jungian scholar Marie-Louise Von Franz notes (1970), archetypes are found in their purest form in fairy tales, so dear to the imagination of the child. As development proceeds, however, an individual—but not individuated—ego consciousness begins to emerge. Slowly, consciousness becomes differentiated from the collective unconscious—that is, the collective unconscious is repressed. A sense of personal identity appears that is heavily structured by the values, ideals, and meanings of the collective consciousness—in short, by the morality of the conventional social world. Parenthood, occupation, and social reputation are the most fundamental expressions of individual ego consciousness. Repression of the collective psyche is the first major stage in the development of individual personality.

In chapter 3 Jung developed this idea through the concept of the persona, his technical term for the adult individual's ego consciousness. By forming a persona, the individual conforms to a social definition of himself: he internalizes the collective ideals or collective consciousness of the community. Such a process is an inevitable aspect of human growth. Jung also believed that an excessive predominance of the persona characterized what he called the rational, extraverted character of modern civilization, or "the man of today." His concept of the persona was also very similar to Freud's notion of the superego, with one exception—that, unlike the superego, the persona was generally understood to be more fully accessible to consciousness. By linking Freud's concept of the superego with the rigid persona of modern man, Jung once again interpreted Freud's system in the light of his own.

But the persona could never constitute, of itself, genuine individuality. It was, as Jung said, "feigned" individuality, for it lacked the inner psychological depth necessary for true selfhood. For this reason the persona—especially the rational and extraverted persona of modern man—is highly vulnerable. The typical Jungian "moment" in therapy occurs, then, when that excessive commitment to collective ideals masking deeper individuality—the persona—breaks down or, as Jung sometimes also says, disintegrates. The dissolution of the persona produces an influx of collective material or involuntary fantasy and the already-mentioned feelings of inflation and inferiority.

While Jung believed that the dissolution of the persona was a fate that especially threatened modern extraverted, rational man, in this essay he also linked it to the analysis of personal repressions by means of Freud's techniques. Presumably Jung meant that a successful Freudian analysis could sometimes maintain the persona, albeit in rigid form; but the analysis of personal repressions could also trigger the emergence of collective material. In the latter case Freud's psychoanalysis became, as it had become in the first essay, a "caustic" that created the need for a Jungian approach. In this sense it was the precipitant for the peculiarly Jungian moment in the process of psychotherapy.

Jung's description of the disintegration of the persona, associated as it was with modern rationality, has been conceptualized in the thought forms of classic psychoanalytic theory by the contemporary psychoanalyst Allen Wheelis (1958). Wheelis describes the process by which modern man can lose contact with his surrounding social environment and become prey to vague inner yearnings and anxieties; he calls this "the decline of the superego." However, from the point of view of the psychology of narcissism—which should not be, as I have emphasized, identified in any simple way with classic psychoanalysis—the dissolution of the persona is a crisis in object relations in which the self loses its cohesion and becomes fragmented, and in which previously formed ideals are rendered questionable. As I shall show at the conclusion of this book, the psychology of narcissism has direct bearing upon the problem of meaning for modern man.

The concept of the persona and its vicissitudes can also be understood in terms of Jung's attempt to give a personal account of the failure of Freud's theories and techniques to monitor successfully the turbulence of his own critical years. During the psychoanalytic period Freud's ideas had become "collective ideals" for Jung. His break with Freud produced disenchantment with these ideals, and, as we know, the break was accompanied by the emergence of what Jung called collective material. This process began immediately after their trip to America in 1909, when Jung first inwardly disagreed with Freud, and continued until it finally entered the center of Jung's consciousness immediately after the final break and during the critical years. Jung underwent his own breakdown of the persona.

Jung concluded his discussion of the persona with the brief fourth chapter, in which he described two ways a person might fail to come to terms with the emergence of archetypal material from the collective unconscious and the experience of inflation it produced. On the one hand, the patient could undergo a "regressive restoration of the persona." In this case he simply turned his back on inflation and its associated collective material and tried to reconstitute himself as he was before the break. As a result of this strategy his personality was diminished—for the collective material, if assimilated, contains the seeds of a deeper individuality—but stable, and he could work at the tasks of his life only in a resigned way far below his actual potential. On the other hand, the patient could naively accept the inflation or godlikeness and erroneously identify with archetypal contents that seemed to provide a wondrous transformation. Jung called this "identification with the collective psyche." It resulted in megalomania and one became a reformer, prophet, or martyr—a flat collective figure. In both cases a person failed to acquire the new and profound sense of his individuality that could have derived from a balanced relation between his ego consciousness and the collective unconscious.

The breakdown of the persona constitutes the typically Jungian moment both in therapy and in development, in two senses—it forms the basis of Jung's attempt to distinguish his theories from Freud's, and it also provided him with the opportunity to introduce his unique psychological ideas, which constitute nothing more or less than a series of qualifications of the individuation process itself. The rest of this essay describes that process in detail. The 1916 essay only briefly mentions several central concepts that are far more fully elaborated in part 2 of the final version—the concepts of individuation, the shadow, the anima and animus, and the final stage of individuation, the formation of the self that occurs in relation to a god-imago. The early essay contains much description of these processes, however, though the concepts themselves are only briefly noted; furthermore, if one reads the early essay in the light of the definitions in *Psychological Types,* one finds that the final version tells little more about the individuation process than do the materials of the creative period, taken together. The final version only organizes the ideas and descriptions of the earlier edition, deepening and clarifying their meaning. All the basic ideas that compose the individuation process are therefore present in the writings of the creative phase of the critical period, although they are more accessible in the final versions of the *Two Essays.*

The individuation process referred, in its broadest sense, to all the life experiences of the individual, from earliest infancy to the encounter with death. But Jung also defined it in a narrower sense as the attempt of the conscious ego, beset by the breakdown of the persona, to come to terms with the archetypal contents of the collective unconscious, and he added that this process usually occurred at the beginning of the second half of life. He developed his discussion in four chapters, which make up part 2 of the second essay. The first, "The Function of the Unconscious," gave an elaborate definition of individuation; the second described the anima, the first collective figure the male ego must confront; the third chapter elaborated the complex psychological processes by which the ego differentiates itself from figures of the unconscious; and the final chapter described the second major archetypal or collective figure—this time male and paternal in nature—from which the ego must differentiate itself. Successful negotiation of this last stage brought into reality the self as the goal or end point of the individuation process. It also required that religion be interpreted psychologically, an issue that will receive careful clarification in subsequent chapters.

In chapter 1 Jung defined individuation first in a general way, then specifically in terms of the persona, and finally as a special kind of relation between the ego and the world as a whole. Individuation meant, he said, a coming to selfhood or self-realization in which one achieved a definite sense of one's innermost, incomparable uniqueness. This profound sense of oneself as distinct from every other person in one's life is therefore a transformation of the persona, in two senses: on one hand the ego is no longer predominantly structured by the collective ideals of the consciously discerned social world but, so to speak, transcends these; on the other hand, the ego is free from the influence of the collective images that beset it as a result of the breakdown of the persona. Domination of the ego either by the collective consciousness or by the collective unconscious produces inflation. Hence, individuation is also a coming to terms with inflation. Finally, individuation signifies that the ego consciousness of the self has become accessible to what Jung called the wider world of objective interests, the world at large that exists beyond personal relations to family and social group.

Each of these facets of individuation bears the marks of a successful struggle with narcissism. To become a unique self entails acquiring some sense of separateness between self and other. Other persons are less likely to be experienced as self-objects. Individuation signifies the overcoming of inflation, which is, as already noted, similar to the condition of narcissistic grandiosity in the self. And, if the self is to become concerned with objective interests in the real world, it must be somewhat free from narcissistic preoccupation with its own ambitions, interests, and goals.

Jung himself experienced some similar sense of release from self-absorption as his critical years drew to a close. His renewed interest in the world of thought, his acceptance of his new role as a much-sought-after psychotherapist, his willingness to be the leader of a new school of psychology, and his readiness to interpret to his contemporaries the nature of modern as opposed to traditional Christian experience all testified that Jung had struggled successfully with his own narcissism. And yet, as the later chapters of the autobiography also clearly show, he was by no means able to renounce an intense preoccupation with the products of his own consciousness.

Having defined the goal of individuation, Jung turned to a twofold description of its actual process: he spoke of the specific archetypes that the individual confronted and of the psychological activity by which these unconscious contents were assimilated. The goal of development was to become free from the parental imagoes. Thus, the first work of self-realization was to come to terms with the contents of the personal unconscious—memories and desires that one experienced and repressed in relation to his immediate family. Once again Jung emphasized the necessity for the "caustics" of Freud and Adler. He believed that the contents of the personal unconscious appeared in dreams and myths in the form of the archetype of the shadow. Although he did not, even in the final version of this essay, devote a chapter to discussing the shadow, it is clear from his many references to it—in the early essay he referred to the "devil dominant"—that confrontation with this archetype denoted a kind of "prologue" to the individuation process. Although it is a collective image, it also refers to the contents of the personal unconscious that derive from one's relationship to one's parents.

Once one has recognized the shadow and come to terms with it, a genuine engagement with the collective unconscious is possible. This takes place through the archetype of the anima, one of Jung's most important and difficult concepts, which he developed in chapter 2. He believed that the first significant personal relationship for a man, once he has freed himself from his parental imagoes, is with a woman. Woman replaces the parents in the immediate environment of the adult, taking on the roles of companion and courtesan. Hence an understanding of this relationship is of fundamental importance for further development. Jung postulated several sources for this relationship: for example, residues of the individual's relation to his own mother and the empirical, observable effects of the actual woman with whom the man is associated. But there is a third: an inherited collective image of woman, independent of real women in the real world. This image is his anima or, as Jung also liked to put it, his soul. Thus, Jung explained in more detail in the next chapter, man naturally tends to project this unconscious, inherited image onto his female companion and in fact chooses her insofar as he senses she is able to receive his projections. Accordingly, a man has to objectivate this image—that is, he has to project it and bring it to consciousness—and then assimilate it. Otherwise he will be unable to move forward in realizing his individuality more fully.

Jung believed that the anima and the persona were related in a balanced or compensatory fashion. The persona is a psychological structure composed of patterns of conformity to social norms. It is the ideal of personality and derives from the individual's father, who provides these ideals. If the conscious ego identifies fully with the persona, then the individual becomes only a role, fully adapted to society and fully rational, and as a consequence the dimension of inner living—the unconscious—is repressed. But Jung believed that no matter how rigid the persona of a man might be, there still existed for him an invisible system of relations with the unconscious. Hence the anima is at one level an archetypal figure with which the ego must contend, but at a more abstract, theoretical level the anima is also a symbol for the existence of the unconscious. To come to terms with the anima is, therefore, to become aware that there is an unconscious. Just as the persona structures adaptation to outer, social reality, so the anima structures adaptation to inner, psychological reality. Accordingly, when the archetype of the anima is assimilated, an autonomous complex is transformed into a function of the relation between conscious and unconscious. The individual has to come to terms with the existence of the unconscious.

Jung's analysis of the structure and dynamics of the anima reflects aspects of the psychology of narcissism at two points. He believed that a man inevitably projected part of himself onto a chosen female figure—that is, a man "saw himself" in the figure of a woman and based his love for her on this likeness. Here Jung described what in effect was a psychic merger in which the woman was experienced as part of the self—in Kohut's terms, as a self-object. What he referred to as coming to terms with the anima was, in effect, a positive developmental process in which the merger is worked through and the self becomes more autonomous and more capable of treating the woman as an object independent of itself. In fact, Jung said as much: "If the soul-image (anima) is projected, the result is an absolute affective tie to the object. If it is not projected, a relatively unadapted state develops, which Freud has described as *narcissism*. The projection of the soul-image offers a release from preoccupation with one's inner processes" (1971, p. 472).

Second, in all this Jung came close to saying that the unconscious of the man had its origins in a very primitive relationship with a female figure. In so saying he anticipated—although he conceptualized it very differently and, I think, less successfully—the views of Kohut and the British school of object-relations theorists who emphasize the priority of the mother over the father in the formation of the infantile self. It may be that what one in later life learns to know as the unconscious is first formed in the earliest infantile relation to the mother.

The concept of the anima is perhaps even more autobiographical in its origins than any of Jung's other originative ideas. During his early years his relationship with his mother was much stronger than his relationship with his father. Jung reported that his critical years contained visions of female figures (which he later interpreted as anima figures), and Hannah has suggested that one of these figures had its origin in Jung's intense involvement with Toni Wolff, his patient, mistress, and companion. It is not surprising, given these circumstances, that in later life Jung's female followers greatly outnumbered his male followers, and his writings on mythology often gave precedence to mother figures. Jung's personal life demanded that his thought give special prominence to the role of woman.

In chapter 3 of part 2 Jung described in detail his techniques for differentiating the ego from the figures of the unconscious. The libido of the collective unconscious can enter consciousness only in the form of fantasy images. Therefore the first step in coping with the unconscious is to allow the unconscious fantasy images to come into one's mind. In this way unconscious contents are initially projected or objectivated—that is, they are experienced as other than the self. Then, with the help of the therapist, the conscious ego actively participates in the images and through interpretation begins to understand them rather than succumbing to them and to the moods of depression and elation they create. Jung called this method active participation or active imagination. Through it the autonomous power of the unconscious is slowly dissolved and transformed. Finally, this process—which we might call an "imaging through" after the fashion of Freud's "working through"—produces a new permanent attitude in the patient, which Jung called the transcendent function. It consists of an enhanced sense of individuality, and because the self is free from collective forces it is capable of a wider and more spacious sense of relation to the world at large.

In the final chapter Jung describes the last stage of the individuation process, subsequent to the anima and coming to terms with it. At this time a second collective figure emerges that Jung referred to in several different ways: as a god-imago, as a mighty man, or as a "mana personality." The dynamics of this final stage, however, are quite similar to those of the preceding stages. Knowledge of the anima and, correspondingly on a more abstract level, knowledge of the existence of the unconscious produces a new surge of confidence and overevaluation in the self. Once again the self becomes inflated and godlike. This inflation is so excessive and so intense that the individual experiences it as if "I and the Father are one." In other words, the patient inwardly feels that he has actually merged with the Deity.

Under such conditions the only solution for the extraordinarily limited and vulnerable ego is to summon up all its previously acquired self-knowledge, in order first to realize that its sense of godlikeness is structured by yet another archetypal image, this time the image of God, and, second, to renounce all claims to power and perfection implied in such an experience. Conscious realization that one has been in the power of an archetypal image leads to differentiation of the ego from the archetype. Jung described this process as a second real liberation from the father, which, when successful, produces a genuine and lasting sense of selfhood and of true individuality. One has at last achieved a balanced and compensatory relation between conscious and unconscious processes. No longer need one be beset by feelings of inflation and inferiority.

But what became of this last and most impressive of all archetypal images? Jung concluded his discussion on a theological or, it would be more correct to say, antitheological note. One could, he said, of course "concretize" this image as "Father in heaven," attributing to it "absoluteness" or what theologians call transcendence, as the Protestant tradition had done for centuries. Such a solution was, however, utterly contrary to all of Jung's hard-won psychological self-understanding. For making concrete the image of God would simply create a new and permanent sense of moral inferiority in the individual, precisely what the Christian church required of those who submitted to its doctrines and practices. It was better, Jung said, to eschew theological solutions to psychological problems. Therefore he not only concluded by defining the self as a "midpoint" or balance between conscious and unconscious processes, but also added that it might equally be called "the god within us." By this he meant that the concept of God was an inevitable product of the natural and spontaneous process of individuation; that it was accessible to all persons who were sufficiently endowed to pursue that process far enough and long enough; and that theological doctrines of God and their associated practices, rooted in sociohistorical institutions and traditions, were distortions of this process. Jung's firm stance against traditional Christianity, and his simultaneous attempt to relate his new psychology to it, will be discussed in detail and clarified in the following chapters, especially chapter 7.

The implications of Jung's final stage of individuation for the psychology of narcissism is clear. The new influx of inflation, associated with the feeling that "I and the Father are one," is really a new phase of narcissistic grandiosity in the self, accompanied this time by a psychic merger with an intensely idealized cosmological

image, the image of the Deity. Jung's solution to the problem—
"destructuring," as it were, the sense of grandiosity into a nonsub-
jective archetypal image and frankly renouncing the wish to believe
so highly in oneself—is really a struggle with narcissism in the self
and with a narcissistic merger relation with an omnipotent, idealized
cultural object. The result is in effect a more cohesive and autonomous sense of self capable of relating to objects in the world as
entities independent of the self.

In fact, the entire individuation process can be understood to a
considerable extent as a struggle with narcissism. The breakdown of
the persona produces feelings of inflation (narcissistic grandiosity in
the self) and inferiority (shame in the self). Then the person goes
through a dialectic in which inflation is reduced by means of
applying the method of active imagination to the archetypes that
accompany inflation. It is not clear, however, whether all archetypes
are experienced as self-objects, although this is certainly so in the
case of the anima and the god-imago. We should remember that,
though Jung described only these two archetypes in the second essay,
he believed there were many more, depending on the individual's
circumstances, and that their dynamics were essentially the same.
The self emerged through a final coming to terms with narcissistic
grandiosity.

Throughout this discussion of Jung's critical years and the
emergence of his core process, I have tried to show connections
between the two—between his personal experience and the construction of his conceptual system. These specific linkages need not
be reviewed here. But one utterly central correspondence between
the two remains unmentioned. Probably the psychologically deepest
phase of Jung's personal crisis was a tripartite experience: his
encounters with a female figure or anima and with a male figure or
wise old man, Philemon, and the resulting sense of having achieved
a new and lasting sense of selfhood. This tripartite experience is
clearly reflected, point for point, in his summary of the individuation
process, which in essence consists in an encounter first with a female
figure or anima, then with the fatherly god-imago, and which
eventuates in a deepened and permanent sense of individuality and
selfhood. In the very act of naming his own personal experiences,
Jung created a unique system of psychological ideas.

Jung's confusion between what is subjective and what is objective in mental life made its way into his mature theory, particularly at the point where he spoke of the ego's need to differentiate itself from the contents of the collective unconscious. At this point I am inclined to agree with the British psychoanalyst Anthony Storr when he states that Jung anticipated the viewpoint of those psychoanalysts who write about an inner world of ''internal objects.'' Jung's descriptions of archetypal images, Storr believes, are closely similar to preoedipal infantile fantasy figures that have been described by other psychoanalysts (Storr 1973, p. 55). That such images are not accessible to an introspective attitude oriented to personal-developmental origins—which was Jung's experience—does not necessarily mean that they are nonpersonal in their genesis. Nor, for that matter, does the conviction that such images might have their origins in very early infantile life imply that one should abandon the hypothesis that they may also be an important psychological factor in comparative mythology. Had Jung retained his earlier interest in infantile fantasy life during the crisis and mature years, he might have come to similar conclusions himself.

In sum, the link between Jung's personal crisis and his creative thought is the psychology of narcissism. Just as his critical years were a struggle with narcissism, so he cast this struggle in terms of a total theory of human becoming. His personal struggle, with all its achievements and failures, became the paradigm for what he would teach during the rest of his life. To say so, however, is to interpret Jung. He did not accept such terminology, of course, for it was not available to him. Whether he would accept it today is another question, beyond the scope of this book, although the evidence is there for Jungians and non-Jungians alike. Given the terminology and language of the times, Jung cast the problem of narcissism in cosmological and ethical language. The idealizations of the self were described as cultural universals, and inflation was, in the last analysis, overcome by an act of will—a person morally renounced overweening grandiosity.

If this is so, in what sense can it be said that Jung advanced our understanding of narcissism? The final chapter of this book takes up the broader cultural implications of narcissism in Jung's psychology. Here it is sufficient to note that on this point his achievement was ambiguous. On one hand, Jung gave much-needed attention to the phenomenon of narcissism. He courageously emphasized the individual self and its relations to itself—the internal relations of human consciousness—as opposed to, for example, Freud's exclusive preoccupation with object love. As a therapist he was, I suspect, more empathic to narcissistic phenomena than was Freud, who shied away from the "narcissistic neuroses." In this he opposed the cultural repression of narcissism just as Freud opposed the cultural repression of sexuality.

On the other hand, Jung also indulged the negative aspects of narcissism to an extraordinary degree. His system of thought, when taken seriously by his readers and patients, placed them at the center of a cosmological epic and encouraged them to view their past traditions and surrounding culture exclusively in terms of the structures and processes of their own consciousness. In doing so he gave them occasion to think endlessly about themselves, and he blunted their capacities for achieving social distance interpersonally and for achieving objectivity in the disciplined study of the religions and cultural objects of the past. Once again, thought and person are related, for Jung's autobiography testifies to the extraordinary degree to which—despite his recovery from his crisis period—he remained absorbed by the endless proliferation of his own consciousness. When Jung remarked that he had resigned from his university post at the onset of his critical years to dedicate himself to the service of the psyche (1961a, p. 192), he committed himself only in part to the discipline of psychology. He also dedicated himself to his own psyche. And his system of thought legitimated this self-absorption, both for himself and for those who followed after him.

### Epilogue: Freud and the Struggle with Narcissism

Although I have argued that a narcissistic transference characterized Jung's relation to Freud and that Jung's original psychological thought thus contained several themes prominent in the psychology of narcissism, this discussion should not be taken to imply that it was Jung alone who was affected. As my analysis of the *Letters* indicated, Freud also was engaged in a psychic merger with Jung. It is therefore reasonable to hypothesize that, as a result of his break with Jung, he too had to come to terms with the interruption of a psychic merger—in other words, that he too underwent a struggle with narcissism (although it was less intense) and with associated narcissistic rage directed at Jung. It is also reasonable to hypothesize that his personal, psychological situation structured his intellectual efforts at the time of the break, as happened with Jung. Although it is not within the purview of this book to document the various psychological and intellectual shifts Freud underwent after the break, several brief remarks must be made about his work at this time and about the bearing of the psychology of narcissism upon it.

Three of Freud's papers—"The Moses of Michelangelo" (1914*a*), "On Narcissism: An Introduction" (1914*b*), and "On the History of the Psychoanalytic Movement" (1914*c*)—all written in the winter of 1913–14, a period Jones has described as "the worst time in the conflict with Jung" (Jones 1955, p. 366), display evidence that narcissism was central to Freud's life at this time. In the first, which was published anonymously, Freud offered a unique interpretation of Michelangelo's famous statue of Moses. Most existing analyses of the statue argued that it depicted Moses coming down from Mount Sinai with the tablets of the law under his arm, seeing the Hebrews dancing around the golden calf, and preparing to rise up in rage against their defection. Freud reversed this view: the statue depicted Moses *after* an outburst of rage, in a state of subsequent calm, the result of having renounced his rage. Freud concluded that as such the statue represented a man's highest mental achievement, "that of struggling successfully against an inward passion for the sake of a cause to which he has devoted himself" (1914*a,* p. 233). Jones (1955) has suggested that Freud identified with Moses and that the unfaithful mob represented the defections of Adler and Jung that Freud had so recently endured, to which we might add that the tablets of the law symbolized the basic tenets of psychoanalysis. Roazen (1975) generally agrees with this interpretation. What is most notable about this scenario, however, is that no oedipal conflict is present. Rather, the "inward passion" is narcissistic rage and the successful "struggle" is the renunciation of narcissistic rage. We may take Freud's analysis of the statue as an effort to work through , in the modality of projection and through the medium of an artistic work, his sense of narcissistic affront or injury occasioned by Jung's defection. The paper is evidence of a struggle with narcissism.

In the second essay Freud turned from a purely projective and dramatic mode of coping with the problem of narcissism, forced upon him by the interruption of a psychic merger with Jung, and engaged it directly—conceptually and intellectually. Several points need to be made about Freud's writing this paper at this particular time in his life. First, before 1914 the term narcissism, though mentioned from time to time in Freud's writings, was peripheral to psychoanalytic theory as a whole. Before 1914 there were very few references to narcissism. But, beginning in 1914 and from then on, the problem of narcissism received frequent attention and reference. Second, the new theory of narcissism became integral to Freud's developing thought in the metapsychological period. According to Ellenberger, the theory of narcissism "was to be the prelude to a complete restructuring of the framework of psychoanalytic theory" (Ellenberger 1970, p. 511). Third, while Freud focused directly on the phenomenon of narcissism, he adopted a moralistic stance toward it, embodying what Kohut has called "the altruistic value systems of the West." This was especially clear in Freud's pejorative attitude toward parental love: "Parental love, which is so moving and at bottom so childish, is nothing but the parents' narcissism born again" (Freud 1914*b*, p. 91). According to Kohut, however, the narcissism of parental love is a legitimate—indeed indispensable —mode of relationship in which the parent invests the child with much-needed esteem, provided, of course, it is intermixed with object love as well.

These features of Freud's thought, which took form exactly at the time he broke with Jung, can be coupled with the observation that Freud had participated in a narcissistic merger transference with Jung. This leads me to hypothesize that the break with Jung forced upon Freud a particular experiential matrix and that the theory of narcissism emerged as a result of introspective reflection structured by his interpersonal situation. Freud may have gone through a miniature version of a second "creative illness" (Ellenberger) as a result of his transference to Jung. I say "hypothesis" because an analysis far more detailed than this one would be necessary to prove it. But if this is true, it appears that their complex encounter led both

Freud and Jung to turn their energies to working out the nature of narcissistic processes—Freud speculating about ego-libido and object libido and Jung about the process of introversion. Interesting too is that each man in his own way took a moralistic stance toward narcissism.

The third important paper of this period also suggests that Freud was undergoing his own struggle with narcissism, but in this case the struggle took sociological, rather than psychological or conceptual, form. As a result of the defections of Adler and Jung and the increased development of psychoanalysis, Freud felt it absolutely necessary to establish a boundary between his science and the positions of the dissidents. In this essay he claimed for the first time that psychoanalysis was his own creation, and with strong emotionality he repudiated the writings of Jung. According to Strachey (Freud 1914c, p. 4), Freud adopted a "far more belligerent tone than in any of his other writings." For example, he spoke of Jung as "relentlessly devoted to the furtherance of his own interests" (1914c, p. 43). As I have already noted, a struggle with narcissism consists in part in distinguishing between the self and an important "other." In this paper Freud came to terms with the interrupted psychic merger with Jung by firmly consolidating his sense of self, now associated with the leadership of the psychoanalytic movement, and thus clearly distinguished his sense of self from Jung. But the belligerent and bitter tone of the essay indicates that this task was an emotional as well as an intellectual one, and that it was not easy for Freud to accomplish.

## Five

# The Role of the Experience of Religion in the Formation of Jung's Thought

The discussion has thus far focused entirely on the psychological origins of Jung's thought and so has attended the adult Jung, partly because this period was the time when his ideas were forming and changing and finally became consolidated. But this is also because, by good fortune, the correspondence with Freud, combined with the supporting evidence from the autobiography's description of the crisis period, provides the best evidence for constructing important psychological features of Jung's personality and its bearing upon his creative ideas. And, from time to time, religion has unavoidably intruded itself upon the events of this period—personally, in Jung's idealization of Freud and his related motivations for writing *Symbols of Transformation;* intellectually, in the contents of that work and, more broadly, in the form of his struggle to come to terms with traditional Christianity, one of the three sociocognitive tensions forming the core process.

But the personal experience of religion was an important factor—far more important than has thus far been indicated—in the genesis of Jung's creative system of thought. Its effects can now be examined, and this must be done in the context of his early and adolescent years, for two reasons. Jung's childhood and adolescent experiences were inseparable from his experience of religion. To study the former is to become preoccupied with the latter. But his experiences of religion were also

deeply psychological in character. We have examined the correspondence with Freud and the autobiography's description of the
crisis period, which together contain the richest evidence for understanding certain psychological features of Jung's life, and have
formed our hypothesis regarding the narcissistic transference to
Freud and the struggle with narcissism in the critical-creative years.
Thus we are now in an advantageous position to generalize retrospectively about Jung's preadult years and to encounter the formidable power of religion in his life. Although the autobiography's
evidence for these years is even more episodic and fragmentary than
for the years with Freud and even for the crisis period, it contains
considerable material that can be illumined by the psychology of
narcissism, and that approach in turn can help clarify Jung's often
confusing experiences of religion.

During his early childhood and adolescence Jung experienced
religion in two very different modalities. On one hand he was
intensely exposed to his father's traditional Protestant Christianity,
institutionalized in the conventions of his Swiss social environment.
On the other hand, he also experienced religion in a modality best
described as "personal-mystical-narcissistic"—personal, because it
was internal and private rather than social; mystical, because it
emphasized a special relation approximating union with a god-
imago; and narcissistic, because in such moments Jung's self-esteem
and need for idealization were intensely engaged. Throughout his
youth each of these modes was a source of personal conflict and,
furthermore, each was in conflict with the other. Then, during his
university and early professional years, he ceased to have these
troublesome experiences of religion. He became more involved in
his immediate social world. But the conflictual experiences of religion reemerged as his relationship with Freud became more strained,
and they became even stronger during the critical years. Jung formed
his core process, in part, to resolve his conflicts with religion.

But how did this resolution come about? It can be understood only
in terms of the interweaving of several factors: the emotional tone of
the early years; the relation between the two modes of experiencing
religion; and the relation of both of these to the experiences with
Freud and the experiences of the critical years. During his early years
Jung repudiated traditional Christianity, and this encouraged the

second mode of his experience of religion, the personal-mystical-     ⌐
narcissistic. As he developed, Jung unsuccessfully attempted to
reconcile these modes to one another and to the circumstances of his
everyday life. Under the influence of his intense emotional and
intellectual relationship to Freud, however, both modes of experiencing religion reasserted themselves, and Jung tried to work
these out, with only partial success, first on Freud and his ideas, then
by writing *Symbols of Transformation*. After the break with Freud
Jung entered his critical years and created his core process. The
individuation process—which culminated in an encounter between
the ego and a god-imago, an encounter that was resolved in the
formation of the self, defined as the "god within us"—enabled Jung
to finally come to terms with the two modes of the experience of
religion. Thus, through a complex process of assimilation and repudiation of religion Jung formed his original ideas.

All the main biographical discussions that interpret Jung's life up
through the critical years—by both Jungians and Freudians—rely
exclusively or in great part upon the autobiography (Hannah 1976;
Jaffe 1972; Van der Post 1977; Winnicott 1964; Stern 1976). Of
these, the two that give the most detailed accounts of outer as well as
inner circumstances are those by Hannah and by Stern, who, despite
relying upon the same central text, give radically different evalua-
tions of the personal quality and significance of Jung's life. Barbara
Hannah joined the Jungian group in Zurich in the late 1920s and
spent the rest of her life there as a practicing analyst, lecturer, and
author. Her intimate knowledge of Jung himself and of the people
and circumstances that surrounded him provides the reader with important details and interesting reminiscences about Jung's life. But
she romanticizes and rationalizes Jung's distressful inner conflicts at
all the major points of his life, converting them all into outstanding
achievements of the great man.

Paul Stern is an American psychotherapist who practices within a
broadly Freudian psychodynamic orientation. The portrait he has
created of Jung is intensely critical and consistently negative. According to him, all his life Jung was egotistical, self-serving, and
opportunistic—in short, Jung was a narcissist in the most morally
pejorative sense of the word, although Stern does not once use this
term to describe Jung. While much of the primary material Stern

uses—the autobiography and the letters—is recognizable to the reader already familiar with it, his book also contains a great deal of additional information and sharply phrased interpretations. Although this material is important and rich in implication, one needs to recognize that none of it is documented.

Taken together, the two books are extremely valuable—provided they are read with their biases in mind. Hannah provides good factual detail about Jung; Stern offers many hypotheses that, even though undocumented, must nevertheless be taken seriously, and he debunks much of the adulation and veneration uncritical admirers of Jung constantly indulge in.[1] The two books jointly provide a detailed outline of Jung's life, but their conclusions about Jung's personality are polarized by the old stereotyped and sterile Freud-Jung debate—for one Jung is always creative, for the other he is always egotistical and confused—and neither recognizes the importance of religion in the development of Jung's ideas. Since such biographical discussions are available, I will not attempt to survey the development of Jung's life as a whole but will instead focus on the emotional tone of his early and adolescent years, drawing upon the psychology of narcissism—which includes both pathology and creativity. And I will emphasize the relation of emotional tone to Jung's personal experiences of religion.

Jung reviewed his memories of the first ten years of his life in the short chapter 1 of his autobiography. Its brevity (eighteen pages) should not obscure the fact that it clearly depicts complex conflicts and linkages between psychological processes and religious ideation. These beset Jung's early life and were carried forward into the later years. Although the chapter is a chronicle of inner events, Jung also gave pivotal information about his early relationship to his parents, and he described two equally important imaginative episodes of a religious nature. These are the most significant features of the first years.

The outstanding psychological theme of Jung's first years was his

1. For an example of such adulation and veneration one need go no further than the first sentence of Van der Post's book: "I have, I believe, known many of those the world considered great, but Carl Gustav Jung is almost the only one of whose greatness I am certain" (Van der Post 1977, p. 3).

personal isolation and loneliness. There is little evidence that Jung's parents or others took emotional, empathic interest in his life and development. This feature of Jung's early emotional life is keynoted early in the chapter, where he reported that when he was three his mother left home to spend several months in a nearby hospital. Jung presumed that the departure was related to difficulties in his parents' marriage. He described the atmosphere of the house a few years later as "unbreathable." He was "deeply troubled" by his mother's absence, and it had a consolidating effect on his early emotional life: "From then on, I always felt mistrustful when the word 'love' was spoken. The feeling I associated with 'woman' was for a long time that of innate unreliability. 'Father,' on the other hand, meant reliability—and powerlessness" (1961a, p. 8). Thus Jung portrayed a situation of early narcissistic vulnerability: a lack of empathic linkage between his parents and himself (they were absorbed with the problems of their marriage) and inability to idealize his father, and a generalized impoverishment of inner self in the face of an indifferent family.

The isolation and loneliness that began with his parents very early in life extended to his relations with other children when he began school. Jung spoke of his "intense sensitivity and vulnerability" and of "the loneliness of my early youth" (1961a, p. 17). He reported that he had looked forward to school because it would provide playmates. But to his disappointment he found that his schoolmates alienated him from himself. When he joined in their games he became, he found, different from the way he had thought he was. He described this wider world as "dubious," "suspect," "obscure," and "hostile" (1961a, p. 19). For him, it seems clear, there was no sense of like-minded sharing of feelings with peers in group play and group solidarity. Neither at this time nor in later adolescence did he develop what Sullivan has called "chum" relationships.

Jung's isolation and aloneness, his narcissistic vulnerability, created by an unresponsive and unempathic personal environment, forced him back into himself. From time to time during his early childhood he experienced overwhelming images, bizarre visions, and vague fears at night. He also reported a number of external events that created a generalized sense of dysphoria throughout these years. It is not surprising, then, that the early Jung was most comfortable and secure when he was alone. He built toy towers and battlefields, which he then destroyed. During these activities he did not want to be disturbed. He enjoyed picture books and looked at them for hours. He reported pleasure at being taken to an art museum, where he could not tear himself away from studying the art objects.

Thus Jung's earliest years were characterized by a profound sense of division between his own inner experience of himself and his perception of the surrounding world's estimate of him—a sense of vulnerability in which the self's relation to another is central. This division might also be considered a precursor to identity-diffusion, in which social estimates of self are at odds with the self's own estimate. This split structured the role of the experience of religion during Jung's earliest years. Indeed, the phenomenon of religion was extraordinarily real for Jung at this time.

Jung's earliest encounter with religion was with the faith of his father, as mediated by his mother (1961a, pp. 9–10). She had taught him a short bedtime prayer that asked "Lord Jesus" to take little children to himself, like "chicks," to protect them from being devoured by Satan. Jung disliked this prayer because the idea of being "taken" by Lord Jesus—whose name had been invoked at burials he had witnessed—had sinister connotations. He began to distrust Lord Jesus. He associated Lord Jesus with clergymen—"the gloomy black men in frock coats, top hats, and shiny black boots" (1961a, p. 10) who gathered at burials. One day a Jesuit passed nearby while he was playing in front of his house. The appearance of the priest frightened Jung so much that he referred to this episode as his first conscious trauma. He also associated Lord Jesus with his father's colleagues and his eight uncles, all of whom were parsons. Lord Jesus came to be a symbol of traditional Christianity. Of all this, Jung concluded: "I made every effort to force myself to take the required positive attitude towards Christ. But I could never succeed in overcoming my secret distrust" (1961a, pp. 13–14). Just as Jung was unable to form a positive idealization of his father, he was equally unable to idealize the pastoral leadership and associated religious doctrine represented by his father and others—he could not idealize culturally transmitted images of the divine. In fact, he actively repudiated them.

Under the impress of personal isolation from parents and peers, and because he could not idealize parental and cultural objects, Jung was forced at times to handle the problem of personal esteem entirely in terms of his own inner life. He managed this during the early years by means of visions, dreams, and rituals. Two episodes of this sort stand out as of great significance. In the first, Jung dreamed, at the age of three, that he was walking in a meadow and came upon a large hole. He climbed down and discovered a lateral corridor, which he followed for some distance. Then he saw, at the end of the corridor, a huge phallus ensconced on a golden throne. The dream terrified Jung. For days he was afraid to sleep lest it be repeated, and it haunted him, he said, for years.

The dream was related in a dynamically negative way to Lord Jesus, the symbol of traditional Christianity. Jung reported that it occurred at the same time as his conscious trauma when he saw the Jesuit. And the dream would reappear in his mind whenever Lord Jesus or other references to traditional Christianity were mentioned. Jung interpreted the dream of the phallus as a subterranean god and, much later in life, as an initiation into the secrets of the earth. But some more dynamic psychological reflection is also available: Gedo has referred to it, building upon previously developed evidence for narcissistic problems in Jung's life, particularly in his relationship to Freud, as "the desperate need to idealize a male figure" (1974, p. 58). Thus Jung repudiated the social and cultural idealizations of the Christianity of his childhood and constructed his own internal object of idealization. This experience took a religious form.

At the close of his first years Jung had another crucial experience of religion. He engaged in a ritual action instigated, he said, by "my disunion with myself and uncertainty in the world at large" (1961a, p. 21). He carved out of the end of a wooden ruler a small manikin, complete with frock coat, top hat, and shiny black boots. He hid this figure in the attic of his house, and over a period of many weeks he would visit it "whenever I had done something wrong or my feelings had been hurt, or when my father's irritability or my mother's invalidism oppressed me" (1961a, p. 21). Jung felt that the existence of this manikin was a great secret that conferred upon him "the feeling of newly won security." He described this secret as "a very powerful formative influence," as "the essential factor of my boyhood,'' and as "the climax and conclusion of my childhood'' (1961*a*, p. 22). This action again portrayed the attempt to idealize a male figure. Unlike the phallus dream, however, it was far more modified by social reality—the coat, hat, and boots likening it to the religious leaders of his community. Primitive and private as this idealization was, it constituted an advance in self-cohesion over the phallus dream, and, although the self-esteem it conferred was self-stimulated, it was nonetheless more realistic in form.

During Jung's early years, then, narcissistic problems (inability to idealize a parental imago and corresponding low self-esteem) were established, and they set the stage for his pattern of the personal experience of religion: the traditional and conventional religion of father and community, which created doubt and distrust, versus the "secret" person-mystical-narcissistic experiences of the manikin ritual, which created an inner sense of well-being and security, and the phallus dream, with its sense of initiation.

In what Jung described as the second period of his life (chap. 2, his "School Years," approximately eleven to sixteen) this pattern underwent considerable development, owing in large part to his increased capacity for conceptualization, although its basic character remained unchanged and in fact deepened. First, Jung's relation to traditional Christianity became more intellectual: he dealt more with religious ideas and not exclusively with feelings about religion. Second, his personal-mystical-narcissistic side also became more articulate and frankly theological. But he was more firmly convinced than ever that the two modes of the experience of religion were utterly irreconcilable. And, as this phase of his life unfolded, his fundamental narcissistic dilemmas persisted and continued to under-gird his religious conflicts. All of this came together in his famous, elaborate fantasy about the destruction of a cathedral.

Jung described his relation to traditional Christianity during this period in many different ways, but with great consistency: "I remember from the time I was eleven the idea of God began to interest me" (1961*a*, p. 27). He took classes in divinity, even though they were "unspeakably dull." He allowed the many parsons in his family to engage him on an intellectual level: "I heard many religious conversations, theological discussions and sermons" (1961*a*, p. 42). In addition to this he read in his father's library,

composed largely of theological books, and listened to his sermons. The culmination of all this was Jung's confirmation and first
communion. This central Christian ritual, with its intellectual preparation, deeply disappointed Jung. Its failure to produce "an experience of grace and illumination" forced him to conclude that "I now
found myself cut off from the church and from my father's and
everybody else's faith. Insofar as they all represented the Christian
religion, I was an outsider" (1961a, p. 56). Thus Jung consolidated
intellectually the pattern he had established emotionally during his
earliest years—he repudiated traditional Christianity.

This increased distrust of institutional Christianity exacerbated
Jung's sense of isolation and loneliness and deepened his need to
possess "secrets" that could in turn serve as a source of much-
desired self-esteem. This trend reached its climax in an episode,
reported in considerable detail, that occurred during Jung's twelfth
year. I refer to it as "the cathedral fantasy." Of it Jung remarked:
"My entire youth can be understood in terms of this secret" (1961a,
p. 41). While returning from school on a bright summer day, he took
special notice of the beauty of the town's cathedral and imagined
God, its maker, sitting regally above it on a golden throne. Immediately he experienced a strong wish to think further about the
cathedral, but the wish was accompanied by an even stronger
inhibition against further thought. The conflict grew to the proportion
of an obsession, and for several days, in a state of mind that at times
approached panic, Jung was only barely able to refrain from thinking
about the cathedral. He pondered with great anxiety who or what
might be forcing him toward these thoughts. Finally, with the
greatest apprehension, he decided it was God's will for him to think,
and that God would side with him even if he had ideas that were
critical of God. He then imagined that a huge turd fell from under the
throne of God, smashing the cathedral to pieces, and simultaneously
he felt a great sense of relief.

Jung's conclusion about the meaning of this fantasy-vision was
easily as remarkable as the fantasy itself, involving as it did some
very heady theologizing—for now Jung demanded intellectual understanding. Why, he asked, did God befoul his cathedral? God,
Jung concluded, sided with this desecrating thought in order to
demonstrate to the questioning Jung that he refused to abide solely by

tradition and that he was not to be limited to the cultural monuments
men had created to him. This view of God was diametrically opposed
to his father's theology: "That was what my father had not understood . . . he did not know the immediate, living God who
stands . . . above his Bible and his Church" (1961a, p. 40). This
experience became the basis of Jung's later reflection that his father's
life had been ruined by a pathetic and shopworn theology, and as a
result of this conclusion Jung pitied him and reported that he had
even tried to help him, but to no avail. His father was unable to
change. Thus Jung believed himself superior to his father in spiritual
matters, a conviction that aggravated even further his already pervasive sense of aloneness and low self-esteem.

Note that, whereas Jung at first reacted to this fantasy with
euphoria (an "indescribable relief"), its lasting effect was quite the
reverse: "The experience also had the effect of increasing my sense
of inferiority. . . . It induced in me an almost unendurable loneliness" (1961a, pp. 40–41). In other words, the experience intensified
Jung's low sense of self-esteem, what I have called his narcissistic
vulnerability. This fact, joined to what is already known of the
centrality of narcissistic organization in Jung's life, permits the
following interpretation. We should, I think, take Jung's word for it
when he remarked that his entire youth could be understood in terms
of this fantasy. In fact, Jungians should accord this fantasy the same
attention that Freud's key dreams in *The Interpretation of Dreams*
have received from historians of the psychoanalytic movement.
Jung's fantasy—especially as the product of the mind of an eleven-
year-old—is remarkable in its effort to penetrate to a dimension of
meaning in his surrounding cultural reality, as well as being rich in
wit and irony.

The "cathedral fantasy" represented a momentary coming together of Jung's two modes of experiencing religion, which had
heretofore been separate in his mind, then a firm repudiation of
traditional Christianity in the interests of his personal-mystical-
narcissistic mode. The image of the cathedral represented the traditional Christianity of his father. Through this ancient cultural object,
so highly esteemed by those in his social environment, Jung attempted once again to idealize his father and all he stood for. But the
attempt was unsuccessful: he could not, the fantasy tells us, idealize

his father and his Protestant religious beliefs and ethics. Instead, he created in imagination a vision of the destruction of these ideas and ideals, by means of setting up a god-imago with whom he had a special and intimate relationship. This was the god of the personal-mystical-narcissistic mode of experiencing religion, which had already appeared several times in Jung's life. Recall that for Jung "father" meant "powerlessness." The component of rage and destructiveness in the fantasy—the shattering of the cathedral—was accordingly not motivated by a desire to competitively destroy his father and his religion. On the contrary, the rage was narcissistic rage, an expression of frustration stemming from the fact that Jung experienced his father and his religion as inadequate objects for idealization. Consequently, he destroyed them in imagination and set in their place the god of his personal-mystical-narcissistic concerns. Thus the personal mode of experiencing religion derived once again—as it had before—from a repudiation of the traditional mode. But in this fantasy the ascendancy of the former over the latter was, for the time being, complete.

Throughout the remainder of his school years Jung emphasized the importance of this personal-mystical-narcissistic mode, especially that it contained a fundamental conflict all its own. On one hand he spoke of this image of God as terrible, incomprehensible, and vindictive. He understood neither the origins nor the nature of his experience of God—his secrets—and this sorely perplexed him. On the other hand, this sense of a special relation to the private, true God gave him a "sense of destiny" and "an inner security" to face the anxieties life imposed upon him at this time: "I had the feeling that in all decisive matters I was no longer among men, but alone with God . . . these talks with 'the Other' were my profoundest experiences" (1961a, p. 48). During his critical years Jung reflected on this mode of the experience of religion, and out of this reflection emerged the concept of the collective unconscious, a key idea in the core process.

Toward the end of Jung's school years and at the beginning of what he called his student years (chapter 3, approximately ages sixteen to twenty-five), a major dimension of experiencing, wholly absent from his life until this time, began to assert itself. This new trend colored all the events, both inner and outer, of this period, and it is this coloration of all events, rather than any single one, that is important. Jung associated the trend most specifically with the beginning of university studies, and it reached its culmination and consolidation when he graduated from medical school and took up his first professional post at the Burghölzli Hospital in 1900, at the age of twenty-five. The description of this period in the autobiography displays a major shift both in emotional tone and in the content of his experiences.

For the first time in his life Jung began to take a sustained interest in the social world about him—not only in his studies but also in vocational planning, friends, and new ideas. His approach to these activities was increasingly active, at times even zestful, and on occasion actually exhilarating. The painful, dysphoric loneliness and isolation of the preceding years began to slowly disappear. And though he continued to have theological arguments with his father from time to time, he was no longer beset by intensely emotional religious struggles. There were no fresh editions of the phallus dream, the manikin ritual, or the cathedral fantasy, and gone was his anguish over the capricious and terrible god of private, immediate experience. All these now slipped into the past. Jung had begun to take cognizance of the social order surrounding him and actively strove to adapt himself to it.

On the basis of this extremely fundamental shift in Jung's pattern of experiencing, we can conclude that his considerable narcissistic vulnerability—his intense feelings of inferiority, low self-esteem, and frustrated experiences of grandiosity, and his associated need to idealize powerful parental imagoes—went into a state of fundamental abeyance or, as Jung himself suggested, were repressed. In Erikson's terminology, Jung was actively and successfully assembling and appropriating elements necessary for a personal sense of identity. Or, since both Erikson and Kohut use the term ''self,'' it could be said that in this period Jung acquired a strong sense of inner self-cohesion. Evidence for this view is pervasive and clear.

Reflecting on the close of his school years, Jung wrote: ''Between my sixteenth and nineteenth years . . . my depressive states of mind improved . . . school and city life took up my time, and my increased knowledge gradually permeated or repressed the world of intuitive premonitions. I began systematically pursuing questions I had consciously framed'' (1961a, p. 68). Jung read works in the history of philosophy, particularly Hegel, Schopenhauer, whom he greatly admired, and Kant. Of this reading he said: "This philosophical development . . . brought about a revolutionary alteration of my attitude to the world and to life. . . . I knew what I wanted and went after it'' (1961a, p. 70). At this time Jung also became concerned with vocational choices and plans: "I had to go forward—into study, moneymaking, responsibilities'' (1961a, p. 88). Jung described his days at the University of Basel, during which he had joined a fraternity, in similar fashion: "My student days were a good time for me. Everything was intellectually alive, and it was also a time of friendships. In the fraternity meetings I gave several lectures on theological and psychological subjects. We had many animated discussions'' (1961a, p. 97).

Jung's mature identity, as has already been suggested, was a threefold one that was consolidated in intimate relation to the formation of the core process. It is no doubt hazardous to speculate on the antecedents of this mature identity, since each of its strands underwent considerable development and change. But it is likely that, because Jung's first real independent access to the social world was cast in terms of serious thinking and spirited debates about the modern world, his identity as an intellectual, social critic, and moralist—explainer of the nature of modernity to modern man—was first formed at this time, during his university years. However, this sense of himself was soon to be superseded, for a brief period, by the professional role of physician.

Jung described many other events toward the close of his student years: his reflections on philosophical materialism, his thoughts on Nietzsche, his initial decision to specialize in internal medicine, his experiences with his young cousin—a medium who became the subject of his doctoral dissertation—and his final decision to become a psychiatrist. All of these have the flavor of positive social adaptation, self-coherence, and an intense involvement with the immediate world of roles and people. This basic shift in Jung's personality organization reached a climax when he began his work as a young doctor: "With my work at the Burghölzli, life took on an undivided reality—all intention, consciousness, duty, and responsibility'' (1961a, p. 112). This positive orientation to the world—so reminiscent of the highly socialized Protestant work ethic—remained essentially undisturbed until Jung's fateful meeting with Freud and the critical years that relationship precipitated.

The role of the personal experience of religion in the formation of Jung's original ideas, which has not been adequately recognized, can now be clarified and understood by inserting the above analysis of Jung's early personal experiences of religion—and their subsequent modification by social adaptation during his university and early professional years—into the already-described interplay between person and thought during the period when his core process was being formed. We have already seen how religion was tangled up in Jung's conflicts with Freud and in his writing of *Symbols of Transformation*. Now, however, we can put that entanglement into a broader context by relating it both to the early experiences and to the core process. When this is done, the significance of religion for the creation of Jung's ideas falls into three easily recognizable stages: the early and adolescent years; the period of conflict with Freud and the writing of *Symbols of Transformation;* and the critical, creative period when new, Jungian ideas emerged. During each of these phases the processes of assimilation and repudiation of religion were at work.

The relatively conflict-free character of Jung's first two years of association with Freud (1907–09) no doubt enhanced a double trend of social adaptation and secularization. Jung had become allied with a great man in a common cause. And he rightly perceived Freud as a secular intellectual and psychoanalysis as a new mode of consciousness in the West, free from traditional thought forms and taking an interpretive perspective upon them.

But the later stage of Jung's relation to Freud did not simply augment the course of his secularization, as might be expected; paradoxically, this became instead a time when Jung's earlier experiences of religion—or, rather, his propensity for personal experience of a religious kind—reasserted itself. During the first two years of their relationship Jung and Freud idealized each other. But after their return from America in 1909 Jung's idealization became excessive. Freud impressed him so strongly that his earlier frustrated need for idealization was reactivated. He temporarily endowed both Freud's person and his thought with divine significance and asserted that

psychoanalysis was the fulfillment of the Christian gospel, a view
Freud firmly rejected. While Jung applied the language of traditional
Christianity to Freud, his idealization was cast in the terms of the
personal-mystical-narcissistic mode of the experience of religion.
Then, simultaneously, he began to report that he was having
"mythological fantasies" and becoming fascinated with the
psychological interpretation of religion.

In all this Jung repeated his earlier patterns regarding the experience of religion. On one hand his references to mythological fantasy
indicated that he was having fantasies—and perhaps dreams and
visions as well—similar to those of his childhood and early adolescence. This time, however, he no longer experienced the fantasies in
a purely passive way. Instead of simply submitting to them, he
brought to bear some modicum of interpretive power, by seeing in
them parallels to the mythologies of the past. According to the
*Letters,* these parallels immensely pleased and excited Jung. In such
fashion the personal-mystical-narcissistic mode of the experience of
religion was reactivated, and in the activity of "seeing parallels"
Jung began to assimilate into his theoretical thinking this mode of the
experience of religion. On the other hand, he was sufficiently
secularized so that he continued to repudiate traditional Christianity.

Jung gave formal expression to this pattern of assimilation and
repudiation—and to the conflicts in his mind between the two modes
of experiencing religion—in *Symbols of Transformation.* The book
was in essence an attempt to put together the two modes of the
experience of religion, albeit in the light of what Jung believed he
had learned from Freud. Although he had revised the libido
theory—to Freud's great displeasure—the book was fundamentally
Freudian in interpreting traditional religion in the light of a secular,
posttraditional theory of the mind. In writing *Symbols of Transformation,* Jung narcissistically and grandiosely attempted to fuse his
own fantasies with the great myths of the past and, at the same time,
repudiated traditional Christianity by interpreting it by the libido
theory. The book was unsuccessful because at the time Jung did not
have adequate control over his inner, mental processes, and instead
of using these as a potential source of insight, he simply projected
them into the text. Still, *Symbols of Transformation* was an attempt
to come to terms with the two modes of the experience of religion,

assimilating to a limited degree the personal mode and strongly repudiating the traditional mode.

The conflict between the two modes of experiencing religion persisted into Jung's critical-creative years, became exacerbated, and was finally resolved by the formation of the core process. Jung remarked that one of the crucial factors precipitating the critical years was his repudiation of traditional Christianity in writing *Symbols of Transformation* (1961a, p. 171). This made him realize that he was in effect faced with a "meaning-vacuum"; that is, he was without a myth to live with in the present. This realization intensified the personal-mystical-narcissistic mode of experiencing religion, augmented in part by the fact that this mode had become a long-term pattern and in part by the loss of a positive relationship to Freud. During the critical years, however, Jung was able to come to terms with this mode of experiencing religion. Remember that the focal point of his fantasies during these years was the biblical figure of Elijah, who became transformed into the image of Philemon, a guru who taught Jung to understand his unconscious processes.

In this fashion the personal-mystical narcissistic mode of experiencing religion structured the experiential matrix of Jung's reflections during his critical years. While writing *Symbols of Transformation,* he had projected similar experiences into the text. But during the critical years he actually reflected on his experiences, gaining some distance from them, and in doing so devised an interpretive schema that would make sense of them. In this way he acquired some mastery over his experiences, instead of either passively submitting, as he had done in the early years, or projecting them into his writing, as he had done during the years with Freud. In this process of experience and reflection he assimilated his personal-mystical-narcissistic experiences of religion into his core process. It was Jung's way of bringing order not just to his interpersonal experience, as the previous chapter suggested, but to his experience of religion as well.

This linkage between the personal experience of religion and the formation of concepts is especially clear in the structure of the individuation process. The end point of that process was the formation of the self—single, cohesive, and whole—and its relation to a god-imago, what Jung called the "god within us." Through this formulation he was able to recast the god of his earlier, private experience in the context of an elaborate conception of human becoming as a whole. By including this concept in his theory he was able to give an account of this aspect of his experience; but, because this god-imago was designated as a natural and spontaneous product of the human imagination, Jung was also able to free himself from the arbitrary control he felt this imago had exercised over him in the past.

Because the "god within us" was natural and spontaneous, it was substantially different from the transcendent and absolute God of traditional Christianity. In his mature years Jung repeated his earlier pattern with regard to religion by constantly interpreting the God of traditional Christianity in the light of his core process. The formulation of the individuation process assimilated the personal mode of the experience of religion while providing the means for explaining the traditional mode. By creating his new system of ideas Jung thus laid to rest a conflict that had plagued him throughout the first half of his life—and at the same time he provided himself with the concepts and problems that were to occupy him throughout the second half.

The preceding discussion has emphasized exclusively one particular dimension or level of the process by which the emergence of Jung's psychological ideas was related to his experience of religion: he assimilated the personal-mystical-narcissistic mode and repudiated the traditional mode. But the work of assimilation and repudiation was not thereby exhausted. Jung's relation to religion, particularly to traditional Christianity, was more complex than this. While it is true that at one level he repudiated it, it is equally important to recognize that, at another level, he also attempted to assimilate elements of it; for that religion was also, in part, the experiential matrix out of which his psychology emerged. A full viewing of the situation requires that we take both levels into account.

How did these two levels work out in relation to each other? The personal-mystical-narcissistic mode served as the fulcrum or axis, so to speak. Jung's intensely negative experiences of traditional Christianity forced upon him the personal-mystical-narcissistic mode of the experience of religion, which he assimilated into his core process, as we have just seen. But all the while he maintained a relationship with traditional Christianity at another level. At this level he attempted to assimilate elements of it during his critical years, but this process of assimilation was structured by the personal-mystical-narcissistic mode. The latter was the "lens" through which the former was viewed. Thus Jung not only experienced religion in two fundamentally different modes; he also had, on the basis of these modes, a double relation to traditional Christianity.

## Six

# Sociological Factors in the Formation of Jung's Thought

The psychological perspective has been extremely valuable for reconstructing how personal experience contributed to Jung's creative system of ideas over a period of nearly twenty years. And hovering over the emergence of Jung's thought and its psychological dynamics was a second influence, that of religion. But psychological conflicts and religious meanings were not the only factors that gave rise to Jung's thought. There were social or cultural influences that can be distinguished from the interpersonal and religious factors—although, as we shall be forced to recognize, no one sphere can be completely separated from the others. .

Accordingly, this chapter inquires into the social and cultural forces that influenced Jung's ideas. This can be appropriately considered a question in the sociology of knowledge or, more precisely, the sociology of *psychological* knowledge. And since social and cultural forces were inseparable from ideational elements in Jung's situation, I refer to the "sociocognitive" forces related to the emergence of his ideas. This aspect of the derivation of Jung's thought has in part already been anticipated in the discussion of the intellectual tensions he first addressed in the writings of his neo-Freudian years. These tensions, I now argue, had their basis in broadly defined social and cultural conditions.

The sociology of knowledge constitutes an amorphous body of literature, not readily adapted to the analysis of psychological ideas. A thorough methodological discussion of such adaptation, furthermore, would be tangential to the task at hand. But discussions of the genesis of Freud's thought provide the means for obviating such a difficulty. It was possible to draw upon the rich literature analyzing the psychological origins of Freud's thought and—because the two men were so intimately related both personally and intellectually—to apply such psychological frameworks to the formation of Jung's thought. There is a small but growing body of literature analyzing the sociological origins of Freud's thought; but there are no similar investigations of Jung's system. It is therefore appropriate to apply the same procedure to this literature: first, to select a sociological analysis of Freud's thought, noting how it makes its case; and, second, to extrapolate from that discussion leading ideas and to apply them, with appropriate modification, to Jung's system.

Although the sociological literature is small (e.g., Buss 1975; Ross 1972; Rieff 1966; Berger 1965; Weinstein and Platt 1973; Cuddihy 1974; Robert 1976; Homans 1974) compared with other genres of sociological inquiry, it is nevertheless extremely valuable here. By giving an account of the rise of psychological ideas that is not simply personal-psychological in nature, it lets us situate personal experience in the wider sociocultural context. Specifically, it lets us link such phenomena as the struggle against narcissism and the identity crisis with sociocultural forces. Yet, in accenting the social basis of psychological ideas, this approach avoids swinging to the opposite and naive extreme of the purely conceptual and ideational orientation—as if psychological ideas were the product of pure ratiocination.

The sociology of psychological knowledge also provides a wider context for understanding the role of religion in the rise of psychological ideas. It lets us place the preceding—admittedly personalistic—treatment of the role of religion in a sociohistorical setting. Some of these sociological discussions make a fundamental distinction between tradition and modernity. They then link religion with tradition and the rise of psychology with modernity and by this means associate the rise of psychology with the decline of religion. Thus the relation between Jung's struggle with the religion of his father, his appropriation of his private personal-mystical-narcissistic brand of religious experience, and the creation of his system of ideas are not to be understood as simply idiosyncratic events. They are also vehicles for the expression of cultural forces. Through this approach it is possible to derive a sense of the interplay between personal, religious, and cultural forces in the formation of Jung's—and, by implication, other psychologists'—leading ideas. Such interplay constitutes the essence of the contextual approach.

### Weinstein's and Platt's Theory of Modernity, the Rise of Psychoanalysis, and Jung's Psychology

Of the several sociological discussions mentioned above, the most important for the purposes of this book is *The Wish to Be Free,* by Fred Weinstein and Gerald Platt. More than any of the others, these authors attend to the details of Freud's theories and at the same time relate them to specific historical movements as they contributed to the rise of modernity out of the Western tradition. According to Weinstein and Platt, Freud's psychoanalysis was the culmination of a long period of evolution in the social organization of the West. The central feature of this evolution was the gradual emergence of more and more freedom from various forms of authority for individual actors. It culminated in the industrial revolution, which created novel social conditions—in particular, it moved the father out of the family circle and into the economic order and segregated the mother from wider social involvement, confining her to the family. These social conditions established as a social fact a new and intense conflict between fathers and sons. Freud exercised great introspective power in the context of this social fact, describing its dynamics accurately and in detail. He ''codified'' social conditions and so created his psychology. Thus four basic elements compose this theory: the nature of traditional societies; the nature of modern societies; the dynamics of the shift from the first to the second; and the role of Freud's investigations in codifying the final phase of the modernization process.

Weinstein and Platt center their analysis upon the relation between authorities and subjects in a variety of spheres—religious, political, economic, and familial. Authority structures in traditional societies are hierarchical—that is, they nurture and protect their subjects and in return demand and receive obedience. Therefore the relation of subjects to authorities is characterized by dependency and exclusion: subjects are dependent upon authorities for nurture and protection, and they are excluded or removed from the sources of power. As a result, traditional societies create an unconscious adherence to the common culture, characterized by a lack of separation between paternal and maternal functions—the child experiences both father and mother as coercive and as nurturant—which in turn blurs any sharp distinction between emotional and abstract mental functions in the mature individual. Thus both authorities and subjects take for granted the moral necessity for dependency relations and arbitrary authority: as long as authorities are nurturant and protective, subjects will not rebel.

In modern societies, on the other hand, the relation between authorities and subjects is one of autonomy and inclusion. Autonomy consists of a rational, calculating approach to all situations in everyday life. The individual is free from dependency upon authority figures—he is self-nurturant and self-protective. Accordingly, he exercises self-control, active mastery of both inner and outer worlds, self-denial, and competitiveness. Autonomous rationality is identical with Weber's descriptions of modern man's worldly activity and commitment to methodical work. In the family of the autonomous individual, paternal and maternal functions are clearly separated, and this produces a capacity for separating emotional and abstract mental functions. Because he is autonomous, the individual demands and receives inclusion: he identifies with and internalizes the values of authority figures, and this permits him to be included in the economic processes that surround him. Modern societies therefore do not display an unconscious adherence to the common culture but instead—by virtue of the collective presence of autonomous, included members—are pluralized and undergo a fundamental separation between public and private morality.

How did the modern capacity for, and commitment to, autonomy arise? The history of the West from the Reformation onward reflects individuals' increased capacity for autonomy and inclusion in relation to different types of authority—first religious, then political, then economic, and finally familial. In these spheres the dynamics of the emergence of autonomy were the same. In each case the authority figures violated the morality that bound subjects to them—they withdrew their nurture and protection. Aggressive wishes for, and fantasies about, freedom from authority were thus for the first time rendered psychologically possible. These aggressive wishes and fantasies were registered in the consciousness of rebellious leaders and their followers, taking the form of a new theory of freedom—be it religious freedom, as in the Reformation and Protestant theology; of political freedom, as in the Enlightenment and the theories of the philosophes; or of economic freedom, as in the rise of the working classes and Marxism. In each case the new theory produced the possibility of autonomy and the desire for inclusion.

The process became relevant to psychoanalytic theory at the time of the industrial revolution. That social upheaval separated the family from the political and economic orders in a very specific way: the father became removed from the family, whereas the mother became functionally located in the routine maintenance of the home. Before the industrial revolution the father both protected and nurtured his children—he was part of their developmental experience during their earliest years, and consequently they related to him according to the modalities of subjection and exclusion. But when the social order drew the father out of the family and into the economy, he no longer could give nurture, and his demands for obedience were experienced as unreasonable and oppressive. The withdrawal of the father permitted—or even required—his sons to entertain aggressive fantasies of rebellion leading to wishes for autonomy and to demand inclusion in the world of the father. Autonomy and inclusion were achieved through identifying with the father and internalizing the values of society by internalizing his values.

Just as past revolutionary situations created new theories of autonomy, this new sociological situation and its consequences for the family called for a new type of reflection, and it was through Freud that such reflection was accomplished. The heart of Freud's theories, developed in *The Interpretation of Dreams* during his self-analysis at the end of the 1890s, consisted of a twofold proposition: the oedipal complex and its unconscious nature. As such it was a theory that made conscious the rivalry between fathers and sons—that centered on one hand upon the son's struggle for autonomy from the coercive power of the father and, on the other hand, upon the son's wish for inclusion in his father's world, the world of public, economic life outside the home. Because Freud's thought became socially accepted and then institutionalized—at least in America and England, the two countries most affected by the industrial revolution—he codified or registered in social consciousness the realities of the new economic situation, thereby providing a "therapy" by which sons everywhere could adapt to the new world of their fathers. Weinstein and Platt quote Heinz Hartmann's well-known observation on the effects of social change: When the social character of the external (social) world changes, creating stress, the ego will attempt to fulfill its organizing functions by increased insight into internal processes. Psychoanalysis codified the rights of the individual within the family, in relation to the father—more specifically, it codified the rights of the ego within the individual personality. It is in this sense that one can speak of the social determination of psychoanalytic theory—that is, the sociology of psychoanalytic knowledge.

But this analysis of the social conditions underlying Freud's psychoanalytic ideas cuts in two directions. It discloses the social basis of what Freud did indeed discover, and it situates him in the social process. Freud's own participation in the socioeconomic situation of his age was the basis for his oedipal discoveries and all they entailed: Freud's own oedipal rebellion against his father led to his liberation from the past and his inclusion in the social order as a middle-class intellectual and a scientist. This was the sociological side, so to speak, of Freud's genius. Since his own father belonged more to traditional than to modern ways, Freud had to forge his own autonomy and inclusion in the modern economic order, and his self-analysis was a crucial instrument in this work. But this very participation blocked off certain other avenues of investigation. In other words, it limited Freud's insights. This limitation was nowhere more pronounced than in his treatment of the feminine world.

Freud considered only the positive libidinal ties of the son to the mother as these centered on his oedipal complex. Except for this he gave exclusive attention to paternal authority and to that process whereby sons become like, or fail to become like, their fathers. He thus ignored females at two points. First, he actively resisted attending to the mother's role in the preoedipal period, when she is the major influence in socialization. During this period the ego-ideal, which later fuses with the superego, is first formed and provides the foundation for the child's positive sense of values and attachments. Put in more recent psychoanalytic terminology, Freud could not expand his focus beyond—or behind—the sphere of object love to include preoedipal object relations. Second, Freud's personal involvement with the industrialized social world also precluded careful study of the daughter. Freud conceived of little girls, and of women generally, as dependent and familial in nature—in short, as unable to break from parents and challenge their authority. Unable to be autonomous, shut off from the economic processes of society, they continued to live in the modalities of subjection and exclusion.

Freud's view of religion also reflected his resistance to introspective reflection upon the preoedipal period—a fact significant for the purposes of this book. Freud's friend, the writer Romain Rolland, once asked him whether an individual's attachment to religion might not be traced to a stage in human life when the subject/object dichotomy did not exist—to that stage, that is, when the infant-mother union was whole and uninterrupted by considerations of object love. Freud, however, persisted in relating religion only to the feeling of helplessness, which was a response to an inability to manipulate the environment in an objective and instrumental manner—in short, to an acute sense of the absence of autonomy. Preoedipal considerations were, Freud said, intangible—too shadowy, too remote.

According to Weinstein and Platt, insight into the preoedipal mother is a function of industrialized societies—really a function of late industrialization—because such insight rests upon recent social and economic change. Before the organization of highly industrialized, technological societies, there existed no sharply differentiated and extended preoedipal period in the development of either the male or the female child. Before the changes imposed by the economic revolution, the father had not been so thoroughly drawn away from the family and into the economic sphere. Hence he participated as an important figure in the child's development much earlier than the oedipal stage. There was therefore no exclusive preoedipal mother in preindustrial societies. The industrial revolution produced the typical modern family, and with it singularly intensive affective relationships centering on the mother-child relationship and excluding the father. The literature on the preoedipal mother thus codifies these sociological changes that are characteristic of late industrial society.

It is possible to extend this sociological analysis to Jung's psychology. The formation of Jung's original psychological system, particularly the dynamics of the critical years and the contents of his core process, clearly indicated intimate linkages between his thought and person and the thought and person of Freud. If Freud's introspective crisis and its ensuing conceptual formulations codified social change, in what sense were Jung's crisis and the following consolidation of ideas also subject to social forces? Applying this perspective, however, produces results even more complex than in the case of Freud. In one sense Jung's psychology is also an appreciation of modernity, and as such it carries forward the codification process begun by Freud. But in a broader and more important sense his psychology must be seen, from the viewpoint of this sociology of modernity, as a regression or failure to meet the socially determined demands of modern life. I myself see Jung's psychology less as a regression than as an attempt to integrate traditional and modern orientations to life. This is the sociological key to its formation.

One of the outstanding features of Jung's system is its awareness and appreciation of the phenomenon of modernity—that is, the modern commitment to autonomy and inclusion. Jung's concept of the persona, particularly the rigid persona of modern man, associated as it was with rationality and the extraverted attitude, matches perfectly the above descriptions of the successful, autonomous person. The person whose ego is fully identified with his persona is completely adapted to the social roles of contemporary life and thereby achieves inclusion in the economic process. Furthermore, the persona-oriented individual is autonomous, for he has achieved the capacity to separate emotional and abstract functions in his mental life. The juxtaposition of persona and anima is a key point in Jungian psychology: consciousness of outer and inner reality are closely interrelated. A rigid persona signifies repression of the anima—of the unconscious instinctual-emotional components of personality. Note in this regard that Jung linked a rigid persona to

Freud's concept of the superego and also to the mode of social adaptation that successful Freudian therapy produces. In all this it may be safely said that Jung's thought, like Freud's, was a response to or codification of those social processes that Weinstein and Platt have described as the essence of modernization.

There is a second point at which Jung can be said to have anticipated the sociological consequences of the modernization process through his psychology. In his lectures, *The Theory of Psychoanalysis,* first published in 1913 when he was beginning to separate himself from the psychoanalytic movement, Jung attempted to describe what are now called preoedipal relationships—he called them "presexual"—between child and mother. And in his description of the role of the anima in the core process Jung not only assigned a central position to the role of woman in the life of man; he also described, as I have already suggested, a clinical situation in which the woman is experienced as part of the self of the man—a type of relationship that precedes object love. At these two points, then, Jung's psychological thought penetrated beyond Freud's exclusive preoccupation with oedipal factors and into a delineation or codification of the child's preoedipal concerns. Paradoxically, Jung, who was so preoccupied with tradition, was in this instance, at least, more modern than Freud.

But, whereas autonomy and inclusion were the goal and end point of Freud's psychology, they were only the beginning of Jung's. He never tired of insisting that oedipal-sexual factors had to be analyzed in any given case before his unique therapy could begin. From a sociological perspective this insistence affirmed the inevitability of modernity as an orienting psychological fact. Thus the rigid persona of the rational, extraverted modern man was the sine qua non of the individuation process. This process is initiated by the breakdown or dissolution of the persona, followed by the emergence of archetypes from the collective unconscious, the differentiation of the ego from these archetypes, and its gradual assimilation of energies associated with them, which leads to the establishment of the self as a "midpoint" between the ego and the collective.

The archetypes of the collective unconscious consist of the oldest and most fundamental psychic contents of mankind. As such, they constitute the essence of tradition. Traditional man—or, as Jung sometimes preferred to say, "archaic man"—insofar as his consciousness was undifferentiated from the archetypes of the collective unconscious, displayed the traits not of autonomy and inclusion, but of subjection and exclusion. Jung's psychology thus contains, alongside its perception of modernity, an even stronger appreciation of tradition. By formulating the concept of individuation, Jung attempted to synthesize or integrate the outstanding features of both modernity and tradition into one unified, consistent process. From a sociological point of view the pressures of modernity forced him to construct a system of thought that would assimilate tradition to modernity. It was as if he had to have it both ways.

The single most general characteristic of modern societies, according to Weinstein and Platt, is the appearance of private morality alongside public morality and the consequent formation of a pluralistic society. The moral codes of traditional societies created an absolute unity between public morality and personal behavior. But modern, technologically complex societies have increased the number of possible legitimate behaviors, forcing a distinction between public and private morality. This in turn has required that individuals acquire the capacity to separate emotional from abstract mental functions. Such rationalized control of affect produces autonomy and, along with it, the possibility of inclusion. Thus individual autonomy and inclusion presuppose a fundamental split between public and private realms of feeling and action.

Freud's psychology fits lock-and-key with this social pattern. The distinction between ego and id is tantamount to a separation between emotional and abstract, and the therapeutic imperative to strengthen the ego in relation to the superego creates the possibility for a private morality sharply differentiated from the public realm, since the individual and cultural superego are closely related. Other examples could be cited. For instance, the distinction between the pleasure principle and the reality principle makes possible in the individual's own mind a separateness between personal, private experience and impersonal, public morality. But in every instance Freud's psychology not only emphasizes the private individual, but also provides, through the theory itself, a way the private self can maintain contact with the public order. Freud's psychology derives from the social situation of industrialization, but it also provides a means of relating to that social situation.

The appearance in a technologically advanced Western society of a fundamental split between private and public morality and its associated pluralization of the social world is also essential for a sociological understanding of Jung's psychology. Unlike Freud's thought, which recognizes the new privacy and autonomy but seeks to create bonds between it and the public sphere, Jung's system locates psychological reality and the nature of the self more within the private sector. Because individuation begins with the rigid persona and proceeds to release the repressed (collective) inner core of the self, it progressively divests the person of his participation in publicly determined roles and behavior. The collective consciousness gives way to the collective unconscious, which is entirely psychical, not social. The end point of individuation is a pure and intensely privatized self, liberated from all obligation imposed from without by the social order. Thus Jung's psychology is an extreme response to the pluralization of modern society, in which the individual, oppressed by the conformity-inducing forces of collective life, eschews these and instead reconstitutes his norms and values from a perspective within the self. Of course the individual self retains its persona, but the persona is secondary when compared with the self.

The central conceptual feature of the argument of *The Wish to Be Free* is the distinction between tradition and modernity. Within this general framework, the authors locate the various resolutions on a historical continuum—first religious, then political, then economic, and finally intrafamilial. In this they associate the rise of Freud's thought exlusively with economic changes and discern no relation between these and the thought they produced, on the one hand, and the personal experience of religion on the other. This is only partly due to their sociological orientation. These authors locate the desire to repudiate religion in a historically earlier epoch and do not consider it could have been an active force at the time Freud created his ideas.

The major historians of psychoanalysis have agreed with this perception, for they have entirely ignored religion as a potential source for Freud's ideas. This has probably been due in part to the vigorous criticism of religion that runs throughout Freud's published writings, as well as to the absence of any introspective reflection upon it in the more intimate and personal documents such as the correspondence and his analyses of his own dreams. But we now know from other sources that Freud spent his boyhood in what was in important ways a traditional Jewish home, and that he received regular instruction in the Jewish religion, and that in later life he never ceased to venerate his teacher, Hammerschlag (e.g., Rainey 1975). And yet Freud, the master of introspection into his own childhood experiences, again and again failed to mention what must have been an important dimension of his early life.

Freud and his close followers needed to protect their discipline from being labeled—and thereby discredited—as a "new religion." But enough time has now passed, and psychoanalysis is sufficiently well established, to permit nonpolemical inquiry into the possible influence of religion on Freud's writings. Now it is possible to take into account the role of both personal experience and religion in Freud's life while remaining within the sociological perspective. Two recent treatments of Freud's thought, by John Cuddihy (1974) and Marthe Robert (1976), have done precisely this and have found that his relation to Judaism was extremely important in the formation of his creative psychological ideas. Cuddihy's study primarily examines religious and social factors, leaving the personal dimension implicit. Robert's discussion, however, not only links social and religious forces but also develops both of them in relation to Freud's personal struggle with his father during his self-analysis. She thereby opens the way to an integration of personal, religious, and social factors as these overlapped in the development of Freud's thought. Her argument can be applied, with careful modification, to Jung's relationship to Christianity.

### Marthe Robert's Theory of the Two Cultures, the "Vague" Father, Psychoanalysis, and Jung's Psychology

It is neither possible nor necessary to summarize Marthe Robert's elaborate documentation of her arguments; but it is possible, and necessary—in order to achieve a deeper understanding of the origins of psychological ideas—to at least review her conclusions, which, unlike her supportive discussions, can be rather succinctly stated. Freud's family belonged, she believes, to a transitional generation of Jews who were caught between "two cultures"—German bourgeois, humanistic culture and the culture of traditional Judaism—and who devoted their lives, and in some cases their exceptional talents, to working out their relations to these two utterly incompatible and irreconcilable orientations to the world. Freud experienced the tension between these two cultures many times and in many different ways throughout his life. But for him the conflict centered with special intensity upon his relation to his father during his crisis period toward the end of the 1890s, which culminated in the discovery of his original, key ideas and in their subsequent publication in *The Interpretation of Dreams*. While psychoanalysis properly achieved the status of an independent science, it had its origins in a conflict with religious forces—the declining Judaism of Freud's time.

Freud's father was a transplanted Jew. He was an Eastern European Jew in his ways and his appearance; Freud described him as coming from a Hasidic background. But Jacob Freud had taken a decisive step away from Orthodox Judaism when he moved his family to the city. In his new environment he preserved within himself sufficient contact with the Judaism of his past to avert a personal sense of uprootedness, but he was not sufficiently committed to it to give his children a firm sense of traditional spirituality. Like many Jewish fathers of the same generation, he demanded of his children a vague fidelity to tradition but, because his own sense of rootedness was weakened, at the same time implicitly consented to their desire to break with that tradition.

But whereas Freud's father was never exposed to, or had to contend with, secular, humanistic culture and was able to sustain his sense of identity by drawing upon his ever-dwindling reserves of Jewish piety, no such solution was possible for his son. Freud's life was squarely situated midway between the two cultures. As a boy he was exposed to his father's residual Jewish piety and received thorough instruction in the Jewish religion (Rainey 1975). As a result he continued throughout his life to speak and think of himself as a

Jew—albeit without the conventional theological commitments. Whenever he wrote about the more serious and painful events in his life he consoled himself by drawing upon Jewish lore for his metaphors and illustrations. But he was also trained in the bourgeois, humanistic culture of the Gentiles. He had a successful German education. He knew Greek and Latin and possessed great familiarity with and love for the classics of Western literature. And in his prepsychoanalytic professional work he became steeped in the rational methods of the physical and biological sciences of the day. From the German humanistic culture Freud derived his dominant ethical, scientific, and aesthetic ideals, ideals that clashed diametrically with those of his Jewish tradition.

Freud's father could not, however, provide his son an adequate model for coming to terms with the tension between these two cultures. Instead he created an ethos of ''vagueness''—vaguely demanding loyalty to the Jewish past but just as vaguely permitting rebellion against it and repudiation of it. This conflict between the two cultures reached a crisis for Freud when his father died, an event that played a decisive part in his self-analysis during his creative crisis, described by many historians of psychoanalysis and recorded in the correspondence with the Berlin physician Wilhelm Fliess. According to Robert, the centerpiece of this crisis was indeed a painful criticism of and rebellion against Freud's father. But the deepest roots of this rebellion did not lie in the fact that his father possessed the oedipal mother, although Freud himself gave this account of his plight. Rather, the source of Freud's conflict with his father was an even more deeply buried wish—entirely unconscious—to disavow his Jewish origins, as imposed upon him by his father, and so to free himself from his religious past and enter the secular, humanistic culture to which he had become increasingly committed. Freud ''wanted to break once and for all with his Jewishness, with all its inner perils . . . and outward disadvantages for an ambitious man determined to rise in the world'' (Robert 1976, p. 97).

The heart of Marthe Robert's argument is her analysis of Freud's dreams and of his feelings toward those about him as they are recorded in *The Interpretation of Dreams* and the Fliess correspondence. She painstakingly shows that the theme of these dreams is not sexuality but ambition. Freud was obsessed by wishes for fame and grandeur. He entertained secret desires to succeed at all costs, to be first in everything, and to eliminate all his rivals. These ambitions were, however, at odds with the values of the Jewish community and eventually settled on Freud's relation to his father. His desire for success in the Gentile world became an accusation of Jacob Freud, a rebellious wish against his father for creating circumstances that held him back, preventing him from becoming a successful member of the secular culture he longed to join. The crux and turning point of the self-analysis was a coming to terms with this accusation. Its resolution freed Freud to explore his early, infantile experience and thereby to reconstruct the first three years of his life and to form a clear picture of the oedipal triangle—freed him, in other words, to make the essential discovery on which his entire science came to be founded.

From this point forward Freud had less reason to feel caught between the two cultures, for he had discovered a dimension of human reality that applied with equal force to Jew and Gentile alike. Now he could in effect say to each: *you* be assimilated to *my* view of the world, for both of you suffer alike from repressed desires and longings, and it is *my* science that explains your innermost secrets. Thus there emerged out of the conflict with traditional Judaism a wholly new way of thinking about the person—"a distinct and independent order of knowledge, which breaks radically with the religious and philosophical tradition of the West" (Robert 1976, p. 134). Psychoanalysis was a bridge or intermediary between the two forms of culture and thought.

There is some evidence that this hypothesis of the two cultures, and to some extent that of the vague father, applies not only to a particular generation of Jews caught in the dilemmas of assimilation—Cuddihy has argued that other creative systems of thought constructed by such eminent Jews as Marx, Durkheim, and Lévi-Strauss also had their origins in the tension between the two cultures—but to Christians as well. At least this was so for some other originative figures in the new discipline of psychology. The historian Dorothy Ross (1972) has shown in great detail how the thought of G. Stanley Hall, one of the founders of American psychology, arose as a result of a tension he felt between his Christian commitments, embodied in his father's view of the world, and the new forces, both intellectual and social, of secularity and modernity. But Hall never forged a successful resolution of this conflict. David Bakan (1966) and Paul Creelan (1974) have called attention to the intimate and conflicted relations between Christian piety and modern science in the life and thought of John B. Watson, founder of American behaviorism. And while the argument has yet to be mounted with regard to William James, it is clear that he too was caught between the Christian piety of his father and the new science associated with secularity and modernity. What was creative and original in James's psychological speculations—at least as regards his psychology of religion—derived from an attempt to synthesize these forces, as each one claimed his loyalty.

Whether the hypothesis of the two cultures and the vague father can be applied across the board to all the originative figures in the rise of psychology must remain an interesting conjecture. But it is no conjecture in the case of Jung. As he told the story of his life, the conflict between the two cultures was central to all his thinking, especially during the crisis period. Jung's early life was steeped in the Christian tradition, and the ethos of his time put him under great pressure to adopt or internalize this orientation to life, despite his persistent criticism of it. But he later encountered the world of modern thought, largely in the form of science, and became strongly attracted to it. Commenting on his studies during his early adolescence, Jung said: "I was powerfully attracted to science, with its truths based on facts" (1961a, p. 72). And again: "My scientific knowledge ... was thoroughly saturated with the scientific materialism of the time" (1961a, p. 74). Later, when describing his anticipation of university study, Jung mused, "I would go to the university and study—natural science, of course" (1961a, p. 84). And when he seriously began to contemplate a medical career, he observed: "More than ever I found myself driven towards empiricism" (1961a, p. 104).

This attraction to science deepened as he took up his medical studies and then became a professional in medical science. One definite point of consolidation was the word association experiments, which were rigorously empirical. But the commitment to science reached its apex in the early years of association with Freud, whose ideas Jung perceived as the epitome of a scientific approach to the

workings of the human mind. Jung's writings during the psychoanalytic years constantly emphasized the scientific character of
psychoanalysis as both theory and therapy. Had not he spoken of his
unconditional devotion to Freud's ideas, and had he not confessed to
Freud that his pre-Freudian views were morally inferior? In so
committing himself, Jung was not simply affirming a new medical
theory of the mind; he was also giving his loyalty to what Weinstein
and Platt have called modernity and what Marthe Robert called the
bourgeois rather than the traditional culture.

Like Freud, Jung also suffered from an association with a
"vague" father in the sociological rather than the psychological
sense. Despite their otherwise extraordinary psychological, cultural,
and religious differences, Pastor Paul Jung did resemble Jacob Freud
at two specific points. First, Jung's father oriented himself toward
life as a whole on the basis of a dwindling reserve of traditional
religious meaning—albeit Christian rather than Jewish. He was
sufficiently a part of this tradition to avoid for himself any sense of
uprootedness, though toward the end of his life he struggled desperately with inner doubts. And he had little contact with or interest in
the secular ethos, with its strong emphasis upon modern science.
Second, for these reasons Paul Jung could only have been experienced by his son as a vague father. On one hand the father, simply
through his vocation and his place in the surrounding social ethics,
drew his son toward Christian spiritual ideals, values, and meanings.
But because of his lack of enthusiasm for these ideals and because of
his own later doubts, he was vague—he was either unable or
unwilling to make a convincing case for Christianity to his son. On
the other hand, he never objected to—and thereby vaguely consented
to—his son's desire to rebel against the Christian tradition and seek a
new place for himself in the emerging secular, modern world.

Jung's autobiography contains considerable evidence of his
father's vague behavior not only toward his own commitment to
traditional Christian culture but also toward his son's relative commitment to the two cultures. The father prepared his son for
confirmation, and during these sessions Jung developed an interest in
the doctrine of the Trinity. But when the time came to discuss it, his
father's response was disappointing: "We now come to the Trinity,
but we'll skip that, for I really understand nothing of it myself"

(1961a, p. 53). This remark epitomized in Jung's mind the plight of his father, who could no longer vigorously believe in what he stood for professionally. Jung referred to him as "my dear and generous father, who in so many matters left me to myself and had never tyrannized over me" (1961a, p. 55). Later, when the two discussed Jung's vocational plans, his father urged the son to avoid his own profession: "Be anything you like except a theologian" (1961a, p. 75). In this context Jung observed: "He had never taken me to task for cutting church as often as possible and for not going to communion any more" (1961a, p. 75). In later adolescence Jung tried to engage his father in theological discussion, but he received only "the same old lifeless theological answers" or "a resigned shrug" (1961a, p. 92). The discussions of Jung's vocational plans continued to the end of his father's life. The year before Paul Jung died he admonished his son, were he to study medicine, not to become "a materialist." Jung's perception of this advice epitomized his sense of a vague father: "To me this warning meant that I ought to believe in nothing at all" (1961a, p. 94).

Thus Jung faced, throughout his adolescence and early professional years, a conflict between two cultures but was without anchorage in either of the two orientations to the world. Nor was he able to derive support for one or the other from his father, who, though ostensibly rooted in the traditional one, could not authoritatively strengthen his son in either direction. This tension between the two cultures and the frustrating presence of a vague father, like the psychological crisis, reached a climax during the critical years. At this time Jung had to come to terms not only with the beliefs of his real father—which in many ways stood for all of his early social as well as intellectual experience—but also with the beliefs of a "second" father, Sigmund Freud, the founder of psychoanalysis, who embodied the spirit of modernity just as strongly as his real father had embodied tradition.

While Jung's autobiographical account of his adolescent and university years supports the view that he experienced the tension between the two cultures and that his father was vague regarding his relation to them, the most important evidence for such a sociological view of the origins of his ideas lies in the opening two pages of the chapter of the autobiography entitled "Confrontation with the Un-

conscious,'' in which he describes the circumstances that precipitated his critical and creative years. These pages indicate that Jung's
crisis years were inaugurated not only by a psychological
conflict—the problem of narcissism in relation to his father, to his
two views of religion, and to Freud—but by a sociological conflict as
well. Jung's crisis also stemmed, the account suggests, from a
double and extremely ambivalent intellectual allegiance: to the
traditionalism of Christianity and to the modernity of Freud.

On the one hand Jung recalled that he had just completed a book
(*Symbols of Transformation*) interpreting psychologically the myths
by which man had always lived. Convinced that he had separated
both modern man and himself from the religious past, he asked
himself in what myth man lived nowadays. Perhaps it was the
Christian myth. But, alas, he was forced to conclude that there was
no myth for modern man, especially himself. At this point he became
uncomfortable and his thinking stopped. In addition to the
psychological distress already described, Jung experienced at this
time a cognitive disorientation, the loss of a prevailing world view,
the loss of traditional Christian sources of meaning. Whereas the
earlier chapters of the autobiography indicate an apparently long-
term and confident repudiation of Christianity, this section clearly
demonstrates that Jung must still have been deeply attached intellectually to traditional religion. But this sense of loss instituted in Jung
an equally powerful urge to create a new vision of the world—what
he called a personal myth, and what would become the collective
myth of those willing to follow him.

On the other hand, Jung wrote of a second factor that brought
about his sense of disorientation at this time—the break with Freud,
which produced ''a period of inner uncertainty.'' The psychological
or affective aspects of this disorientation have already been explored
in detail; but Jung's uncertainty was cognitive and intellectual as
well. From the psychological point of view Jung's task at this time
was to form a cohesive sense of himself in the light of his narcissistic
merger transference to Freud. But from the sociological point of
view—which, as I will argue at the end of this chapter, supplements
rather than contradicts the psychological analysis—Jung had, in
committing himself to Freud's psychoanalysis, in effect committed
himself to the values of autonomy and inclusion; that is, to the

secular, modern culture that stood in opposition to the traditional culture of the past. Consequently, the break with Freud was not just a problem in psychological separation; it also imposed upon Jung the task of rethinking the values and ideals he had affirmed during the psychoanalytic years.

Any attempt to reconstruct the social forces that influenced Jung's critical and creative years should refer, when appropriate, not only to autobiographical statements but to his formal work as well. The contents of his writings composed during the neo-Freudian years, at the onset of the crisis period, and those written during the creative conclusion of that crisis have already been reviewed. The first group of works clearly supports the view of the autobiography—namely, that Jung was deeply preoccupied with the tension between traditional Christianity and the emerging psychoanalytic theory of Freud. But these works also indicate that a third tension or source of conflict was at work in Jung's mind. This was his growing perception of modernity—of modern man as mass man and of modern society as mass society. Jung began to indicate that he sensed modern society to be traditionless, authoritarian, and excessively rational, thus creating a depersonalized consciousness in the typical modern man. Thus three tensions or forces were operative at the beginning of the critical period, although the autobiography mentions only two—Freud and Christianity.

*Symbols of Transformation* contained—in addition to its revision of the libido theory, its interpretation of Miss Miller's fantasies, and its grandiose attempt at a comprehensive psychology of world mythologies—a personal quest. In it Jung sought to reconcile what he felt was the conflict between traditional Christianity and Freud's psychoanalysis. But this conflict had made him sensitive to a third issue, the problem of modern man—the problem of "our time." Hence Jung said in his book that he sought to construct a stable point of view outside our own culture that leads to an objective understanding of that culture. This search received its clearest and most direct formulation in the 1912 essay, "New Paths in Psychology." In it Jung spoke of cultural forces as the root of clinical problems— urbanization, industrialization, the division of labor, and the like had created a new and ominous psychological crisis. They had in effect created modern or mass man, a new species of human being to be sharply distinguished from traditional Christian man. At the time, however, Jung had no thoughts on how the psychological needs of modern man—or, for that matter, the tension between traditional Christianity and Freud's thought—could be resolved.

That Jung should allude, in his opening description of the conditions underlying the inception of his critical years, to his sense of separation both from traditional Christianity and from Freud's psychoanalysis, and that he should speak in his formal writings of the same period of the cultural crisis of modern man, permits a series of conjectures regarding the sociological origins of his creative system of ideas, his core process. Jung found himself, it seems, beset by a realistic dilemma, one that many thinkers after him have also attempted to resolve. He had sensed the power of the Christian myth to organize personal and social life in the past, and he had been, more than he realized, committed to his own Christian heritage. But in more recent years he had come to be just as genuinely committed to Freud's psychology, which contained the essence of modernity, although during the psychoanalytic years he had succeeded in putting religion and Christianity behind him. And he had come to sense the problem of modern man as mass man.

But now, at the onset of his crisis—roughly 1912—he not only sensed the power of these orientations but also recognized that they were unreconcilable. Unable to affirm either Christianity or psychoanalysis, he was equally unwilling to abandon either entirely. His creative thought therefore emerged as an attempt to ease the tension between the values of traditional Christianity and those of Freud's thought, in the light of his emerging perceptions regarding the problem of modern man. His system is not, therefore, as Freudians polemically argue, simply an attempt to Christianize the leading ideas of psychoanalysis—it is not, that is, a regression to religion. Jung's perception that the Christian myth had run its course was too strong to permit this. Nor is it, as some theologians fear, simply an attempt to psychologize Christianity. Jung's objections to what he believed to be Freud's reductionistic orientation toward religion were too adamant on this point. Despite Jung's stated conviction that at this time he had put aside both Freud's psychology and traditional Christianity, he was still heavily invested in both. His system is, rather, a genuine alternative to both Christianity and psychoanalysis but draws aspects of these orientations into a fresh synthesis. Jung found himself forced to create a conceptual system that would serve as a vantage point for viewing classic psychoanalysis, traditional Christianity, and the plight of modern, mass man.

How might such an interpretation work out in relation to specific central concepts of Jung's core process, as he derived these during the creative phase of the critical years? We can speculate with regard to three leading Jungian ideas. First, Jung had clearly become convinced that Freud's concept of the unconscious was an integral one, and he wished to retain it in some form in his own thinking. But he also wanted to affirm Christianity's view of a realm of being and power that transcended man's consciousness of himself and was favorable to him. Yet he was convinced that modern man could not accept any form of belief at a public, institutional level. He resolved these tensions by formulating his ideas of the archetypes and the collective unconscious. Second, Jung believed that excessively rational, modern man was in need of a personal transformation, and he recognized that the Christian tradition provided one such model for that process, even though it had become meaningless. Freud's psychology provided a conception of personal transformation through its delineation of psychosexual development. But Freud's theory was reductionistic and thus unacceptable. Under the impress of these tensions, Jung forged the notion of individuation.

Third, Jung was convinced that Christianity had lost its power to provide a sense of tradition and consequent personal uniqueness, and that as a result modern man had become mass man. He believed Freud had to some extent recovered a sense of inner depth and historicity for the modern person, although he also believed that Freud had compromised this sense of depth through conformity to rational social norms. To provide modern man with a living relation to himself and to his past, Jung devised the concept of a pure self that stayed in touch with tradition (the archetypes) but also transcended the erosive social and political forces of modernity. In each of these three instances Jung created a new psychological idea by mediating between selected elements of psychoanalysis, Christianity, and his view of modernity as a mass society.

These observations or interpretations must be called conjectures, for there is no autobiographical evidence that Jung was self-consciously synthesizing these three trends in the way suggested. Nor is there, for that matter, any direct evidence that Freud self-consciously concerned himself with "codifying" the intrafamilial effects of the industrial revolution, or that he thought of his new system of ideas as building a bridge between the two cultures, or that he conceived of his self-analysis as a struggle to come to terms with a vague Jewish father. To expect such evidence is to parody the sociological approach to the origin of psychological ideas. For the essence of such an approach is that it seeks to account for psychological ideas in terms of broadly defined social and cultural forces that the originative psychologist does not submit to self-conscious introspective clarification. There is a "sociological unconscious" just as there is a psychological unconscious. ✓

The crux of the argument here is that there is evidence that Jung was centrally preoccupied with each of the three sociocognitive trends at the onset of the critical years. And at the end of his critical period he had devised a system of ideas expressly devoted to integrating these trends—his new system of thought took a perspective that provided the means of interpreting Freud's psychoanalysis, traditional Christianity, and the dilemmas of modern man as mass man. I thus postulate a connection between the sociocognitive forces that precipitated the crisis and the product of its resolution—namely, the core process. This connection is not, however, a causal one, or even a dialectical one. Rather, I postulate a fundamental symmetry between the sociocognitive forces influencing Jung's thinking at the inception of his critical years and the contents of his core process. One thing is clear: the core process is entirely given over to resolving exactly those tensions present at the onset of the critical years.

But while it is on the whole true that there is no clear evidence that Jung self-consciously constructed his system of ideas in order to reconcile these three forces, this is not entirely so. In chapter 4 I attempted to demonstrate that Jung's ordeal was an identity crisis and that his emerging central ideas, associated with its resolution, constituted a new ideology. Jung described his crisis not only as an inner, psychological one, but also as an attempt "to find an entirely new and different orientation" (1961a, p. 193). He wanted, he said, "to convey to my intimates a new way of seeing things" (1961a,

p. 195). While the first remark could possibly be construed to refer simply to a new therapeutic orientation, the second clearly goes beyond this and refers, as I have already suggested, to ideology. In this passage Jung failed to specify what "things" were old and what he saw in a new way. But the above sociological analysis brings some specificity to this cryptic but also highly revealing remark. The old way of seeing things referred, I suggest, not only to Freud's ideas and therapy, but also to traditional Christianity and to a lesser extent to the emerging phenomenon of mass man. The "new" way was to be a creative system that could bring order out of the conflict between these and so provide modern man with a functional equivalent of traditional religion, which would both incorporate and transcend the insights of classic psychoanalysis.

It is possible to conclude these speculations by extending them to their limits, in which the sociological interpretations are combined with those regarding the role of psychological and religious factors in the formation of Jung's original ideas. Such a procedure creates a model or "paradigm" that embodies—albeit in a highly compressed and abstract way—the many processes and factors I have described in detail and thus summarizes the contextual approach to Jung's thought. Such a paradigm telescopes into one sequence the many personal, religious, and social experiences that contributed to Jung's psychological ideas, from his earliest years through his creative period. While the validity of this paradigm is necessarily restricted to Jung's life and thought, it can in principle be generalized—or at least tested—with appropriate modification, in relation to the emergence of other systems of original psychological ideas.

(1) The process began with an initial loyalty to religious ideas, their associated social ethos, and the forms of personal experience they prescribed. (2) Then tension developed between loyalty to religion, with all this implied, and an emerging loyalty to the conditions of secularity or modernity. The religious orientation came to be experienced as oppressive—that is, as ideationally rigid, as demanding social immobility, and as restricting inner, imaginative variation at the level of personal-psychological experiencing. Secularity or modernity, on the other hand, was experienced largely as science (ideational flexibility), as social mobility, and as the possibility of imaginative variation in the sphere of personal experience.

(3) This tension, which created a sense of being between two orientations, forced a heightened self-consciousness, a new inwardness, an intense, introspective preoccupation with self, rich in narcissistic overtones. And it forced a crisis in thought as well—something new in the intellectual sphere was needed to conceptualize the introspective consciousness and to bridge the gap between the religious orientation and the attractiveness of secularity or modernity. (4) The crisis was resolved by the emergence of a new form of thinking that was neither wholly scientific, in the sense of experimental science, nor wholly religious, in the sense of traditional religion, but that was instead "psychological." This form of thinking supported the new introspective orientation; and it allowed Jung, the innovative thinker, to separate himself from, and also relate himself to, both the old world, organized by religion, and the new world, organized by modernity or secularity. In such fashion did Jung first repudiate traditional religion, in the light of his narcissistic struggle, and then assimilate those portions of it that supported that struggle.

Since the interpretive frameworks used in the contextual approach to Jung's thought were drawn from analyses of the genesis of Freud's ideas, and since Jung's system differs from Freud's in significant ways—both in content and in genesis—it is important to note the similarities and differences. In one sense the first three stages were essentially the same in both cases. As a boy Freud was nurtured in the traditional Judaism of his father's household. Then, as his education proceeded, he moved more and more into the secular, humanistic German culture. He experienced increased tension between these two cultures, which came to a focus in his relation to his father during the self-analysis, creating a heightened introspective self-consciousness. And out of this crisis there emerged Freud's original system of ideas. But, unlike Jung's thought, this system was fully independent of the traditional religious culture; and, despite Freud's wish to associate it with the scientific orientations of his time, it was equally independent of those. As Paul Ricoeur (1970) and others have pointed out, while it is possible to claim the mantle of science for Freud's psychoanalysis, his psychology was not an "observational science" in the same sense as nineteenth-century physics and biology. Rather, it was a bridge discipline that provided an independent perspective not only upon traditional religion but also upon the secular culture of the times.

The emergence and status of Jung's system differ from those of Freud's system on two points. First, Jung met Freud after Freud's original system of ideas had been formed—partly just because he was almost twenty years younger. But while he encountered the same scientific and humanistic culture that Freud had faced, he also came to see Freud as an instance of this modern, secular culture during his critical years. Thus the tension between the two cultures was for him, especially during the crisis years, a tension between Freud's ideas and those of traditional Christianity. Second, whereas Freud created a system of thought wholly independent of the two cultures, Jung developed a set of ideas that not only would allow him to be separate from his two cultures, but would also let him synthesize them into his own new system of ideas. Jung's need for continuity and order between perspectives initially perceived as unbridgeable was far greater than Freud's. Freud proudly and triumphantly asserted the independence of his views; Jung wanted to see—and succeeded in seeing—continuity between the two cultures and his own ideas.

Consequently Jung was always, first in his creative period and later at great length throughout his mature thought, continually attempting to show that his system was the logical and psychological fulfillment or completion of Freud's psychology; that it was the antidote par excellence for the plight of modern man as mass man, and that it was a means for reinterpreting traditional Christianity. The three sociocognitive tensions present at the onset of the critical years were resolved by the core process, and that process became given over to interpreting Freud, modernity, and Christianity. This threefold interpretive effort became the thematic essence of Jung's mature thought. Specialist appropriation has, I believe, distorted this fundamental feature of his system, a feature the contextual approach discloses. This view of Jung must be corroborated in a more thorough analysis of his mature thought, which is the burden of the following chapter.

But before turning to that discussion, it is important to consolidate an earlier statement that the sociological interpretation of the origins of Jung's thought complements rather than contradicts the psychological analysis. Doing so also gives some specificity to the paradigm and anticipates the concluding chapter of this study. Personal-psychological, religious, and sociological factors were intimately related in the genesis of Jung's thought, and all share the process of idealization.

Jung's early psychological situation was characterized by the frustrated need to idealize, a facet of his struggle with narcissism. In his life, idealization was closely related to religious meanings. In repudiating traditional religion and affirming—that is, idealizing—his personal-mystical-narcissistic mode of experience, he was unable to idealize the cultural objects of traditional religion. His phallus dream, his manikin ritual, and especially his cathedral fantasy all dramatically illustrated this. Later he idealized Freud and his ideas. But when the relation became too intense it activated his earlier conflicts with religion; thus his struggle with narcissism during the critical years, although it had a religious dimension, was an attempt to cope with the problem of idealization. His core process emerged as a solution to this problem, for through it he created ideas, ideals, values, and meanings he deemed worthy of the lifelong commitment of his energies. He blended his work as originative psychologist with the role of social critic and prophet into the all-encompassing role of ideologist. While at one level these were separate enterprises, Jung constantly strove to bring them together. The drive for order, continuity, and coherence was extremely strong thoughout his mature life.

The problem of narcissism and the associated process of idealization can be seen—so this discussion has in effect implied—in a sociological context. It is the personal-psychological side of the problem of tradition and modernity—that is, of the problem of the two cultures and the vague father. From this point of view narcissism arose and became problematic for Jung during the critical years because he was caught between the two cultures and could not idealize the values of either one. His plight was substantially reinforced by his vague father, who could neither evoke the idealizations of his son nor redirect them toward the emerging secular and modern culture. Thus the combination of the tension between two cultures and the vague father provided the necessary social or cultural conditions that reinforced the possibility of narcissistic crisis in

Jung's life. He could either, as he said of his father's warning about materialism, believe nothing at all; or else he could enter into the painful, creative work of developing a new system of ideas and ideals that would make sense of his dilemma.

# Seven

## The Structure of Jung's Mature Thought: Its Three Themes

Over the period 1900 to 1918 Jung underwent an incredible series of changes in both his personal, inner life and his thought. These changes reached a climax during 1912–16 and were consolidated in the brief creative period from 1916 to 1918. At the end of this period Jung underwent a double integration. In his personal life he came to terms with the myriad and complex psychological, religious, and sociocognitive forces that had driven him into the crisis, creating for himself a new sense of inner coherence of self and, at a broader and more general level, a new sense of personal identity. And in his creative thought he constructed an entirely new, distinctive system of psychological ideas. The keystone in this synthesis of person and thought was Jung's emergent threefold identity as originative psychologist and critic of Freud, as social critic (explainer of the nature of modernity to modern man), and as prophet (reinterpreter of Christianity in the light of psychoanalysis and the problem of mass man in a mass society).

At the end of the creative period, with its double consolidation of personality and thought, Jung had achieved a permanent sense of closure in both spheres. From this time forward his personal life remained stable and consistent. To be sure, there were many new experiences and personal relationships, and there was continued reflection on both. But there were no more radical shifts in any sense comparable to those of the critical years. Jung's later personal life was marked by continuity rather than discontinuity. Having the core process in hand, he could interpret the various inner events of his later life in terms of it. Of the critical period Jung himself said, "The years when I was pursuing my inner images were the most important in my life—in them everything essential was decided . . . the later details are only supplements and clarifications" (1961a, p. 199). And, in like fashion, there were no changes in intellectual formulation in any way similar to those of the critical period. Jung's creative years not only were the occasion of his personal integration, they were also the source of all his later thinking. Jung's work produced after this period—which I call his mature thought—was only a deepening of what had been established during the critical period.

At precisely this point—the character or structure of Jung's mature thought—there is considerable divergence of opinion in the available (and all too often unquestionably accepted) literature on Jung, as I have already pointed out in detail. But none of these prevailing approaches to Jung have opened themselves to assessing the import of his thought as a whole, apart from their specialist agendas. Nor have they engaged the even more important question of origins and derivation. These two questions, however, are related: analyzing the origins of Jung's thought can shed considerable light on its structure—on the question of what it is all about. While the specialists are all in part right, by ignoring the question of origins they have deprived themselves of an important source for reflecting on structure. Also, they have ignored Jung's own observation that the critical years were indispensable to understanding the import of all his later work. Since origins cue structure, they can provide important clues to the central intellectual themes of the mature Jung. After the critical years, Jung turned back upon the three tensions that stimulated his thought and interpreted them in the light of his core process, thus giving coherence to his work.

### The First Theme: Jung's Interpretation of Freud's Psychoanalysis and His Own Theory of Therapy

The literature embodying Jung's estimate of Freud—and to a lesser extent the Freudian literature on Jung—is considerable. It begins with the *Letters* and is further enhanced by both men's comments on each other in their published writings. And the cudgels have been taken up by members of both the Jungian community and the psychoanalytic movement. Most of the followers' remarks occur in the context of other concerns, so that few full-scale studies exist of the two men's estimates of each other. And, invariably, the disciples have deferred to their masters' views on all essential matters, establishing more firmly than ever the "either/or" polarization. Two of the best-known studies of Freud and Jung, Edward Glover's *Freud or Jung?* (1956) and Liliane Frey-Rohn's *From Freud to Jung* (1976), illustrate this pattern clearly and vigorously.

Glover's book displays the mind of the classic psychoanalyst at work, not simply illuminating Freud's tenets but defending himself absolutely against even the slightest progressive innovation of the master's metapsychological maxims. His is truly a study in what I would call "psychoanalytic fundamentalism." To him Jung is an obscurantist psychologist of consciousness who unsystematically undermined every advance Freud made. Speaking for the other side, Frey-Rohn, though less polemical, is no less devout. The overarching assumption of her entire study is that everything Freud asserted merely anticipated the full and correct truth of Jung's final formulations.

Both books make good points. Jung was moralistic about the personal unconscious. He believed the patient could come to terms with it by means of a little thought and willpower. But his view of the collective unconscious was extraordinarily dynamic, a fundamental point Glover misses entirely. And Frey-Rohn is also right: Jung did see his theories as a fulfillment of Freud's views. But she attends little to Freud's lasting contributions. More to the point, however, both studies fail to ask what the contextual approach has revealed as a central question: What was Jung's mature estimate of Freud, and did it differ from the view of the critical years? And, even more important, how pervasive was Jung's preoccupation with Freud during the mature years? Did such preoccupation rightfully stand out as a theme in his thought? The questions are closely related, but to ask them requires setting aside the polemics of the Freud-Jung polarization.

Joseph Wheelwright (1976), a senior Jungian analyst trained by Jung, has remarked that Jung told him that throughout his life he

never ceased trying to understand what had gone wrong in his
relationship with Freud. This remark is generally contradicted by the
autobiography. According to that document, when Jung broke with
Freud during the critical years, the separation was final and complete. The portions of the autobiography describing the mature years
rarely mention Freud at all, and then only incidentally. But Wheelwright's remark can be extended beyond the person of the mature
Jung to the sphere of his thought. Jung's mature writings are rich in
allusion to Freud; in fact, they portray a mind deeply preoccupied
with the status of Freud's psychoanalysis. Throughout his mature
years Jung again and again sought to determine the position, rele-
vance, and significance of Freud's thought in relation to his own.

This conclusion is not on the whole accepted by Jungians, who
prefer to follow Jung's autobiographical remarks intimating that the
break during the critical years was final not only interpersonally but
also intellectually. Nor is it considered important by Freudians, who
believe that Jung's significance lies entirely in his defection from
psychoanalysis, and who therefore see no reason to study Jung's
work. But such a conclusion is not so surprising if one recalls
Freud's prominence in all the contexts that gave rise to Jung's
system. Freud was psychologically central to Jung as part of his
struggle with narcissism. Before his critical years Jung had temporarily idealized Freud and his system, viewing the latter as a
culmination of the Christian gospel, and his task during the critical
years was to separate his sense of self from his merger with Frued.
Freud's psychology, embodying as it did a vision of modernity, was
one of the three sociocognitive forces Jung had to integrate into his
core process. Only an extraordinarily self-destructive act of repression could mitigate these circumstances. Freud was bound to be a
key figure not only in Jung's later life, but also in his thought.

There is considerable evidence that the significance of Freud's
thought was a central intellectual theme throughout Jung's mature
work. Unfortunately, lack of biographical evidence precludes our
examining the extent to which his extensive and intensive preoccupation with Freud's thought expressed his earlier struggle to free
himself psychologically from personal involvement with Freud, but
it seems likely that the extent was considerable. The *Two Essays*
illuminate not only the nature of the core process, but also Jung's

assessment of Freud. Jung could not separate an assessment of Freud from his clearest and most representative exposition of his theories. In his mind the one led quite naturally and inevitably to the other. Not only do the definitive *Two Essays* mark out Freud's thought as central to understanding the significance of Jung's ideas, but the other volumes of Jung's *Collected Works* (with the exception of the books on alchemy), spanning the full range of Jung's mature years, contain substantial references to Freud. In the midst of this steady stream of allusion one volume stands out: *The Practice of Psychotherapy* (1954) contains twelve papers written over the period 1928–51. Despite the title of this volume, none of its essays provide concrete instances of therapeutic technique; and though they span more than twenty years there is little development or change in the content of the ideas. In an important sense the essay "The Transcendent Function" (1958), written in 1916 during the creative years, remains the best statement of the principles of Jungian treatment. Once Jung had formulated his core process, his ideas underwent little change.

Many of these papers contain detailed and elaborate criticism of Freud, but all of them, even those few that do not mention his ideas specifically, make it clear that the thrust of the Jungian argument emerges from a critique of Freudian concepts and principles. Those that refer explicitly to Freud are remarkably repetitive. First Jung summarizes Freud's theory of therapy; then he often mentions Adler's deviant position; then he argues that both are one-sided and hence in need of his own more impartial point of view; and finally he presents the ideas that constitute his view. To a lesser extent the same pattern holds for most of the papers in *The Development of Personality* (1964*b*).

Finally, Jung wrote three papers (1931, 1934, 1939) in which he directly addressed the cultural and historical significance of Freud's work. Thus he approached Freud not only in his own role as originative psychologist, but also in terms of his personal identity as an interpreter of modernity and contemporary cultural life and, as we shall see in a moment, in his role as the reinterpreter of traditional religion. All this stands in sharp contrast to Freud's writings on Jung. After 1914, Freud referred to Jung for the most part only when alluding to his break with the psychoanalytic movement—although there are a few scattered accusations that Jung smuggled a world view into his clinical writings.

Brief and cursory as it is, this review of Jung's later references to Freud clearly indicates that Freud occupied a central position in his mind. Three observations are in order. First, Jung's discussions of Freud are not really comparative analyses of the relative orientations and merits of the two systems of psychological thinking. Rather, they are interpretations—that is, they employ the core process to assess conclusively the significance of psychoanalytic ideas. Once he had the core process, Jung could integrate Freud's thinking into his own wider scheme. Second, Jung interpreted Freud's thought at two levels; first in terms of clinical process, then at the level of historical and cultural significance. And, third, Jung could not separate his estimate of Freud from the other two themes of his mature thinking—the view of modernity and his reinterpretation of traditional Christianity. What exactly was the content of Jung's interpretation of Freud?

The essence of this interpretation lies in Jung's explication of his core process in the *Two Essays,* and in particular in his description of what I have called the typically Jungian moment in therapy (interpretation at the level of therapy) and the dynamics of the persona (interpretation at the level of culture). But the inception of both lies in the theory of types: Freud was an extravert, Adler an introvert, and both described the same clinical situation. Thus in its early stages therapy proceeded as both men described it. A transference relationship developed and had to be analyzed in terms of the parental imagoes of childhood experience. But the time came when such analysis produced not a resolution of the transference, but fantasies and attitudes of a more extravagant kind: inflation or godlikeness and the view of the therapist as savior or demon. This situation could be understood only through Jungian terminology: the archetypes of the collective unconscious, their interpretation by means of the constructive-synthetic method, and the individuation process. In these formulations lies the origin of Jung's interpretation of Freud's theory at the clinical level.

But Jung extended his discussion to the cultural level by using the concept of the persona. The typically Jungian moment in therapy is also described as the breakdown of the persona. Its weakening led to the influx of collective material and called for the Jungian method of treatment. Jung's concept of the persona, which he equated with excessive rationality and extraversion, was his diagnostic term for the ills of modernity. He also associated a rigid persona with Freud's superego and with successful Freudian therapy. Thus, through the concept of the persona, the ground was prepared for a cultural interpretation of Freud.

Without essential modification, Jung expanded these clinical and cultural estimates of Freud into a full-scale interpretation in his subsequent thought. The clinical papers already mentioned (1954) evince very little, if any, progression or development of ideas, and no one paper is given over to any particular concept. Instead, interpretations of Freud and associated Jungian ideas are scattered throughout. But a nucleus of argumentation can be abstracted from them. Freud reduced all psychological processes, Jung said, to infantile imagoes and their origins in infantile sexuality. This reduction was nowhere more evident than in his technique for handling transference, and his recommendations consequently could not resolve it. In this Freud rendered normative the extraverted type, which was an expression of his own personal psychology. Thus his attitude was one-sided and therefore dogmatic, rigid, and fanatical. In short, Freud ignored the central feature of the psyche, that it was collective as well as personal, and the corollary of this, that the unconscious— and neurosis as well—was not limiting only but also creative and thus a source both of illness and of health.

Jung elaborated on this view of Freud by developing a series of polarities juxtaposing his own ideas to Freud's. Thus it was important to distinguish between fantasy, associated with the personal unconscious, and the archetype, which was really a collective fantasy; between treating dreams as mere symptoms and valuing them as symbols; between sexual energy and psychological energy in general; and between the reductive approach to mental productions and the synthetic method. Jung emphasized the real importance of values in the psychological life of the patient and so in effect created a distinction between Freud's emphasis on the ego and his own readiness to accept a broader psychological structure, the self. Many of his patients, he said, were in the second half of life, a phase that had no place in Freud's psychology; hence he distinguished between psychosexual development and the "life span" concept of individuation. And, finally, Jung believed the therapist had to adopt an attitude of personal participation in his patient's life, which he contrasted with Freud's method, in which the psychoanalyst hid behind the authority of his role as doctor.

But Jung's strongest, most critical interpretations are found in the three papers (1931, 1934, 1939) addressed explicitly to Freud's more general significance. Just as he found Freud's clinical theories relative to Freud's person, so his cultural assessment of Freud was based on relativism. Jung's argument in each of these papers is essentially the same and consists of several closely related assertions: Freud lived in an era saturated with scientific materialism and Victorian hypocrisy, and his theories were expressions of this ethos. Consequently, Freud employed materialistic premises to destroy the idols of his age, especially in the spheres of sexuality and religion. But in doing so he adopted a "nothing but" attitude: he rejected all possibilities for a positive evaluation of the human predicament. Hence he was unable to replace what he had destroyed, thereby leaving modern man bereft of any authentic consolation. In this he did not respect man's need to repossess the religious attitude. Jung concluded that Freudian psychology, because of its dogmatic clinging to the doctrine of scientific materialism, was more akin to a religious movement than to science, and that Freud was a prophetic figure.

While Jung's mature thought was organically connected to the forces that produced it, it was also in part free from those forces, largely owing to the core process. Still, it is important to recognize these originating forces whenever they assert themselves, even in the later writings. This is nowhere more apparent than in Jung's memorial essay (1939), published a week after Freud's death. This essay contains no ideas about Freud that Jung had not expressed on other occasions. What strikes the reader is its tone. In all the other commentaries on Freud, Jung managed to remain relatively objective; but this one is a rambling, disorganized essay in a tone of bitter repudiation that at times borders on the rude or even the abusive. It is reminiscent of the closing months of their relationship, as recorded in the *Letters,* before the final break.

Jung began by belittling Freud. Freud was, he said, "first and foremost a 'nerve specialist' . . . by training he was no psychiatrist, no psychologist, and no philosopher'' (1939, p. 41). Then he rehearsed the origins of psychoanalysis, tracing them to the work of Charcot and Breuer. Jung deprived Freud of originality by stating that Breuer's discovery of psychological trauma "laid the foundation of all Freud's theories'' (1939, p. 42). Returning to Freud's clinical work, he asserted, "he constantly had the clinical picture of neurosis before his mind's eye—the very attitude that makes people ill and effectively prevents them from being healthy'' (1939, p. 45). Freud's clinical attitude was demonically obsessive. Toward the end of the essay Jung rehearsed his view of the cultural relativism of psychoanalysis and picked up again, sarcastically, the theme of Freud's philosophical innocence: "Freud's psychology moves within the narrow confines of nineteenth century scientific materialism. Its philosophical premises were never examined, thanks obviously to the Master's insufficient philosophical equipment'' (p. 47). Freud's psychological method was "dangerous and destructive . . . like every fanaticism, it evoked the suspicion of an inner uncertainty'' (1939, p. 47). He concluded by invoking the analogy of a relay race in which Freud had passed the baton on to Jung: "each of us carries the torch of knowledge only part of the way'' (1939, p. 47). Thus Jung's psychology was, as ever, a corrective fulfillment of Freud's.

Unlike most memorial essays, which tend to overestimate the achievements of the deceased, Jung's article vehemently denounced Freud. The reason for this is not difficult to come by, given some knowledge of the complex history, especially in its early phases, of the Freud-Jung relationship. It is likely that Freud's death momentarily stirred these old conflicts to life, though almost twenty-five years had elapsed since they had agreed to break off their relationship. Freud's death must have activated earlier painful wishes to idealize Freud and to merge with him, as well as the even more painful narcissistic rage that occurred in response to Freud's dismissing of Jung's idealization and rejecting his innovative ideas. The reference to Freud's psychology as making people ill and preventing them from becoming healthy is almost an undisguised accusation and may derive from Jung's earlier frustration because Freud and his theories were unable to help him as his critical years developed. Some such emotional charge must have given the memorial article its bitter tone; otherwise Jung could have simply stated his theoretical objections in a quiet, dignified manner. And he might even have allowed some of his earlier profound admiration to round out the picture.

While it is beyond the scope of this book to review at length Jung's many, repeated objections to Freud and to evaluate them, two such points call for comment, for they anticipate Jung's understanding of religion. The first is his interpretation of Freud's concept of the personal unconscious. The most important differences between the two men can be traced to the distinction between the personal and the collective unconscious, and Jung associated the latter with religion. Jung's thought was extremely moralistic at this point. He assumed that the personal unconscious, which Freud had devoted his life to understanding, could be successfully analyzed, worked through, and integrated by moral effort and willpower. For example, on the opening page of the final version of the second essay Jung briefly summarized Freud's theory of repression, then added: "According to this theory, the unconscious contains only those parts of the personality which could just as well be conscious, and have been suppressed only through the process of education"; and he concluded that "the removal of repression ought to endow a person with a prodigious memory which would thenceforth forget nothing" (1966a, p. 127; see also 1966a, p. 77, and 1963a, p. 75). But it was precisely Freud's point that the forces of infantile sexuality could never be mastered in a simple, voluntaristic fashion but that the patient could at best only reduce the strength of the instincts through insight and constantly had to renew his struggle with his own unconscious—the struggle of a lifetime. But throughout his mature writings Jung persisted in advancing this highly moralistic interpretation of Freud.

A more important aspect of Jung's estimate of Freud was his mature opinion that the founder of psychoanalysis had introduced religious factors into his psychology. In 1931 Jung wrote of Freud's concept of the father: "This father-complex, defended with such stubbornness and oversensitivity, is a religious function misunderstood, a piece of mysticism expressed in terms of biological and family relationships. As for Freud's concept of the superego, it is a furtive attempt to smuggle the time-honored image of Jehovah in the dress of psychological theory" (1931, p. 339). And in the autobiography he accused Freud of being personally religious about his ideas: "Freud, who had always made much of his irreligiosity, had now constructed a dogma; or rather, in the place of a jealous God whom he had lost, he had substituted another compelling image, that of sexuality . . . the 'sexual libido' took over the role of . . . a hidden or concealed god'' (1961a, p. 151).

Why did Jung persist in viewing Freud's theories as religious and Freud as a religious man? This estimate on Jung's part has always struck me as a bit like the pot calling the kettle black. There were at least three reasons for this strategy. First, the accusation of religiousness must be seen as an accusation of narcissistic grandiosity. Narcissistic struggle was an important part of the relation between the two men, and it is not unlikely that Jung sensed in Freud a kind of grandiose certainty that characterizes many truly great men—an absolute confidence in the validity of their own ideas. After all, Freud was profoundly convinced of the truth of his ideas—ideas that at the time had not been validated by many others or by the scientific community. Second, each man carried within himself a strong resentment toward the other after their break, and each claimed his own work was truly scientific. In the ethos of their time the accusation of religiousness was a commonplace means of discrediting an opponent who made claims to scientific truth—and it still is, even today. Jung had often been accused of being religious, and he may have wished to turn this back on Freud. Furthermore, whereas today a generalized accusation of religiousness or of being ideological is enough to discredit an opponent, during the late Victorian era when Freud and Jung met and parted such accusations were cast in terms of specific religions. Hence they thought of each other not simply as religious or irreligious, but as Jew and Christian. And, finally, Jung may have sensed the sociological fact that, as Erikson has put it, the psychoanalytic movement provided its early practitioners not only with a new science but also with a "psychoanalytic identity"—that is, he may have sensed the ideological element in Freud's psychoanalysis.

In two papers on psychotherapy written relatively late in his career—"Psychotherapy Today" (1946a) and "Fundamental Questions of Psychotherapy" (1951)—Jung developed his clearest and most articulate statement of the cultural significance of both Freud's system of treatment and his own. In doing so he demonstrated how inseparable in his own mind were the three themes of his mature work. Each implicated the others: Freud's therapy was closely related to the predicament of modernity; that predicament was defined as the loss of traditional religious meaning; religion had to be reinterpreted in light of the character of modernity. Then Jung went on to show that his own system of psychology was especially suited to interpret this central cultural problem successfully. The first paper contains the essence of the argument, and the second supplements it.

In early development, Jung surmised, the child lives in relation to the images of his parents, but in adolescence he must somehow resolve this relationship. The parental imagoes cannot simply be withdrawn; they cannot be worked out in a personalistic way in relation to immediate social others, such as the psychotherapist—an implicit criticism of Freud. Traditionally, religious ritual served to permit a transition from the world of childhood to the world of the adult. Thus religion did not, for Jung, destroy the parental imagoes; rather, it changed and exalted them. This was particularly so in Catholicism, wherein the pope takes on the image of the father and the church the image of the mother. As long as the individual remained in touch with these collective beliefs—described by Freud under the rubric of the superego and by Lévy-Bruhl with his concept of "collective representations"—his psychic balance was maintained. But, Jung asked, "how fares it with men and women who have been uprooted and torn out of tradition?" (1946*a*, p. 99). This uprootedness led to a lack of disposition of the parental imagoes and to "endless isolation within the ego" (1946*a*, p. 100). While Freud's therapy could bring to consciousness the parental imagoes, his analysis of them could not resolve the isolation uprootedness produced.

Uprootedness and isolation constituted the predicament of the contemporary psychiatric patient, and for this patient Jung adduced his core process. Isolation in pure ego consciousness produced impersonal collective contents; the ego was released from the parental imagoes and, if the person was in therapy, from the personalistic ties of transference. Thereupon "a healthful, compensatory operation comes into play which each time seems to me like a miracle'' (1946*a*, p. 101). There arises a countering action in the unconscious, which produces a kind of centering and, subsequently, a self rather than an ego. Thus the process of individuation could, when it occurred, heal the wounds created by the false starts of Freudian therapy, by the loss of ties to traditional religious symbols, and by the subsequent rise of modernity as a cultural situation.

### The Second Theme: Jung's Interpretation of Modernity as Mass Man in a Mass Society

Commentaries, interpretations, and applications pertaining to Jung's mature thought have often given a central position to his relationship either to Freud or to Christianity, thereby creating the impression that these were his major concerns. There are very few discussions of his thought in relation to contemporary social, political, and cultural phenomena. And when Jung's psychology has been applied to culture at all, it has been to high culture, in the mode of humanistic inquiry, such as the study of ancient myths or modern literature. These studies are noted for selecting materials in which social and political concerns are secondary to internal psychological processes. The few studies of Jung's social thought are on the whole disappointing. They attempt to show a strong positive relation between the self and social and political processes. Actually, the notion of a "Jungian sociology" seems almost a contradiction in terms. This trend in the literature on Jung no doubt reflects the fact that his psychology, even more than Freud's, was one of the inner life, in which socialization remained an extremely muted concern. I will evaluate this very important feature of Jung's psychology in the concluding chapter.

It is a mistake, however, to think that the great emphasis on internal processes found in the primary and secondary literature, and the unconvincing character of sociological applications of Jung's thought, signify that he had no interest in, or theory of, the relation of the self to the social order. There are two reasons for taking a different position on this issue. First, the contextual approach, which argues that origins cue structure, suggests that, because Jung's core process emerged out of a struggle with a particular perception of the social order, his mature thought would probably contain substantial reference to such a view. And, second, a definite but often neglected body of Jungian writing does address the subject of modernity. Thanks to the editors of the *Collected Works,* these writings, scattered over the period 1918 to 1959, have been gathered under the sociologically suggestive title *Civilization in Transition* (volume 10 of the *Collected Works,* 1964*a*). The title, organization, and contents of this volume highlight the point that Jung's mature thought does in fact analyze the contemporary cultural situation. The question, therefore, is not Was Jung concerned with modernity and the nature of the social order? Rather, it is What was his theory of the social order? What role did it play in his mature thought? And does it bear as essential a relation to his core process as do the writings on Freud and on religion?

Sociologists and political scientists have given a great deal of attention to how the psychoanalytic tradition bears upon the forms of social and political life. This developing tradition has been fundamentally open to such speculation: Freud's concept of the permanent character of the cultural superego and Erikson's emphasis upon identity as a link between the ego and social institutions, for example, have provided social scientists a means of integrating psychological and social phenomena. Jung's psychology, in contrast, permits no such "integrative" or "synergic" approach. But this does not mean he ignored social processes. Rather, he simply had a different theory of the proper relation between self and society—in effect, his psychology articulates with a different orientation within sociological thinking. I believe Jung's psychology fits lock-and-key with an enormous and incredibly amorphous body of sociological literature that has been subsumed under the rubric "the theory of mass society." It is this theory, with its particular image of the prevailing social order, which Jung's psychology assumes; and his core process is addressed in a fundamental way to this specific vision or diagnosis of contemporary sociality.

Along with Marxism, the theory of mass society is the most prevalent and widely known theory of modernity. As such, it is really more of a conceptual leitmotiv that runs through many different types of modern thought—at times drawing them together— than it is a series of easily definable sociological propositions firmly anchored in a specific framework. It is really an "umbrella" term that describes a view of the modern world and its relation to traditional Western culture. It has been ably summarized, both historically and systematically, by the sociologist Salvador Giner (1976), who describes it as a "total outlook" that lies somewhere between a religion and an ideology. As such, it not only presents a vision of the history of Western man but also purports to explain modern politics, culture, and community life. Accordingly, versions of it can be found in such otherwise diverse intellectual trends as contemporary literary criticism (the tradition of Matthew Arnold and T. S. Eliot), in classic German sociology (the writings of Ferdinand Tönnies) and current viewpoints influenced by that tradition (such as the work of C. W. Mills), and in existentialist philosophy (the writings of Karl Jaspers and Paul Tillich).

Although the theory of mass society has its roots deep in the history of Western political philosophy, in the modern period it has taken a distinctive turn. The modern version did not begin to develop until the late 1920s, and it was only after the Second World War that the theory really reached its fullest articulation as a general account of the state of modern man, in the form of a theory of mass society, mass politics, and mass culture. Giner has shown that Max Scheler, José Ortega, and Karl Mannheim were the modern originators of this theory, and that each figure contributed a key concept that was employed and embellished by later writers. Scheler devised the term "massification," Ortega coined the phrase "mass man," and the concept of "mass society" is attributed to Mannheim.

The writings of Max Scheler were decisive, according to Giner, in their explicit conception of modern society as a mass society. Scheler believed that contemporary Western culture was in the midst of a moral and cultural crisis and that the root of this crisis was a vast process of equalization that produced a homogeneous and monotonous society only superficially integrated by political and state mechanisms. In a 1927 lecture Scheler spoke of his own time as one of "social levelling," by which he meant that "individuals are now becoming less and less different from each other (that is, less and less individual)" and that "the broad elements of social differentiation between groups, collectivities and institutions are getting weaker" (Giner 1976, p. 74). Later, Scheler called this leveling "massification,'' by which he meant that ''modern man's basic difference from his predecessors stems from the fact that . . . he is ceasing to be an individual. He is only part of the mass . . . and not a relatively free and autonomous part of a structured whole . . . he is emotionally unstable, capricious and hysterical'' (Giner 1976, pp. 74–75). Thus Scheler launched the theory of mass society with his concept of ''massification.''

In 1926 José Ortega coined the term ''mass man'' for what both he and Scheler recognized as the depersonalized, lonely individual of modern society. According to Giner, Ortega's main preoccupation was ''the demise of the individual under the relentless pressure of 'the fearful homogeneity of situations'' (Giner 1976, p. 76). This homogeneity breeds a new type of man, the mass man, whom Ortega described as ''man previously emptied of his own history, lacking a memory of his past . . . he is the shell of a man . . . he lacks an inner self, an intimacy . . . a self that cannot be revoked'' (quoted by Giner 1976, p. 76). Mass man, Ortega said, is ''any man who does not value himself, who feels instead that he is like everybody, who has no anxiety, and who feels satisfied in being identical to others'' (quoted by Giner 1976, p. 77). Consequently, mass man takes the state for granted. But the state, now separated from its historical roots, concentrates only on controlling contemporary life and so destroys individuals and their private institutions. This state of affairs can only result in the total submission of the masses to the all-powerful modern state.

In 1929 Karl Mannheim published his famous book *Ideology and Utopia*. While this work is often taken as a forerunner of the sociology of knowledge, and while Mannheim does not explicitly discuss the concept of mass society, nonetheless it contains many elements of the theory, in particular an account of how such a society emerged in the West. First, Mannheim argued that medieval life, more than any other period in Western history, provided a strong, firm, and mutually supportive relation between social solidarity and epistemological and ontological consensus. A single, generally accepted view prevailed as to what constituted objective reality, in both an ultimate and a practical sense. This consensus permitted considerable stratification of groups within society without restricting common loyalties. Second, this continuity between social order and a common view of reality was broken at the time of the Reformation and the Enlightenment. The breakdown of social stability went hand in hand with a corresponding fragmentation of the shared sense of objective truth. The Reformation was therefore a preparation for the later formation of a mass society. Third, these sociological and ontological changes affected corresponding shifts in the pattern of integration between self and society—forcing the burden of personal integration away from institutionalized mechanisms and placing it more on the individual. Fourth, this shift, in which a traditional world view no longer organized men in a wholesome manner, created the conditions of modern, mass society.

Mannheim attempted to describe the features of the emerging mass society by the term "massification" (presumably borrowed from Scheler). By this he meant, according to Giner, "the total loss of individuality and the total identification of individuals with their collectivity or group . . . the emergence in the mass of the qualities of mass man: traditionlessness, aimlessness and above all lack of individuality. Through group identification individuals lose all sense of being different." Mannheim implied that "the growth of the mass society involves regression and not progress" (Giner 1976, p. 125).

We can further summarize this synopsis by noting that the three originators, taken together, stress three major interlocking features that form the core of the theory of mass society. First, they all argue that modern man has lost contact with the past and thus is uprooted and traditionless. Furthermore, at least Scheler and Mannheim regarded the Christian faith as a viable and wholesome source of a sense of tradition. This loss of tradition is closely associated with the process of massification. Second, because he is uprooted from his traditions, modern man has become depersonalized—he has lost his autonomy, separateness, and distinctiveness. He is a cog or unit in contemporary society. He is, in short, "mass man." Third, depersonalized or mass man relates to the social order in one of two ways, neither of which is conducive to individuality and rootedness. Modern man either is isolated and alienated from the social order or else is submissive to its authoritarian political and social structures. A mass society is, therefore, that type of social order that creates isolation or submission.

The literature on the theory of mass society is far more extensive, complex, rich, and sophisticated than this brief survey suggests. Readers concerned with its ramifications can consult Giner's careful and thorough review, which also contains an excellent critical discussion. My purpose in introducing the theory is not to present a full-blown portrait of it, nor for that matter to argue its merits. Rather, I wish to show that it is integral to Jung's core process and to his mature thought. Jung's system assumes a diagnosis of modernity identical to that of the theory of mass society; and, even more important, Jung's core process served as a "cure" or "therapy" for the ills of modern, mass man. This preoccupation with the plight of modern man constitutes a fundamental theme in Jung's mature thought and is inseparable from the two others—his concern with Freud's psychology and his reinterpretation of traditional Christianity.

Jung's first published diagnosis of modernity appeared, as I have already noted, in the 1912 essay "New Paths in Psychology." At that time he assessed the clinical situation as a cultural problem—the problem of "our time," of modernity—and thus stated, albeit in his own words, a diagnosis of modern society as mass society. But the "cure" had not yet been formulated. The essay was revised in 1917 to become one of the two major texts describing the core process. That process not only assumed that modern man was mass man living in a mass society but also contained Jung's remedy for the predicament of modernity. Modern man was characterized by a rigid persona that Jung associated with extraversion and excessive rationality. The cause of such rigidity was that modern man was separated from or alienated from his roots in the past. He had, in other words, lost touch with the archetypes of the collective unconscious, the source of all tradition. And the social consequences of a rigid persona were total and uncritical adaptation and submission to the roles and expectations dictated by the state. In this way Jung cast in the language of analytical psychology the equivalent of what mass society theory expressed by such terms as massification, mass man, and mass society.

But Jung's core process was not simply a diagnosis of modernity—it was much more fundamentally a therapy or cure for its ills. The breakdown of the persona, the emergence of archetypes from the collective unconscious, their interpretation by the synthetic method, the assimilation of collective material, and the gradual emergence of a self as opposed to a merely rational ego—in short, the whole process of individuation—all were understood by Jung as a remedy for the rigid persona and all its sociocultural implications. Thus Jung's concept of individuation was not designed just as a psychotherapeutic strategy, isolated from its social context. It was addressed with equal seriousness to the problem of modernity, understood as mass man in a mass society.

After the core process took form, toward the end of the decade of 1910, Jung's personality and thought consolidated, and he embarked on the lifelong process of exploring his major intellectual interests more deeply and with finer nuances. Among his writings were many occasional essays on modern man, which always emphasized his uprootedness in relation to traditional, ancient, and archaic patterns of experience; the importance of religion as a point of anchorage for such experience; and the power of analytical psychology to bridge the gap between the two. Jung produced a steady stream of literature on this subject, assembled in *Civilization in Transition* (1964*a*). From time to time throughout these essays he sparingly used such terms as mass man, the mass, and mass movement to describe the contemporary situation. But his fundamental understanding of both diagnosis and cure did not change.

The best evidence for the view that Jung assumed a diagnosis of modernity identical to that proposed by the theory of mass society is a long essay written only four years before he died (but included in *Civilization in Transition*), the English title of which is ''The Undiscovered Self'' (1957). The significance of this essay lies not in any new estimate of modernity—it follows the familiar Jungian form—but rather in the fact that here Jung openly adopted the vocabulary of the theory of mass society and wove it into his already well-established patterns of thinking. Thus the essay indicates explicitly what had before been implicit. Furthermore, it gives great emphasis to the intimate, causative relation Jung saw between the rise of mass man and the decline of traditional religion, as well as to the powers of analytical psychology to remedy the situation by reinterpreting traditional religion.

Jung began by analyzing what he called the plight of the individual in modern society. Because the rise of the scientific attitude has forced the individual to think of himself as a statistical average, and because the authoritarian modern state has robbed the individual of his dignity, modern man has succumbed to what Jung called "mass-mindedness." Jung also spoke of "mass rule," "the blind movement of the masses," "the infantile dream state of mass man," and "mass psychology." By such terminology he meant that modern man had lost contact with the ancient and largely unconscious resources of tradition whereby he could think of himself as autonomous and self-regulating, responsible for his own existence in the world. Instead, he had become a collective being, dependent upon socially based authority structures—in short, he had allowed himself to be defined by collective ideals.

To explore the origins of this plight Jung turned to religion. Religion had traditionally been the central resource protecting man's individuality. Dependence upon God, he argued, was a point of reference outside the collectivities of rationalism and communalism. Religion organized and gave wholesome symbolic form to the irrational facts of personal experience. It consisted of inner, transcendent experience "which alone can protect him [the individual] from the otherwise inevitable submersion in the mass" (1964*a*, p. 258). In contemporary life, however, religion had crystallized into dogmas, creeds, and beliefs and so it had itself become rationalistic, like science, and its organizations had become authoritarian, like political totalitarianism. Thus Jung saw no difference between the offerings of the Christian church and the creeds of communism and scientific materialism. To make his own case even stronger, he spoke of the futility of demythologization.

In the remaining sections of his essay he offered his solution to the predicament of mass man, under the rubrics of self-understanding and self-knowledge. Modern man's consciousness was caught up in a conflict between natural, archaic, and instinctual endowments—which found expression in the form of traditional religion—and his contemporary need to adapt to rationalistic and collectivistic norms. This conflict is the essence of neurosis, not as Freud had defined it, in his one-sided, personalistic sense, but as Jung had defined it, in terms of the collective unconscious. Analytical psychology was therefore a diagnostic tool for the problem of modernity and, correspondingly, contained the only possible cure for modern man.

Hence the remaining sections of the essay consisted entirely of a series of explicit references to the various therapeutic concepts and the general thrust of analytical psychology. Mass man was characterized by a rationalistic commitment to collectivity—what Jung in other places called a rigid persona and an extraverted attitude—a psychological situation for which individuation provided a unique remedy. Jung unabashedly offered the creative ideas of his unique psychological system as the only reasonable antidote for the predicament of modern, mass man. By doing this he gave an interpretation of one of the forces that had initiated his critical years and at the same time fulfilled the portion of his personal identity that expressed itself in his activities as moralist and social critic.

An examination of Jung's writings makes it patently clear that he adopted the theory of mass society, but why he did so is by no means so obvious. Jung had extensive knowledge of Freudian and Adlerian theory, and he had immersed himself deeply in various types of philosophical and religious thought. But there is no corresponding debt to the mass-society theorists, who had begun to write in the 1920s and whose work became more and more well known after the Second World War. Except for an occasional reference to Le Bon,[1] Jung did not attend to this growing genre of social commentary. Still, several speculations can be offered. First, the theory fit in with that aloofness from the European world that characterized the Swiss. Jung had a deep fear of countries larger than his own—which meant he feared almost every country he was familiar with. In 1945 he wrote: "We have only to multiply the population of Switzerland by twenty to become a nation of eighty millions, and our public intelligence and morality would then automatically be divided by twenty in consequence of the devastating moral and psychic effects of living together in huge masses" (1945, p. 200).

Second, many of the dynamic psychologies assume in varying degrees the theory of mass society (e.g., Giner 1976, pp. 64–65; Homans 1974). Third, Jung was deeply influenced by the thought of Nietzsche, and, as Giner has pointed out, Nietzsche was one of the

1. For example: "One need only read what Le Bon has to say on the 'psychology of crowds' to understand what I mean: man as a particle in the mass is psychically abnormal" (Jung 1946b, p. 239).

most powerful spokesmen for the theory of mass society (Giner 1976, pp. 54–57). Finally, it can be observed that the forces of industrialization—particularly urbanization, mass transportation, and mass communications—were extremely threatening to intellectuals and social critics in the first half of the twentieth century, and Jung clearly thought of himself as a member of this group. For all these reasons he would find the theory of mass society congenial.

This review of Jung's interpretation of Freud and his psychotherapeutic theory, and of Jung's interpretation of modernity as a mass society, shows how difficult it was for him to separate these issues from religion. This opens up the most basic question of all regarding the fundamental status of his mature thought: Just what exactly was the relation of Jung's system of psychological ideas to historical Christianity? And this question raises the third and most privileged theme in all of Jung's written works.

### The Third Theme: Jung's Reinterpretation of Traditional Christianity

To the reader only moderately familiar with Jung's writings, and to anyone guided by the secondary literature, it may not have seemed obvious that the themes of Freud and modernity are central to Jung's mature work. Hence, in discussing these themes I have been forced to argue actively for their preeminence. But no such argument is needed for the role of religion in Jung's thought. That religion was a central theme in his mature writings is a point on which both the casual reader and the careful critic—regardless of his "position" on Jungian psychology—can agree. Religion was, as we have seen, crucial to the core process: the last stage in individuation consisted in the successful resolution of an encounter with a god-imago. Jung never abandoned this conviction. In his mature years he wrote about religion again and again from different points of view: primitive religions and archaic man; Eastern religions; the relation of psychotherapy to the work of the clergyman; but above all about Christianity and Christian dogma, in particular the dogma of the existence or transcendence of God.

This feature of Jung's mature thought is fully supported by the contextual approach. Just as he himself remarked that he had never ceased trying to understand his relation to Freud—a point I have expanded to include his thought—so he never in his later life stopped thinking about religion. For religion was present at every important stage of his personal and intellectual development. The personal experience of religion pervaded his turbulent childhood and early adolescence. Religious concerns colored his relation to Freud and the writing of *Symbols of Transformation*. During his critical years he assimilated his personal-mystical-narcissistic mode of the experience of religion and at the same time struggled with the tension between Freud and modernity on the one hand and traditional Christianity on the other. After Jung had formed his core process, he turned back upon the phenomenon of religion, which had vexed him throughout so much of his early life, and interpreted it—or, as I will explain shortly, *re*interpreted it—according to his unique system of psychological ideas.

So the question regarding Jung's relation to religion in the mature years is not whether it was a bona fide theme. Rather, given the fact that religion was a central theme, the question is, What was Jung's view of it? This question contains a central issue in understanding Jung's thought as a whole, one that has created most of the polarization among critics of Jung, and can be stated as follows. Did Jung, like Freud, develop a set of interpretive categories by means of which he could "see through" and thereby explain away traditional Christianity? Or did he, in devising his system of unique ideas, conceive of a way to translate traditional Christianity into terminology acceptable to modern man without appreciably altering the traditional doctrines? In other words, was Jung a Christian or a post-Christian psychologist?

The correct response to this question—which I will illustrate below with a discussion of Jung's best-known text on religion—is that both aspects of it must be answered yes, but that neither one constitutes his whole approach. Jung did not opt exclusively for either of these alternatives. His thought on religion is a complex attempt to synthesize both. By applying his core process to traditional Christianity, Jung in effect created a double movement of reduction and retrieval of meaning. In one sense he *was* reductive: he interpreted the totality of Christian faith in the light of analytical psychology. This psychology became for him the key for "seeing through" its otherwise opaque character. All the major tenets of Christianity were interpreted as instances of archetypes in the collective unconscious. The individuation process was the lens through which Jung viewed the Christian faith. It was a new set of categories, derived from his researches and his contact with Freud, completely foreign to the Christian tradition. Without this psychology that faith simply did not make sense. Jung's interpretation of Christianity was in this sense very different from Christianity's own self-interpretation. In this sense his psychology embodied what Paul Ricoeur has called a "hermeneutics of suspicion" (1970). This feature of Jung's stance toward religion corresponds to the mood of repudiation that has already been emphasized at various points.

But Jung's psychology contained a second movement that built upon the first, in which he attempted to retrieve religious meaning from the Christian tradition and incorporate it into his psychological theory of the person. Once the reductive movement had been made—once the psychological meaning of doctrine had been disclosed—then Jung proceeded to clothe these constructs with positive meaning and value, arguing that they were in fact essential if modern man, uprooted and dissociated from his traditional roots, was ever to relate himself again to Christian tradition. Hence he claimed that the archetypes and the individuation process, though not part of the vocabulary of the traditional Christian, nevertheless captured the hidden essence of that tradition. Thus Jung's psychology contained within it, alongside its hermeneutics of suspicion, what I call a "hermeneutics of affirmation," corresponding to the mood of assimilation we have discussed.

To emphasize the double movement in Jung's psychology, in which both rejection and affirmation were present, I call his approach a *re*interpretation rather than simply one more interpretation. In all this, Jung gave expression to the third facet of his personal identity—which existed alongside that of originative psychologist and social critic—that of prophet or reinterpreter of traditional Christianity.

In proposing that there was a double movement in Jung's approach toward traditional Christianity, I take issue with existing discussions of Jung's view of religion—the literature of specialist appropriation. The positively toned theological interpretations—such as those of

Cox (1959), Schaer (1950), and White (1952)[2]—have not given
attention to the massive evidence that supports Jung's lifelong
struggle to repudiate Christianity—to free himself from its oppressive claims upon him. Nor do they see the great extent to which
Jung, in his mature writings, found traditional Christianity utterly
incomprehensible. To say that a particular doctrine or tenet of faith is
"really" an archetype of the collective unconscious is to assign to it
a meaning quite different from that which the Christian tradition
gives it.

On the other hand it is equally necessary—in order to achieve a
correct and full sense of Jung's stance toward religion—to oppose
the anti-Jungians such as Hostie (1957), Philp (1958), Rieff (1966)
and Johnson (1974). These critics have ignored the element of
affirmation. They have not seen how classical Christian experience
provided an absolutely essential matrix, or "field," out of which the
individuation process took its peculiar shape. Thus, for Jung, the
traditional beliefs in God, Christ, the Trinity, and the church were all
necessary background for the modern individual if he was to understand himself in a new way. Traditional Christianity was the indispensable context for individuation. Paradoxically, it was there in
order to be put aside. In Jung's mind, analytical psychology evolved
out of the Christian tradition, in a historical sense, and the end result
was just as religious—but not theological—as the context out of
which it emerged.

To clarify this argument further, it helps to point out that Jung's
psychology really comprised three types or images of man. First,
there was the good Christian, either Catholic or Protestant, who
believed unquestioningly in the tenets of his faith and for this very
reason did not need psychology. For such people, traditional doctrine
successfully organized their unconscious processes and hence protected them from becoming neurotic. But Jung was primarily interested in a second type, the so-called modern man, who was fully
self-conscious, rational, and extraverted, who was oriented to science and the modern state, and who, because he was unconnected

---

2. Victor White, after writing at length about the similarities between the Christian
life and Jungian psychology (1952), eventually withdrew this conviction. His slow
change of mind is recorded in Jung's correspondence with him (Jung 1975).

with the past, was vulnerable to the unconscious. And then there was what I call "Jungian man," who was modern in that he rejected the literalism and authoritarianism of traditional Christianity but was also in part traditional, in that he was ready to reinterpret Christian symbols in the light of analytical psychology. Thus Jung's view of religion was complex: during his mature life he tried to reconcile the tension between tradition and modernity, and his psychology is an attempt—through its double movement of reduction and affirmation—to close what most people consider the unbridgeable gap between two orientations to the world. Jung's need for continuity between these orientations must be heavily emphasized. It had its roots in his inner, psychological need for self-coherence, which he transposed to his intellectual work.

This estimate of Jung's view of religion is clearly confirmed by the delineation of his core process in the *Two Essays,* which I have already summarized. In that statement he defined the final stage of individuation as an encounter with a god-imago that had a distinctly Christian cast. The consolidation of the archetype of the anima created a new sense of inflation, a merger with the Deity that produced the feeling "I and the Father are one." To come to terms with this merger the patient could, Jung said, concretize or absolutize this image of God as "Father in heaven." This would be the traditional Christian solution. But he cautioned against such a move, for it would only produce a new sense of moral inferiority and oppression—a fundamental prerequisite of traditional faith. In saying this Jung repudiated the Christianity of tradition and took the side of modern man, suspicious of all commitment to theological dogma.

But he did not stop here. He went on to introduce the archetype of the self and to apply this concept interpretively to the theological situation. He spoke of the self not only as a midpoint between conscious and unconscious, but also as "the god within us." And he defined the emergence of the self as a natural and spontaneous process, not dependent on traditional theological dogma. Thus, by using the categories of analytical psychology Jung was able first to repudiate traditional Christianity, then to affirm the formation of the self as a genuine result of evolution out of the prior theological situation.

Throughout his mature writings Jung never deviated from this approach to religion. He did write a number of short articles on Eastern religions, but his purpose was to emphasize what the West lacked. He did not share the interests of the historian of religion. Rather, he was predominantly concerned with the Christian faith. Through analytical psychology Jung reinterpreted traditional Christianity, first by repudiating its formulations, then by going on to show how classic faith provided the experiential matrix out of which the individuation process could evolve.

Now, with this understanding of Jung's strategy firmly in hand, let us turn briefly to his explicit writings on religion. While the basic strategy is present throughout all his many and varied analyses of religious questions and provides a unified perspective upon their otherwise great diversity, it is particularly evident in his best-known work on the subject, originally written in 1938, "Psychology and Religion" (1963b). This text focuses Jung's central and lifelong preoccupation with Christianity: the psychological nature of the Christian doctrine of God. At the very beginning of the book Jung set the stage for his basic strategy with regard to religion by distinguishing between religion on the one hand and dogmas or creeds on the other. He defined religion as "a careful consideration of certain dynamic factors that are conceived as 'powers': spirits, demons, gods, laws, ideas, ideals" (1963b, p. 8). Religion, he wished to make clear, was an experience of a particular type—it was immediate, subjective, and therefore psychological. He equated it with what the Protestant theologian Rudolph Otto meant by "the numinous"—suggesting awe and reverence toward a supreme object. And later in the book he spoke of religious experience as "immediate experience," by which he meant the irruption into an overly rational ego consciousness of collective, archetypal material—an experience that in its own way inspired awe and dread or fear. In contrast to religious experience, Jung juxtaposed dogmas and creeds. These were, he said, "codified and dogmatized forms of original religious experience" (1963b, p. 9). A dogma is formed when the immediate religious experience congeals into a rigid and elaborate structure of ideas.

Thus, at the very outset of his book, Jung prepared the reader for his unique approach to religion. Dogma was the language of traditional Christianity, whereas religious experience was the target of analytical psychology. Jung's task was to unearth the structures and processes of religious experience that dogma had obscured and repressed. By exposing the hidden roots of dogma, Jung would reductively interpret Christianity; but then, by demonstrating the underground source of dogma in universal religious experience, he would affirm and reinterpret traditional Christianity. The key to this double movement was the new system of ideas known as analytical psychology and, in particular, the individuation process.

To carry his argument forward, Jung presented his reader with details of a practical case, several dreams of one of his psychotherapy patients. The life situation of this dreamer was an important piece of Jung's argument, for he embodied Jung's concept of modern man: a scientifically minded intellectual who, because of his commitment to modernity, could no longer believe in creeds and dogmas and who, like most moderns, identified religion entirely with such creeds and dogmas. Jung then analyzed these dreams and demonstrated that they contained images of the archetype of the quaternity—what he called a mandala. Such dreams reflected, he argued, the presence of immediate experience, of the numinous, and were religious in nature. They were, in fact, when properly interpreted, "symbols of God." Jung gave two further reasons for this conclusion. First, the comparative method had shown that ancient thinkers had associated quaternities with God. But Jung also suggested that mandalas were expressions of a religious attitude because the people who dream them link this symbol to the highest value in their personality. "Religion," he said, "is a relationship to the highest or most powerful value . . . that psychological fact which wields the greatest power in your system functions as a god" (1963b, p. 81).

Having established that dreams and visions of quaternities and mandalas were evidence of the presence of God in the experiential life of the subject, Jung was forced to reflect upon traditional formulations of the nature of the Deity. He rightly turned to the doctrine of the Trinity as the privileged form in which the character of deity had been expressed in Christian faith. And he concluded that the Trinity, with its exclusive emphasis upon three rather than four elements in the divine life, was excessively rational and one-sided. The doctrine of the Trinity had repressed the principle of evil and the principle of femininity in the nature of God, and hence also in the consciousness of man. The quaternity, on the other hand, made room for these elements and as such was a more complete and also fully natural symbol of the godhead. But Jung's major concern was not simply with the doctrine of the Trinity per se—he discussed this at length in a separate essay on the subject—but also with what mandalas presaged for the fate of the image of God in the modern world. In traditional Christianity the image of God existed outside the believer's psyche, and he submitted to and was reconciled with that imago. But in the mandala dreams of modern man, Jung said, "the place of the deity seems to be taken by the wholeness of man" (1963b, p. 82). Jung called this wholeness or totality of man the self, the end result of the individuation process. The emergence on the modern scene of mandala dreams signified, it seems, the disappearance of the traditional view of God and the appearance of the self.

Once again Jung had brought into play what I have called the strategy of a double movement. Using the categories of analytical psychology, he was able to interpret psychologically the key Christian theological formulation of the nature of God. The image of God embodied in the Trinity was repressive, and it distorted psychological reality accordingly. Thus Jung reduced Christian theology to psychology in the spirit of a hermeneutics of suspicion. But then he went on to show how the reality of the Deity, though no longer an object of traditional faith, continues to live in the form of a structure of the self, undergirding "the wholeness of man." His point here was identical to his concept of the self as "the god within us" found in the *Two Essays*. By virtue of the interpretive power of analytical psychology, the Jungian self was a new emergent, evolving out of the matrix of traditional faith. But the movement of retrieval was based upon, and was never separate from, the prior movement of reductive interpretation.

Toward the end of the book Jung introduced one of his most important concepts, "the withdrawal of projections," which illustrated more clearly his strategy of a double attitude toward traditional Christianity (1963b, pp. 83, 87). Primitive man lived in a state of almost total projection: he projected inner emotions onto external objects and persons and consequently lived in a condition of relatively minimal self-consciousness and self-knowledge. But as Western history progressed, changing circumstances brought about the gradual withdrawal of projections and a consequent increase in consciousness and knowledge of both self and world. Physical science caused the withdrawal of "the most distant" projections. Echoing Max Weber's concept of disenchantment, Jung referred to this as the first stage in the despiritualization of the world. The early discoveries of modern science became the foundations of the modern outlook, shaping as they did an entire world view. According to Jung, it was the essence of modern man to examine all his projections. Modern man "cannot project the divine image any longer" (1963*b*, p. 95)—he is no longer able to believe in the existence of God as described by the traditional dogmas of the church. Although Jung did not mention Freud in this context, it is clear that Freud's psychology of religion epitomized this stance. Hence the impasse of modernity: modern man can no longer believe—he has withdrawn his projections. But when he does so he becomes an isolated ego consciousness. Jung resolved this conflict by adducing analytical psychology: "If we want to know what happens when the idea of God is no longer projected as an autonomous entity, this is the answer of the unconscious psyche" (1963*b*, p. 96).

The "answer of the unconscious psyche" was of course the answer of the entire individuation process, and it bore a double relation to the predicament of modernity. Analytical psychology focused primarily on the affects and images (instincts and archetypes) that undergirded the traditional doctrines and the loyalty believers brought to them. As such it in effect counseled the withdrawal of projections. Jung continually insisted throughout his diverse writings on religion that insofar as he could, especially in his role as psychotherapist, he always returned the believing Catholic or Protestant to his traditional faith; but this was largely a matter of practical therapeutic strategy. For it is just as clear that his analytical psychology "saw through" the projections of traditional believers. He in effect postulated an archetypal infrastructure—what I would call "the archetype beneath the doctrine"—to traditional belief. Thus, though the good Catholic or Protestant may not know it, his religious faith is motivated by the forces analytical psychology describes. The conceptualization of these forces constitutes a system of ideas and a corresponding reality very different from traditional faith. To say "I believe in God the Father" and to say "I am at this moment stirred by an archetype" are two very different explanations of a particular inner state. In all of this the thrust of analytical psychology is against traditional Christianity. It is a hermeneutics of suspicion, an unmasking process, a reductive approach, in which dogmas and creeds—the sole modes of conceptualization of traditional faith—are repudiated.

But the withdrawal of projections was only the first part of the double movement. Jung believed he had discovered a natural healing process that occurred when projections were withdrawn—a healing process that would replace or, rather, carry forward the projective process. In the dreams and visions of his patients, especially when they took the form of mandalas, Jung saw at work a process that was remarkably similar to those he believed undergirded the most traditional belief systems. His theory and techniques simply brought these processes to a higher level of self-consciousness than they had attained under the conditions of traditional faith. The withdrawal of projections activated new psychological forces, unknown to the traditional believer, that were then raised to a new level of awareness and integrated into self-consciousness. In this sense—but in this sense only—Jung ascribed to his own system of ideas a significance functionally equivalent to traditional belief systems. As he had put it in an essay written several years earlier: "It is as though, at the climax of the illness, the destructive powers were converted into healing forces. This is brought about by the archetypes wakening to independent life. . . . As a religious-minded person would say: guidance has come from God. With most of my patients I have to avoid this formulation, apt thought it is, for it reminds them too much of what they had to reject in the first place. I must express myself in more modest terms and say that the psyche has awakened to spontaneous activity. And indeed this formulation is better suited to the observable facts. . . . To the patient it is nothing less than a revelation" (1932, p. 345).

Thus Jung attempted to retrieve meaning from traditional Christianity. But, because his hermeneutics of affirmation was preceded by a thoroughly reductive and repudiative movement, his psychology cannot be identified in any simple way with the contents or intentions of ancient faith. Nor is it—for the same reason—a simple repudiation of the religion in which he was nurtured and which he struggled against all his life. Rather, his psychology is a genuine alternative to classic Christianity, evolving, however, out of the matrix of experience that long ago produced the original doctrines. In such fashion did Jung reinterpret traditional Christianity in the light of his core process.

# Eight

## Conclusion: Jung, Psychological Man, and Modernization

### Jung and Psychological Man

In this brief concluding chapter, I shall reflect upon the foregoing analyses of the origins and structure of Jung's thought in the light of broader cultural trends. For Jung's work is not simply an idiosyncratic set of materials isolated from cultural surroundings; rather, it embodies a wider series of phenomena that lie beyond the vicissitudes of his life and the contents of his thought.

I began by situating this study in the context of what has come to be called the rise of psychological man, a new and increasingly dominant image of humanity that is achieving more and more prominence in contemporary life. In Chapter 1 I suggested that Jung's psychology was a particularly apt instance of psychological man. I reviewed the better-known literature on this topic and summarized the outstanding marks of psychological man as follows: the decline of the power of traditional religion to organize personal and social life; a diffuse and heightened sense of personal self-consciousness, in which consciousness tends to be structured and meaning realized primarily in the context of personal, private, and psychological experiencing; and an emerging split between personal self-consciousness and the social order, eventuating in a devaluation of the social structure as a source of and object for personal commitment. The detailed analyses of the events in Jung's life and of the formation and structure of his thought allow us

193

to reflect with some specificity upon how the several features of psychological man—in this case, "Jungian man"—came into being. In so reflecting, I give more precision to the hypothesis of psychological man and open the way, if only in principle, to generalizing that hypothesis to the sphere of other originative psychologies. How do the three marks of psychological man appear in Jung's odyssey, and how does that journey illumine the nature of psychological man?

Existing discussions of the emergence of psychological man, and of the psychological ideas that support this new image of the person, almost always associate it in some way or other with the decline of the influence of traditional religion. But despite such recognition of religion's importance, these discussions do not specify in detail the relation between the decline of religion and the rise of psychological man and psychological ideas. Instead, they in effect postulate the equivalent of a "meaning vacuum" at the broad sociocultural level: the removal of religion creates an empty epistemological space that is then filled by psychology. However, the careful and detailed study of Jung's person and thought clarifies how, at least in his case, this shift came about, for it provides a "microsociological" perspective on what can only be called a "macrosociological" generalization. I formulate this process by means of an extremely awkward—but also, I hope to show, warranted—assertion: Jung interrupted "the Protestant psychologic," and so threw into motion the forces that led to the creation of his psychology as an outstanding instance of the rise of psychological man.

By using the phrase "the Protestant psychologic" I wish to emphasize that classical Protestantism—which structured the sociocultural ethos in which Jung spent his life, especially his early life—created a unique and highly effective solution to the universal psychological needs for idealization and merger. Protestantism synthesized these needs with viable and appropriate cultural objects through its doctrine of the transcendent existence of God, which met the need of the self for idealization, and through the evangelical doctrine of the believer's oneness with Christ—I am in Christ and Christ in me—which nurtured the believer's associated need for merger with a supreme cultural object. In this way Protestant Christianity articulated with the narcissistic needs of it followers. In all this I think the psychology of narcissism provides a better foundation for a psychology of religion than does the oedipal, object-love orientation of classic psychoanalysis. The former describes the psychological grounds for belief itself, whereas the latter is more suitable for an analysis of the dynamics of the relation between man and his god, once belief in the god's existence has been established.

Jung "interrupted" the Protestant psychologic—he could not idealize those cultural objects that his surrounding social ethos had endowed with supreme value. As a consequence he repudiated traditional Christianity, although throughout his life he remained at war with it. This struggle began with his earliest suspicions of Lord Jesus; it was embodied in his childhood dreams, rituals, and visions, in particular his fantasy of the destruction of the cathedral, which expressed his inability to invest the Christian doctrine of God with idealizing affect; and it took mature form in *Symbols of Transformation,* wherein he sternly dismissed Christianity, and in his later criticisms of the repressive nature of the doctrine of the Trinity. There is a long but straight line from the childhood experiences of Lord Jesus down to the 1938 essay "Psychology and Religion."

When the Protestant psychologic loses its organizing power, the result is the emergence of narcissism—a diffuse and heightened form of immediate self-consciousness—and Jung's life and thought were largely energized by this phenomenon. From his earliest years and throughout the first half of his life he was confronted by the need to find new objects of idealization and by problems of self-esteem and grandiosity. His struggle with narcissism was further exacerbated because he stood midway between the emerging modern, secular culture and the culture of traditional religion. As a result of these psychological and sociological forces, Jung in effect broke with the altruistic value systems of the West, which were embodied with extraordinary intensity in Protestant Christianity and which denied or repressed the unconscious desire to give attention to the grandiose self. Then, during his critical years, he finally developed a system of ideas that could structure his inner diffuseness and social ambiguity. At the same time it provided him with a meaningful set of values to idealize, epitomized by the goal of individuation and the attainment of the true self, and also gave him some perspective upon his esteem needs, grandiosity, and social location. In such fashion was the "decline of religion" related to the "rise of psychological ideas."

The result was an incredibly ingenious system of thought, combining a genuine break from the Protestant tradition with an attempt to relate it to the new system of ideas. Jung's writings, both autobiographical and formal, provide the most detailed and systematic account I have found in modern intellectual history of the struggle of an individual who was unable to accept the Christianity in which he was reared but at the same time unwilling to let it completely pass him by.

The emergence of the theme of narcissism in Jung's life and thought, coinciding with the breakdown of the power of the Christian doctrine of God to integrate into itself his narcissistic needs for idealization, articulates with an emerging trend in contemporary culture. I call this trend "the cultural shift to narcissism." It constitutes the second mark of psychological man and gives specificity to my generalized description of that image as a diffuse and heightened sense of personal self-consciousness wherein meaning tends to be realized in the context of private rather than public experience. A number of writers specializing in very different areas have noted that narcissism is rapidly becoming one of the central problems of contemporary society. Rieff's reconceptualizing what he had originally called psychological man as "the therapeutic character type" conveys the strong implication that this new type displays important aspects of narcissism. In fact, Rieff has been criticized (Beldoch 1975) for implying that Freud in effect proposed a narcissistic stance toward life. Freud of course did quite otherwise; he counseled object love and believed that this psychological organization existed in inverse relation to narcissism: the more object love, the less narcissism, and vice versa. More to the point, however, as readers of Rieff know well, is the fact that he saw in Jung's thought an outstanding example of the therapeutic type. We need not argue with Rieff's polemic oversimplification of Jung's relation to traditional Christianity—he ignores the intensity of Jung's struggle with his own unbelief and his associated efforts to affirm traditional Christianity—in order to note that there is a linkage between psychological man, Jung's ideas, and the emergence of narcissism as a cultural trend.

Kohut captured much clinical speculation when he remarked that the narcissistic character disorders have largely replaced the classical neuroses (obsessive-compulsive states and hysteria) as the predominant psychopathology of contemporary life. In effect, the problems of our age are becoming largely those of self-esteem, inner emptiness, the absence of values to idealize, and grandiosity with the self—which now exist alongside the classical problems produced by aggressive and erotic conflicts in the oedipal sphere of object love. Writing from a sociological viewpoint in a volume of essays whose title is itself significant—*The Narcissistic Condition: A Fact of Our Lives and Times* (Nelson 1977)—Ann Braden Johnson has argued that the youthful radicals of the late 1960s were motivated by unresolved narcissistic concerns and that they came to populate the psychoreligious cults of the early 1970s, all the while perpetuating their narcissistic dilemmas. Jung, we must note, is a congenial figure to some of these cults. In his recent book *The Fall of Public Man,* the social historian Richard Sennett (1974) has suggested that people in contemporary society are less and less able to relate actively and vigorously to impersonal social structures, producing a collapse of the public sphere of life. He believes that this inability to establish a wholesome sense of social distance is due to the emergence of narcissism as a social trend. And the popular critic Tom Wolfe's well-known characterization of the mid-70s as the ''me generation'' is in effect a statement that narcissism has become a major cultural fact.

The growing body of commentary suggesting that contemporary society shows a significant trend toward narcissism has by and large emphasized what could be called its ''hazards.'' The accent is upon negative moral consequences. So it is argued that people are more preoccupied with themselves and less energetic in investing others and the otherness of life; that they feel their lives are empty and meaningless; that they are more frankly grandiose and self-seeking; that they search out, more than ever, powerful authority figures to idealize; and that they gravitate more closely to cults and ethnic groups that display a strong in-group/out-group polarization, thereby providing the opportunity to express narcissistic rage. While all these observations are supported by the psychology of narcissism, as it has been derived from clinical observation and research, it is also possible that social critics can put such assertions at the service of the altruistic value systems of the West, which are grounded in the repression of narcissism rather than in its transformation. In such cases the psychology of narcissism becomes just one more tool in the hands of perennial doomsayers who never cease to argue that people these days are more selfish and self-seeking than ever before. In short, the very real hazards of narcissism can become the occasion of a new moralism.

Partly for this reason, but primarily for reasons intrinsic to the theory itself, we need to consider not only the hazards of narcissism but its hope as well; for the phenomenon of narcissism is double-edged. Kohut has emphasized the fact, almost always ignored by social critics, that narcissistic phenomena have their own independent line of development. They do not bear an inverse relation to object love. Rather, the vicissitudes of the narcissistic phase of personality development (the development of the self) contain the seeds of important developmental achievements in later life. The crux of the matter really is whether narcissistic phenomena are repressed or transformed. If they are transformed, then the propensity to idealize the parent imago gradually becomes converted into realistic ideals, goals, and values. This stage serves as the basis for guides to action and commitment. And the tendency toward grandiosity is gradually transformed into realistic and wholesome self-esteem and self-concern. Both these developments lay the groundwork for what Kohut calls therapeutic transformations of narcissistic personalities, by which he means an increase in the capacity for object love, for creativity, for humor, and for wisdom. All these essentially human virtues derive not from the oedipal sphere but from the narcissistic realm of human experience. The emergence of narcissism as a cultural trend therefore embodies, along with its many hazards, the hope and promise of a deeper appreciation of the inner life of the self. As Ernest Wolf has argued (1976), this sector of experience has been repressed for some time in Western cultural and social life.

Everything we have learned about the origins of Jung's thought suggests that his system should be understood in the context of the double-edged character of narcissism. His early years and critical years displayed narcissistic processes with great intensity, and his core process emerged from a struggle to come to terms with them. Accordingly, as might be expected, that system of ideas itself displays both the hazards and the hope of narcissism. It embodied hazards, for it authorized not only Jung, but also his patients and followers, to become endlessly preoccupied with their own inner life, making it the perspective from which to judge all social and cultural events. But Jung's psychology also contained ideational equipment whereby the clinical phenomenon of narcissism could be recognized and to some extent mitigated. His thought is therefore neither merely narcissistic nor in any sense simply creative: it is a mix of both. The presence of both facets links his thought to the emerging cultural shift to narcissism understood as a specific instance of the related phenomenon of the rise of psychological man.

The interruption and breakdown of the Protestant psychologic and the consequent emerging cultural shift away from object love and into the sphere of narcissism create the third mark of psychological man—his particular understanding of the relation of the self to its surrounding social order. This is perhaps the most outstanding—at least it is the most often emphasized—feature of psychological man. The rise to prominence of narcissistic processes creates a deep suspicion of the demands for commitment that institutions make upon the individual. The result is a generalized devaluing of social structure in the interests of a private self. Psychological man tends to view the social order as destructive of personal, inner integrity rather than as a means of fulfilling and completing that integrity. Consequently, he turns away from socially prescribed values and instead attempts to construct value and meaning in terms of his own self-consciousness. And he sees his private values as constantly threatened by the meanings and values of society. This pattern is particularly clear in such humanistic psychologies as those of Gordon Allport, Carl Rogers, and Abraham Maslow, in the therapies of the human potential movement, and in the psychoreligious cults that have recently come upon the social scene.

Carl Jung's life and thought exemplify this feature of psychological man in what can only be called an extraordinarily precise and all-encompassing way. Throughout his life he was deeply suspicious of the social order. The central experiences of his childhood and early adolescence forced upon him an intense awareness of an irrevocable split between his inner experience and the norms of the religiously authorized social order in which he developed and convinced him that private experience took primacy over the paradigms offered by society. This trend persisted alongside his more conventional socialization experiences of late adolescence and young adulthood. In fact, Jung went so far as to distinguish two personalities, which he called "number one" and "number two" (1961a, pp. 86–87), the former referring to a socially adapted self and the latter to a self that existed before and independent of the social order. Then during the critical years he was again cut off from many social contacts—except for his family, his patients, and Toni Wolff—and within the context of this isolation he created his core process. And while he definitely had friendships in later life, he was for the most part caught up in the intricacies of his evolving work and in his self-identity as an originative thinker, so that his relationships with friends were defined in terms of these factors. Swiss carefulness reinforced his lack of connection with the social world.

Once again the linkage between person and thought, between origins and structure, is instructive. For Jung's thought followed the pattern laid down by his life experiences: it authorized a deep suspicion of the social order as a source for authentic living. At the heart of Jung's system lies a firm distinction between the persona, collective ideals, and the collective consciousness on the one hand, and the individuation process and all it involves on the other. Authentic selfhood lies in the capacity to separate a matrix of personal individuality from the demands of the collective. In Jung's system the cardinal sin is identification of the ego with the persona, and the outstanding virtue is the discovery of the self that by definition exists apart from the collective consciousness of society. The individuation process begins with the discovery that the persona is not all and ends with the establishment of the self, defined as that which transcends the social order. In all fairness to Jung, we should recognize that he always specified that individuation presupposed a firm commitment to social ideals, and Jungian therapists nowadays speak of the need to strengthen the persona. But in spite of these caveats, the force of the Jungian system on the whole moves against the social order and commends a self that is free from its compelling influence and power. Jungian therapy is for people who choose not to adapt entirely to the world of social convention.

In all this, Jung rendered normative a lack of meaning in the public sphere. He spoke against the institutional structuring of the personal sector of life, creating in effect a doctrine of the private self. All the social, political, and religious structures that formerly existed apart

from the individual self were reinterpreted as psychological processes. The three themes best exemplify this trend: Freud's cultural
superego, the political structures of mass society and the state, and
the mystery of God's transcendent reality were all rendered into
psychological form. In the world of Jung's thought, the mind became
society and church—a world within a world.

## Jung and Modernization

To reflect adequately upon the details of Jung's life and thought as an
instance of the emergence of psychological man, it is valuable to
situate them in the broadest possible context—contemporary life as a
whole—for both Jungian man and psychological man dwell within
this context. The key to so situating Jung's thought (and by implication other psychologies as well, and Freud's psychology in particular) is the notion of modernity or, more precisely, modernization. I
discussed the tension between tradition and modernity and its relation to Jung's psychology in chapter 6, using Weinstein and Platt's
theory of modernity and Marthe Robert's view of the two cultures.
But both these analyses, useful as they are for clarifying aspects of
the origins of Jung's thought, are deficient in giving an appreciation
of its overall significance. First, they do not analyze modernization
explicitly in terms of consciousness; second, they possess no
categories that can account for the novel elements in Jung's attempt
to synthesize tradition and modernity into a genuine third alternative.
The sociology of knowledge, as it has been applied to contemporary
life by writers such as Peter Berger (1973), provides one insightful
framework for a broader analysis of Jung's ideas, although, as I shall
shortly argue, it too needs to be expanded to fully comprehend his
thought's uniqueness. Berger assumes that all analyses of modernity
must begin with the phenomenon of modern consciousness, and his
three trends or ideologies, when applied to Jung's theory, provide an
account of its novelty.

Berger centers his analysis of contemporary life upon the modernization of consciousness. It is the essence of modern consciousness
to be irrevocably structured by the technological aspects of industrial
production. The individual of today transfers the engineering ethos
of modern technology and bureaucracy to his personal consciousness

and emotional life. This ethos, characterized by mechanicalness, reproducibility, and measurability, produces in consciousness the traits of abstraction, functional rationality, and instrumentality. Modern consciousness is therefore capable of a degree of self-analysis and self-abstraction never before achieved. As such it is separated from traditional sources of feeling and meaning—it is, in effect, ''homeless.''

This modernization of consciousness has produced two contrary movements in thought and society. First, it has created an intense nostalgia for the integrative symbols of the past, resulting in a traditionalism that defensively reaffirms ancient symbols of community. Berger calls this movement ''counter-modernization.'' But the modernization of consciousness has also produced an attempt to oppose modernity's emphasis upon the anonymity and abstraction of rationalistic individuality by creating new values and a new sense of community that cannot be derived from a sense of tradition. Berger calls this trend ''demodernization'' and finds it best expressed in contemporary youth culture, the counterculture, and the antirepression psychologies of such writers as Norman O. Brown and R. D. Laing. The principal affirmation of demodernization is the conviction that modern people must rediscover a real, ''naked'' self that exists beyond institutions and roles—a metainstitutional self—and that the sources for this new self lie in the future creation of fresh and new values. Thus the trend in the direction of demodernization is even more privatized than is the modernization process itself.

Viewed in terms of this tripartite analysis of modernity, Freud's psychology clearly belongs to the first: it is a form of thought that introduces the forces of modernization into the sphere of consciousness itself. But it is not ambiguously so; it in fact consists of a double movement in which consciousness is both modernized and demodernized, although modernization eventually wins out. On one hand, Freud clearly supported the application of the principle of instrumental, functional rationality, drawn from the scientific world view of his day, to the sphere of personal consciousness itself. His methods of investigation and his clinical and therapeutic techniques brought this principle to bear upon the dynamics of personal consciousness. Freud's theory and therapy thus supplied the means for a weakened ego to strengthen its sense of autonomy and independence in relation to surrounding social structures, thereby adapting to them more strongly and participating in them more actively. This facet of Freud's thought is well captured by the oft-quoted maxim he offered regarding the purpose of life: to love and to work. In this sense Freud was the great modernizer of consciousness, and his psychology can be seen as extending into the depths of consciousness itself the Protestant ethic, with its emphasis upon hard and rewarding work and, through that work, upon adaptation to social conditions.

On the other hand, Freud did not simply apply the principle of functional rationality to personal consciousness. His psychology also contained a second feature—even more important than the first—that rendered far more complex its relation to the modernization of consciousness: Freud discovered a new dimension to consciousness. By freeing dreams and associations from conventional moral restraints, by his nonmoralistic stance toward symptoms, and by his neutral attitude of evenly hovering attention, he opened up for modern men a sphere of consciousness that had heretofore been inaccessible—one that could be integrated into rational consciousness, thereby rendering personal consciousness richer, deeper, and more meaningful and liberating it from the coercive control of the social order. This dimension of Freud's psychology displays a trend toward demodernization, a movement against what can be called the repressive effects of instrumental, functional rationality. In this sense—which emphasizes Freud's empathic discovery of the unconscious, not his avowed scientific-ascetic techniques for analyzing it—Freud's psychology is not so much an extension of the Protestant ethic as the beginning of the end of the Protestant ethic. However, Freud's purpose in emphasizing the existence of a sphere of personal consciousness, formerly captive to the social order but rightfully belonging to the individual, was not to overthrow the social order, but rather to return the individual to it refreshed and more in charge of himself than before. Thus Freud's psychology moves against modernization in order to serve that trend more adequately. There is more than a little irony to the fact that such groups as the human potential movement, which owe so much to Freud's original discovery of psychodynamics, should have exploited so egregiously its limited support of the process of demodernization.

Jung's psychology bears a more complex relation to Berger's three trends than does Freud's, for it articulates substantially with all three, although in the final analysis I am inclined to place the accent upon the third, demodernization. Jung's system takes full cognizance of the modernization of consciousness by affirming that modern man must accept that collective ideals and collective consciousness form the persona, an essential ingredient of his personality. Jung's descriptions of modern man as mass man embody well the principle of functional rationality. The consciousness of modern man was for him truly "homeless." But, as I have already emphasized, this state of affairs was only the beginning of individuation. The breakdown of the persona activated the archetypes of the collective unconscious and called for their assimilation into the ego, thereby broadening the scope of modern man's consciousness and alleviating his condition of homelessness. The archetypes might well be called structures of tradition. As such their existence and the need for their assimilation constituted the dimension of countermodernization in Jung's psychology: they are symbols rooted in the ancient past that unify modern consciousness and overcome its homeless condition.

But Jung's psychology does not stop here. He did indeed counsel a return to the past, yet only so that the past might be surpassed. The modern ego must, as it were, travel through the past, on its way to the future. If individuation is allowed to continue uninterrupted, the assimilation of the archetypes of the collective unconscious results in the formation of the self, a core of essential, personal uniqueness that exists beyond institutions and roles—in short, a truly metainstitutional self. As such, the self cannot be defined entirely in terms of conformity either to modernity or to tradition; it constitutes a genuinely new structure, not simply an amalgam of the two. The Jungian self assimilates the past, by means of the archetypes, but it also repudiates it, for it "sees through" the claims of tradition by penetrating to their archetypal infrastructure. Thus the emergence of the self, the final state of the individuation process, while it is built in part upon modernizing and countermodernizing processes, also attempts to go beyond these in the direction of demodernization, a view of the person that is entirely new, being neither simply modern nor simply traditional. Jung's psychology is therefore an attempt first to codify and then synthesize all three of these trends as they exist in present-day social and intellectual life, blending them into one unitary system of thought.

While it is true that Berger's tripartite diagnosis of modernity provides a conceptual framework within which the main features of Jung's thought can be understood, it is also possible to illumine Berger's analysis by means of the preceding discussions of the origins of Jung's system. The key to such an effort consists in establishing a linkage between the concept of demodernization and what I have called the cultural shift to narcissism. Such a linkage provides a psychological perspective on demodernization. Perhaps the outstanding feature of psychological man is his deep suspicion of the social order as a source of obligation and personal commitment. Consequently he tends to construct, as Jung did and as other psychologists have done, a sphere of value and meaning within the private, personal sector of experience. Berger accordingly calls this tendency demodernization, for it eschews deriving norms either from contemporary social structure (modernization) or from traditional social structure (countermodernization). But a more concrete and less abstract perspective sees this trend as a form of the struggle with narcissism. We know that this struggle tries to overcome suspicion of the social order by establishing a relationship with the otherness of life, especially with social others, and that it also includes an attempt to construct realistic ideals, values, and meanings. Furthermore, this linkage between demodernization and narcissism allows us to infer that in demodernizing systems of thought the problems of idealization, self-esteem, and grandiosity are central—a point wholly absent from Berger's discussion. For these reasons it is illuminating to view the trend toward demodernization in broader psychological terms as well as seeing it as a struggle with narcissism.

There can be little doubt that Jung's psychology belongs in the most general sense to that genre of thought whose overall aim is to reflect critically and innovatively upon the problem of modernity and tradition and that his system thus is well understood in terms of frameworks such as Berger's, addressed precisely to this problem. But since I wish to situate Jung's psychology in as broad a cultural context as possible, and since Berger's analysis focuses upon modernity and tradition in the West—though he does draw examples from primitive and non-Western cultures—it is appropriate to conclude with a brief exploration of the even broader perspective of cultural anthropology.

Jung's psychology submits readily to the categories of analysis provided by the anthropologist Victor Turner in his well-known study *The Ritual Process* (1969). Such an analysis suggests that Jungian psychology is an expression of massive cultural change, but that the conditions for such change, far from being restricted to the modern period in the West, can be found in other times and other places as well. Like Berger's sociology of knowledge, Turner's analysis is suggestive not only for the significance of Jung's psychology but also for the concept of psychological man and for the rise of the discipline of psychology.

Turner analyzes cultural change in the context of what he believes are two fundamental modalities of human relatedness, which he designates as social structure on the one hand and liminality or communitas on the other, although he is almost entirely absorbed by the nature of the latter. Structure refers to the form of social relatedness characterized by heavily institutionalized norms, roles, and status positions. These produce an ethos of differentiation and hierarchy, and people view themselves in ways assigned to them by law, custom, convention, and ceremonial. From time to time, however, people withdraw from these normal modes of social interaction and enter a structureless or liminal phase in which the customary rules of social organization no longer apply.

This new type of social organization differs point for point from the old. First, the conditions of liminality produce intense comradeship and egalitarianism that involve the whole man in relation to other whole men, creating an overarching sentiment of humankindness. Second, whereas social structure is highly routinized and practical, liminality is charged with affect, immediacy, and spontaneity. Third, such social relatedness generates myths, symbols, rituals, and philosophical systems. These newly produced systems of imagery and thought serve as a way to declassify men's relation to nature, society, and culture as these were conceived under the more orderly conditions of social structure. Finally, the members of communitas together submit to the general authority of ritual elders.

Jung's psychology portrays a form of liminality or communitas.

This becomes clear if it is viewed as in essence describing the individuation process, and if that process is considered as a cultural process including the experiences and principles of psychotherapy, not simply as a system of ideas. Individuation begins with a withdrawal from normal modes of social action, epitomized by the breakdown of the persona. Such a withdrawal activates the transference relationship, which is accompanied by the patient's intense desire to be encountered as a whole person. Jung repeatedly recommended a therapeutic attitude of forthrightness and directness, advising his followers to treat their patients as whole persons—otherwise, how were they to truly become whole? Such an attitude meant eschewing the conventional role of physician. Individuation produced intense spontaneity and affective immediacy, but central to the process was the creation, at the level of fantasy and mental imagery, of myths, rituals, and philosophical systems. Again and again Jung emphasized the potential of the collective unconscious to create, in the form of archetypes, alternative views of reality, views that were necessarily at odds with the ethos of the conventional world from which the patient came. And of course the Jungian therapist serves the function of a ritual elder, a wise man who understands the process of passage from the conventional world to that of the new self. He is therefore capable of serving as a guide for those undertaking the experience of individuation. And, as with liminality, much of the imagery of individuation expresses the themes of birth and rebirth. It seems inevitable that such a motif would appear in the mental life of persons who experience themselves as "betwixt and between"—in transition from one order of reality to another.

But Jung's psychology also departs from Turner's analysis of structure and liminality, and this departure illumines its most important and outstanding feature. According to Turner, all liminality must eventually dissolve, for it is a state of great intensity that cannot exist very long without some sort of structure to stabilize it. This dissolution occurs in one of two ways: either the individual returns to the surrounding social structure—energized, to be sure, by his own new experiences—or else liminal communities develop their own internal social structure, a condition Turner calls "normative communitas." But neither of these alternatives applies to Jung's system, nor do they adequately characterize the community of Jungian patients, therapists, and teachers. The individuated self of the committed Jungian returns to the social order only in an extremely instrumental manner, and the social organization of the Jungian community is very loose and unstructured, although there is some hierarchy in the contrasting positions of, say, a lay Jungian and a supervising analyst. For these reasons it is more correct to say that Jung's psychology presents the student of cultural change with a form of "permanent liminality" in which there is no need to return to social structure or to generate a social structure internal to the community. Instead, the individuated person simply continues to interpret himself and the world about him in terms of Jungian categories. For the Jungian—be he patient, therapist, or teacher—the problem of social order ceases to exist at all: it has been replaced by the problem of inner, psychological order.

This shift of the locus of meaning and order from the social to the personal, psychological sphere is the central conceptual leitmotiv that runs throughout Jung's personal life and his system of thought, unifying the two, and it constitutes both the positive achievement and the major limitation of his work. We saw this motif in the deep personal suspicion of social norms that characterized his life beginning in early childhood. This reluctance to internalize social norms informed his perceptions of religion and was present in his reactions to the sociological forces of modernity. It constituted an essential ingredient of his core process, and it appeared again and again in each of the three themes of his mature work. To account for its presence, I have interpreted this central motif in a number of ways. Foremost among these was the psychology of narcissism, which depicts the self as struggling to relate both internally, to itself, and also to ever-widening ranges of sociality beyond itself. I then broadened this analysis by situating it in the context of social processes: Jung's accent upon the private self derived also from his sense of entrapment between the modern secular culture and the culture of traditional religion. Still further, this emphasis is to be understood culturally as the process of demodernization or, even more broadly, as an instance of permanent liminality. Jung's rich structuring of the inner diffuseness that accompanies suspicion of the social order is his greatest achievement. But in eschewing the social order his thought also faces its greatest limitation: he did not see the necessity—so convincingly emphasized by current social science— for institutional organization of the private sector. Thus the final assessment of Jung's work must remain a double one.

Can anything be said regarding the appeal of Jung's thought—why it is so popular? This study of its origins, structure, and general significance suggests that Jung went through a series of life experiences that many people today see as representative or paradigmatic— in their general form, of course, not in their specific details— and which they feel reflect their own lives. Thus, many people today struggle with narcissism; they struggle with Freud's counsel to adapt to the miseries of practical, everyday life and, more broadly, with the potential of newer forms of psychotherapy to reduce these miseries; they struggle with the haunting fear of becoming mass men in a mass society; and they struggle with unbelief in the face of the declining power of traditional religion. But far more than that, Jung's formal system of ideas codified his personal experiences and provided a systematic and plausible interpretation of them all. Narcissism, psychotherapy, modernity, religion—all are interpretively organized in the formal system of writings. By creating his unique system of ideas Jung has given many people a means of conceptualizing, ordering, and reflecting meaningfully on their own inner struggles.

# References

Abell, W. 1966. *The collective dream in art*. New York: Schocken Books.

Bakan, D. 1966. Behaviorism and American urbanization. *Journal of the History of the Behavioral Sciences* 2:5–25.

Beldoch, M. 1975. The therapeutic as narcissist. In *Psychological man*, ed. R. Boyers, pp. 105–23. New York: Harper and Row.

Berger, P. 1965. Toward a sociological understanding of psychoanalysis. *Social Research* 32:26–41.

Berger, P.; Berger, B.; and Kellner, H. 1973. *The homeless mind*. New York: Random House.

Berger, P., and Luckmann, T. 1967. *The social construction of reality*. New York: Doubleday Anchor.

Billinsky, J. M. 1969. Jung and Freud. *Andover Newton Quarterly* 10:39–43.

Bodkin, M. 1934. *Archetypal patterns in poetry*. London: Oxford University Press.

Boring, E. G. 1950. *A history of experimental psychology*. New York: Appleton-Century-Crofts.

Buss, A. R. 1975. The emerging field of the sociology of psychological knowledge. *American Psychologist* 30:988–1002.

Campbell, J. 1956. *The hero with a thousand faces*. Cleveland: World Publishing Company.

Cox, D. 1959. *Jung and Saint Paul*. New York: Association Press.

Creelan, P. 1974. Watsonian behaviorism and the Calvinist conscience. *Journal of the History of the Behavioral Sciences* 10:95–
118.

Cuddihy, J. M. 1974. *The ordeal of civility.* New York: Basic
Books.

Ellenberger, H. 1970. *The discovery of the unconscious.* New York:
Basic Books.

Erikson, E. H. 1958. *Young man Luther.* New York: W. W. Norton.

———. 1959. *Identity and the life cycle.* New York: International
Universities Press.

———. 1963. *Childhood and society.* New York: W. W. Norton.

———. 1964. The first psychoanalyst. In *Insight and responsibility,*
pp. 19–46. New York: W. W. Norton.

Freud, S. 1914a. The Moses of Michelangelo. In *Standard edition,*
13:211–36. London: Hogarth Press, 1953.

———. 1914b. On narcissism: An introduction. In *Standard edition,* 14:73–102. London: Hogarth Press, 1957.

———. 1914c. On the history of the psychoanalytic movement. In
*Standard edition,* 14:3–66. London: Hogarth Press, 1957.

Frey-Rohn, L. 1976. *From Freud to Jung.* New York: Dell Publishing Company.

Frye, N. 1957. *The anatomy of criticism.* Princeton: Princeton
University Press.

Gedo, J. E. 1974. Magna est vis veritatis tuae et praevalebit:
Comments on the Freud-Jung correspondence. Unpublished
manuscript.

Giner, S. 1976. *Mass society.* New York: Academic Press.

Glover, E. 1956. *Freud or Jung?* Cleveland: World Publishing
Company.

Hall, C. S., and Lindzey, G. 1978. *Theories of personality.* 3d ed.
New York: John Wiley.

Hannah, B. 1976. *Jung: His life and work.* New York: G. P.
Putnam's Sons.

Heidbreder, E. 1933. *Seven psychologies.* New York: Appleton-
Century-Crofts.

Henderson, J., and Oakes, M. 1963. *The wisdom of the serpent.*
New York: George Braziller.

Hillman, J. 1975. *Revisioning psychology*. New York: Harper and Row.

Homans, P. 1974. Carl Rogers' psychology and the theory of mass society. In *Innovations in client-centered therapy*, ed. D. A. Wexler and L. N. Rice. New York: John Wiley.

Hostie, R. 1957. *Religion and the psychology of C. G. Jung*. New York: Sheed and Ward.

Hughes, H. S. 1958. *Consciousness and society*. New York: Alfred A. Knopf.

———. 1975. *The sea change*. New York: Harper and Row.

Jacobi, J. 1967. *The way of individuation*. New York: Harcourt, Brace and World.

Jaffe, A. 1972. The creative phases in Jung's life. *Spring* 1972:162–90.

Johnson, W. A. 1974. *The search for transcendence*. New York: Harper and Row.

Jones, E. 1955. *The life and work of Sigmund Freud*. Vol. 2. New York: Basic Books.

Jung, C. G. 1902. *On the psychology and pathology of so-called occult phenomena*. In *Collected works*, 1:3–88. Princeton: Princeton University Press, 1970.

———. 1903. On simulated insanity. In *Collected Works*, 1:159–87. Princeton: Princeton University Press.

———. 1904. On hysterical misreading. In *Collected works*, 1:89–92. Princeton: Princeton University Press, 1970.

———. 1905*a*. Cryptomnesia. In *Collected works*, 1:95–106. Princeton: Princeton University Press, 1970.

———. 1905*b*. Experimental observations on the faculty of memory. In *Collected works*, 2:272–87. Princeton: Princeton University Press, 1973.

———. 1906. Psychoanalysis and association experiments. In *Collected works*, 2:288–317. Princeton: Princeton University Press, 1973.

———. 1907. *The psychology of dementia praecox*. In *Collected works*, 3:1–151. Princeton: Princeton University Press, 1972.

———. 1908*a*. The content of the psychoses. In *Collected works*, 3:153–78. Princeton: Princeton University Press, 1972.

————. 1908*b*. The Freudian theory of hysteria. In *Collected works*, 4:10–24. New York: Pantheon Books, 1961.

————. 1909. The analysis of dreams. In *Collected works*, 4:25–34. New York: Pantheon Books, 1961.

————. 1910*a*. Psychic conflicts in a child. In *Collected works*, 17:1–35. New York: Pantheon Books, 1964. An English translation of the original lecture first appeared as "Experiences concerning the psychic life of the child." In *Analytical psychology*. New York: Moffat Yard and Company, 1916.

————. 1910*b*. A contribution to the psychology of rumor. In *Collected works*, 4:35–47. New York: Pantheon Books, 1961.

————. 1911*a*. A criticism of Bleuler's theory of schizophrenic negativism. In *Collected works*, 3:197–202. Princeton: Princeton University Press, 1972.

————. 1911*b*. Morton Prince, "The mechanism and interpretation of dreams": A critical review. In *Collected works*, 4:56–73. New York: Pantheon Books, 1961.

————. 1912. New paths in psychology. In *Collected works*, 7:245–68. New York: Pantheon Books, 1966. This paper is the first version of the first essay of the *Two essays on analytical psychology*.

————. 1913*a*. General aspects of psychoanalysis. In *Collected works*, 4:229–42. New York: Pantheon Books, 1961.

————. 1913*b*. The theory of psychoanalysis. In *Collected works*, 4:83–226. New York: Pantheon Books, 1961.

————. 1913*c*. A contribution to the study of psychological types. In *Collected works*, 6:499–509. Princeton: Princeton University Press, 1971.

————. 1914. On psychological understanding. In *Collected works*, 3:179–93. Princeton: Princeton University Press, 1972.

————. 1916. The structure of the unconscious. In *Collected works*, 7:269–304. New York: Pantheon Books, 1966. This paper underwent subsequent revision and appeared in final form as the second of the *Two essays on analytical psychology*.

————. 1917. The psychology of the unconscious processes. In *Collected papers on analytical psychology*. London: Baillière, Tindall and Cox. This paper is the second version of the essay "New paths in psychology," originally published in 1912, and, after further revision, became the first of the *Two essays on analytical psychology*.

―――. 1921. *Psychological types*. In *Collected works*, vol. 6. Princeton : Princeton University Press, 1971.

―――. 1931. Freud and Jung: Contrasts. In *Collected works*, 4:333–40. New York: Pantheon Books, 1961.

―――. 1932. Psychotherapists or clergy. In *Collected works*, 11:327–47. New York: Pantheon Books, 1963.

―――. 1934. Sigmund Freud in his historical setting. In *Collected works*, 15:33–40. New York: Pantheon Books, 1966.

―――. 1939. In memory of Sigmund Freud. In *Collected works*, 15:41–49. New York: Pantheon Books, 1964.

―――. 1945. After the catastrophe. In *Collected works*, 10:194–217. New York: Pantheon Books, 1964.

―――. 1946*a*. Psychotherapy today. In *Collected works*, 16:94–110. New York: Pantheon Books, 1954.

―――. 1946*b*. Epilogue to *Essays on contemporary events*. In *Collected works*, 10:227–43. New York: Pantheon Books, 1964.

―――. 1951. Fundamental questions of psychotherapy. In *Collected works*, 16:111–25. New York: Pantheon Books, 1954.

―――. 1953. *Psychology and alchemy*. In *Collected works*, vol. 12. New York: Pantheon Books, 1953.

―――. 1954. *The practice of psychotherapy*. In *Collected works*, vol. 16. New York: Pantheon Books, 1954.

―――. 1957. The undiscovered self. In *Collected works*, 10:245–305. New York: Pantheon Books, 1964.

―――. 1958. The transcendent function. In *Collected works*, 8:67–91. New York: Pantheon Books, 1960. Originally written in 1916.

―――. 1959*a*. *The archetypes and the collective unconscious*. In *Collected works*, vol. 9, part 1. New York: Pantheon Books, 1959.

―――. 1959*b*. *Aion: Researches into the phenomenology of the self*. In *Collected works*, vol. 9, part 2. New York: Pantheon Books, 1959.

―――. 1960. *The structure and dynamics of the psyche*. In *Collected works*, vol. 8. New York: Pantheon Books, 1960.

―――. 1961*a*. *Memories, dreams, reflections*. New York: Random House.

————. 1961*b*. *Freud and psychoanalysis.* In *Collected works,* vol. 4. New York: Pantheon Books, 1961.

————. 1963*a*. *Psychology and religion: West and East.* In *Collected works,* vol. 11. New York: Pantheon Books, 1963.

————. 1963*b*. Psychology and religion. In *Collected works,* 11:3–105. New York: Pantheon Books, 1963.

————. 1964*a*. *Civilization in transition.* In *Collected works,* vol. 10. New York: Pantheon Books, 1964.

————. 1964*b*. *The development of personality.* In *Collected works,* vol. 17. New York: Pantheon Books, 1964.

————. 1965. *Psychology of the unconscious.* New York: Dodd, Mead. Published in English in 1916 as a translation of the original 1912 edition of *Symbols of transformation.*

————. 1966*a*. *Two essays on analytical psychology.* In *Collected works,* vol. 7. New York: Pantheon Books, 1966.

————. 1966*b*. *The spirit in man, art and literature.* In *Collected works,* vol. 15. New York: Pantheon Books, 1966.

————. 1967*a*. *Symbols of transformation.* In *Collected works,* vol. 5. Princeton: Princeton University Press, 1967.

————. 1967*b*. *Alchemical studies.* In *Collected works,* vol. 13. Princeton: Princeton University Press, 1967.

————. 1970*a*. *Psychiatric studies.* In *Collected works,* vol. 1. Princeton: Princeton University Press, 1970.

————. 1970*b*. *Mysterium coniunctionis.* In *Collected works,* vol. 14. Princeton: Princeton University Press, 1970.

————. 1971. *Psychological types.* In *Collected works,* vol. 6. Princeton: Princeton University Press, 1971.

————. 1972. *The psychogenesis of mental disease.* In *Collected works,* vol. 3. Princeton: Princeton University Press, 1972.

————. 1973*a*. *Experimental researches.* In *Collected works,* vol. 2. Princeton: Princeton University Press, 1973.

————. 1973*b*. *Letters.* Vol. 1. Princeton: Princeton University Press.

————. 1975. *Letters.* Vol. 2. Princeton: Princeton University Press.

Kohut, H. 1966. Forms and transformations of narcissism. *Journal of the American Psychoanalytic Association* 14:243–72.

————. 1971. *The analysis of the self.* New York: International Universities Press.

————. 1972. Thoughts on narcissism and narcissistic rage. *Psychoanalytic Study of the Child* 27:360–400.

————. 1975. The future of psychoanalysis. *Annual of Psychoanalysis* 3:325–40.

————. 1976. Creativeness, charisma, group psychology: Reflections on the self-analysis of Freud. In *Freud: The fusion of science and humanism*, ed. J. E. Gedo and G. H. Pollock, pp. 379–425. New York: International Universities Press.

Lifton, R. J. 1968. Protean man. *Partisan Review* 35 (no. 2):13–27.

McGuire, W., ed. 1974. *The Freud-Jung letters*. Princeton: Princeton University Press.

Maddi, S. R. 1968. *Personality theories: A comparative analysis*. Homewood, Ill.: Dorsey Press.

Miller, D. 1974. *The new polytheism*. New York: Harper and Row.

Murphy, G. 1949. *Historical introduction to modern psychology*. London: Routledge and Kegan Paul.

Nelson, M. C., ed. 1977. *The narcissistic condition: A fact of our lives and times*. New York: Human Sciences Press.

Neumann, E. 1962. *The origins and history of consciousness*. New York: Harper and Row.

Nisbet, R. A. 1966. *The sociological tradition*. New York: Basic Books.

Philp, H. L. 1958. *Jung and the problem of evil*. London: Rockliff.

Rainey, R. M. 1975. *Freud as student of religion: Perspectives on the background and development of his thought*. Missoula, Mont.: Scholar's Press.

Read, H. 1965. *Icon and idea*. New York: Schocken Books.

Ricoeur, P. 1970. *Freud and philosophy*. New Haven: Yale University Press.

Rieff, P. 1959. *Freud: The mind of the moralist*. New York: Viking Press.

————. 1966. *The triumph of the therapeutic*. New York: Harper and Row.

Riesman, D. 1950. *The lonely crowd*. New Haven: Yale University Press.

Roazen, P. 1975. *Freud and his followers*. New York: Alfred A. Knopf.

Robert, M. 1976. *From Oedipus to Moses: Freud's Jewish identity*. New York: Doubleday Anchor.

Ross, D. 1972. *G. Stanley Hall: The psychologist as prophet.* Chicago: University of Chicago Press.

Schaer, H. 1950. *Religion and the cure of souls in Jung's psychology.* New York: Pantheon Books.

Schultz, D. 1974. *A history of modern psychology.* New York: Academic Press.

Schur, M. 1972. *Freud: Living and dying.* New York: International Universities Press.

Sennett, R. 1974. *The fall of public man.* New York: Alfred A. Knopf.

Shils, E. 1972. Mass society and its culture. In *The intellectuals and the powers,* pp. 229–47. Chicago: University of Chicago Press.

Singer, J. 1972. *Boundaries of the soul.* New York: Doubleday.

Stein, M. 1976. Narcissus. *Spring* 1976:32–53.

Stepansky, P. 1976. The empiricist as rebel: Jung, Freud and the burdens of discipleship. *Journal of the History of the Behavioral Sciences* 12:216–39.

Stern, P. 1976. *C. G. Jung: The haunted prophet.* New York: George Braziller.

Storr, A. 1973. *C. G. Jung.* New York: Viking Press.

Strout, C. 1968. William James and the twice-born sick soul. *Daedalus* 97:1062–82.

Tolman, E. C. 1966. Psychological man. In *Behavior and psychological man,* pp. 207–18. Berkeley: University of California Press.

Turner, V. 1969. *The ritual process.* Chicago: Aldine Publishing Company.

Van der Post, L. 1977. *Jung and the story of our time.* New York: Random House.

Von Franz, M.-L. 1970. *An introduction to the interpretation of fairy-tales.* New York: Spring Publications.

———. 1975. *C. G. Jung: His myth in our time.* New York: G. P. Putnam's Sons.

Weinstein, F., and Platt, G. 1973. *The wish to be free.* Berkeley: University of California Press.

Wheelis, A. 1958. *The quest for identity.* New York: W. W. Norton.

Wheelwright, J. 1976. The Freud and Jung correspondence. (Series title, Freud and Jung: An historical perspective.) New York: Psychotherapy Tape Library.

White, V. 1952. *God and the unconscious*. Cleveland: World Publishing Company.

Whitmont, E. C. 1969. *The symbolic quest*. New York: G. P. Putnam's Sons.

Winnicott, D. W. 1964. Review of *Memories, dreams, reflections*. *International Journal of Psychoanalysis* 45:450–55.

Wolf, E. S. 1976. Saxa loquuntur: Artistic aspects of Freud's "The aetiology of hysteria." In *Freud: The fusion of science and humanism*, ed. J. E. Gedo and G. H. Pollock, pp. 208–28. New York: International Universities Press.

Woodworth, R. S. 1964. *Contemporary schools of psychology*. New York: Ronald Press.

# Index

Active imagination, 92, 107
Active participation, 69, 92, 107
Adler, Alfred: and Freud, 93, 95, 96; and Jung's theory of
  types, 72, 93, 95, 96
*Aion,* 26
Alchemy, 27
Alter ego transference, 41. *See also* Narcissistic transference
Altruistic value systems (Kohut), 97, 113, 195, 197
Ambition: in Freud's dreams, 146; in Jung's life history, 88
Ambivalence, in Bleuler's theory, 59
America: Jung's success in, 61; trip to, 49, 52, 53, 53 n, 54,
  55, 57
Amsterdam conference, 51
Anima: described in *Two Essays,* 103, 105–6; Jung's experience
  of, 82, 106; relationship to persona, 105; as symbol for
  unconscious, 105
Anthropology, cultural, 206–8
Anti-Jungian view of Jung, 17, 19, 185
Archaic man, 142
Archetypal criticism, 18
Archetypal psychology, 19
Archetypes: emergence of, in therapy, 98, 101–2; in fairy
  tales, 99; and Freud's thought, 154, 167; Jung's experience
  of, 80–84; and parental imagoes, 82–83; relation to Chris-
  tianity and modernity, 154; traditional dimensions of, 141,
  190; in *Two Essays,* 98. *See also* Collective unconscious
*Archetypes and the Collective Unconscious, The,* 26
Art and the anima, 82
Attention, evenly hovering, 36
Authority, and society, 3, 135–37
Autobiography, Jung's: as basis of biographies, 28, 117–18;
  and contextual approach, 15, 23; discussion of Freud in,
  29–30; life stages in, 25, 29
Autonomy (Weinstein and Platt), 136–37